Affinity Designer Workbook

Learn digital design and
illustration with Affinity Designer

By the Affinity Team

Foreword

Based in Nottingham in the UK, Serif was founded in 1987 with the aim to develop low-cost alternatives to high-end publishing and graphics packages for PC. In late 2009 we took the major decision to return to our indie development roots, and formed a dedicated team to imagine new, amazing, professional-grade software. Serif Labs was born, and these developers and designers have created Affinity, for Mac, PC and iPad.

The creation of Affinity has arguably been the most exciting period in the history of the company. Since we put Affinity Designer on the Mac App Store in October 2014, followed by Affinity Photo, we have achieved more than we dreamed possible—from the recognition of an Apple Design Award in June 2015, to the amazing reviews from the global media, and the creative people like you who have joined us on this journey. The response has been overwhelming and humbling.

The Affinity vision was to create a trio of apps encompassing graphic design, image editing and layout which would not only develop into class-leaders in their own right, but also work together in a way never seen before. The launch of Affinity Publisher in 2019, and the unique integration between the different strands of the Affinity package, represent the culmination of the first part of our journey.

We approach our official Workbooks with exactly the same creative freedom and dedication that we apply to our software. As well as covering the basic interface and core skills, we enlisted the help of the very best illustrators and designers to show you how they use Affinity Designer. The Workbook is not intended to be a traditional manual, rather we hope it will inspire you to explore the boundaries of your own imagination, as you discover just how much the app is capable of.

We say it all the time, but it really is true, we couldn't have done any of this without the people who have supported us, by buying the software and the books, as well as acting as evangelists for us out online and in the real world. To all of you, we thank you.

Ash Hewson
Managing Director

Contributors from Team Affinity

This book has been conceived and created by the following members of the Affinity team.

Editors	Andy Capstick and Kate Musgrove
Technical Writers	Andy Capstick
Art Direction	Neil Ladkin, Kate Musgrove and Ian Cornwall
Artworkers	Ian Cornwall and Ian Upcott

Illustration and design contributors

Everything we add to our software is designed around the needs of creatives like you. To this end we work with some of the finest designers and illustrators to show what is possible in Affinity Designer—and this book has been no exception.

We have been so lucky to welcome the following contributors (in order of appearance) to create the projects in this book, and we would like to take this opportunity to say a big thank you to them for sharing their expertise in Affinity Designer.

Ben the Illustrator—With vast experience as an illustrator, creative director, and animator of music videos, Ben is one half of the impressive multidisciplinary creative studio, Huddle Formation. Ben's an award-winning designer based in Somerset, England and has been a full-time illustrator for over 10 years.

Check out Ben's project The Panther on p. 128 and find out more about Ben and his work at bentheillustrator.com

Romain Trystram—Parisian illustrator and graphic designer based in Morocco. Romain is a well-respected illustrator, who previously worked on an animated series and as a colourist for comic books. His work is loved for its use of reflections of big-city lights shown in glorious colours.

Learn to use Affinity Designer like Romain in his project Reflected Skyline on p. 152. To see more of Romain's work, visit romaintrystram.myportfolio.com

Paolo Limoncelli—Italian-based Paolo is a UX/UI Designer and illustrator. Paolo also creates amazing brush sets designed using real media under the brand **DAUB Brushes**.

Paolo walks you through brush creation and combining vector and raster illustration in The Whittler on p. 186. Follow Paolo on Twitter @paololimoncelli to be the first to find out when he releases new brushes for Affinity.

Kevin House—aka Kevin Creative is a Canadian illustrator and logo designer who has had an ongoing affair with paths and pixels for over 25 years. Working in 2D and 3D, Kevin also loves all things isometric.

Create an isometric illustration with Kevin in Wine Cellar on p. 236 and see more of Kevin's portfolio at kevincreative.com

Jonathan Ball—Head of famed pokedstudio, Jonathan is an illustrator, animator and character designer based in Cardiff, Wales. Incredibly cute 2D and 3D characters in sometimes surreal environments with vivid colours showcase Jon's vision with beautiful detail.

Learn how to create a 3D style illustration in Affinity Designer with Jon's project The Fisherman on p. 264. Check out Jon's work at pokedstudio.com

Neil Ladkin—Illustrator, designer and thrill-seeker, Neil has been a designer and creative lead for many years and now heads up creative direction at Affinity.

Learn about creating brand collateral, logo design and designing for print from Neil in the design projects Lace Frame Galleries 1 & 2 on p. 308 and p. 340. You can also see more of Neil's design and illustration work at behance.net/neilladkin

Tom Koszyk—CEO and lead designer of Polish design agency Hologram. Tom is a multidisciplinary designer focused on digital products design & strategy. Throughout his 10-year long career he has so far had the privilege of working with startups, software houses and digital agencies from around the world.

Learn about UX/UI design and icon design with Tom in Tix App 1 & 2 on p. 364 and p. 416. Check out more of Hologram's work at hologramdesign.co

TABLE OF CONTENTS

Welcome

Chapter 1 : Interface Tour

Chapter 2 : Core Skills

Inserts

Chapter 3 : Illustration Projects

Chapter 4 : Design Projects

Index

WELCOME

Affinity Designer Workbook

Welcome to the Affinity Designer Workbook. This workbook has been been created with a host of creative contributors to help you either get started with Affinity Designer, or hone your illustration and design skills within the app.

In this introductory section, learn more about us and how to get the most out of your experience with Affinity.

ABOUT AFFINITY

Affinity is revolutionising design, photography and publishing with a trio of powerful, professional apps which work together in a unique way. Created to harness the full power of the latest hardware, their development has been driven by the demands of real-life work environments. Affinity is fast becoming a new global standard with more than 1.5 million users and over 10,000 5-star reviews worldwide.

Our trio of apps comprises:

- **Affinity Designer**—professional graphic design software, available on Mac, Windows and iPad

- **Affinity Photo**—professional photo editing software, available on Mac, Windows and iPad

- **Affinity Publisher**—professional desktop publishing, available on Mac and Windows

Designer
for Mac

2014

Designed for cross-platform creatives

Affinity software is developed with full feature parity and total cross-platform compatibility in mind. Every Affinity file you create can be opened by any app in the Affinity suite, and on any of our supported platforms. That extends to shared history too!

True multi-discipline, mixed-media designing is finally here. It's how we think a creative software suite should be.

The story so far

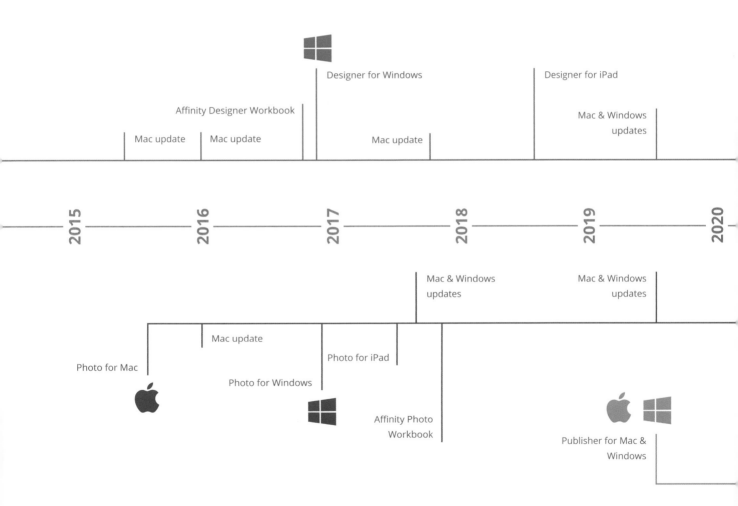

Designer for Windows

Affinity Designer Workbook

Mac update | Mac update | Mac update

Designer for iPad

Mac & Windows updates

2015 — 2016 — 2017 — 2018 — 2019 — 2020

Mac & Windows updates

Mac & Windows updates

Mac update

Photo for iPad

Photo for Mac

Photo for Windows

Affinity Photo Workbook

Publisher for Mac & Windows

ABOUT
AFFINITY DESIGNER

Affinity Designer is the fastest, smoothest, most precise vector graphic design software available. Whether you're working on branding, websites, icons, UI, or creating concept art, Affinity Designer will revolutionise how you work.

And you don't have to take our word for it. Affinity Designer was Mac App Store's Editor's Choice from day one, featured as one of the best new apps of 2014, and received the highly coveted Apple Design Award at WWDC in June 2015 for its incredible performance and capabilities.

> *Affinity Designer is a smooth, precise, high-performance graphics design app for creative professionals that's available on the Mac... this is an excellent example of what a state-of-the-art Mac app should be.*

Apple.com
Apple Design Awards 2015

Key Features

Built for your workflow

With core principles of performance, stability and lack of bloat, Affinity Designer has been meticulously crafted for a professional workflow.

It's fast. Really fast

Pan and zoom at 60fps and see all adjustments, effects, transformations and brushes in real time.

Incredible accuracy

You can zoom to over 1,000,000%. Enough said.

Work in any colour space

RGB, LAB, Greyscale (8/16 bit) and CMYK colour modes. End-to-end CMYK workflow with ICC colour management.

Unsurpassed file compatibility

The best PSD import engine available and full support for SVG, EPS, PDF, PDF/X and FH files means injecting Affinity Designer into your workflow is painless.

Regular updates, no subscription

In its first year of launch, Affinity Designer received three major updates, including hundreds of new features and improvements. All delivered to Affinity Designer owners for free.

Design tools redefined

All the tools you need in a professional vector design app, from an incredibly precise pen tool to a supersmooth gradient tool. All carefully considered and meticulously developed, they just work—in precisely the way you want them to.

Key Features Cont.

Transform

Scale, rotate and shear objects (and node selections) by eye or with the Transform Panel for absolute precision.

Pixel perfect control

With real-time pixel preview in standard or retina resolution available with a single click, you can always see what you're going to get and still edit while previewing.

Non-destructive effects and adjustments

With a huge library of adjustment layers, effects and blend modes—combined with support for masks and clipping layers—Affinity Designer offers the most advanced layer controls available.

Flexible workspaces... and workflows

With a focused, fully customisable workspace, including light/dark UI, docked/floating UI modes and multiple designs to view, Affinity Designer lets you work how you want. Plus, with savable history, unlimited undo and non-destructive adjustments you can always go back and change your mind.

Grid layouts

Adopt a square grid or isometric grid with easy plane switching and drawing directly to plane. Take things further with custom axonometric grid creation from a transformable cube model.

Focus on UI/UX

Make designing for UX and UI fast and unencumbered with feature-rich Symbols and the best in class Constraints.

Natural brushwork

Combine Force Touch, stylus pressure, and tilt with stroke stabilisation for natural-looking artwork. Edit vector brush strokes as cleanly and easily as regular curves, and add raster brushwork—on its own or with vector art—to add depth and high-quality organic textures. Rotate the canvas, blend colours, edit brush parameters, add symmetric/mirrored brush strokes, create your own brushes and nozzles, and import .abr brushes.

Throw some shapes

Affinity Designer offers controls for adjusting geometry with corner settings and smart snapping indicators. The Corner Tool rounds any shape's sharp corners. A full set of Boolean geometry operations, non-destructive compound shapes, and full node editing means you can create beautiful complex geometry in no time.

Just your type

Add artistic text for headlines, text frames of any shape, or text that follows any vector path. Apply sophisticated styling and ligatures, previewing all your available fonts and style sets in on-screen panels. All the controls you need are built in, including leading, kerning, baseline shift, tab stops—as well as the convenience of spell checking and quickly adding placeholder text.

Professional print controls

Affinity Designer features full professional print output. Pantone® support, end-to-end CMYK and ICC colour management are just part of it. You can also open, edit and output PDF/X files, set overprint controls, use spot colours, and add bleed area, trim and crop marks.

Powerful export

In Export Persona you get a complete workspace dedicated to image export. Select areas, layers or objects to export, controlling each item's output settings independently. For efficient web and UI design, you can automatically create new files whenever your design changes including standard and retina versions (2x and 3x) of everything in one go.

Common Affinity file format

Mixed discipline design is as it should be with a shared file format across Affinity apps. Open any native Affinity file in any Affinity app and just keep working—benefit from shared history, undo options and seamless app switching.

Incredibly powerful artboards

Create an unlimited number of different design variants and sizes with artboards—laying them out in one document to see them all at once. When you come to export you get full control over what artboards to output and with what settings, dramatically simplifying your workflow for responsive and app design.

Fully customisable shortcuts

Enhance productivity with a huge library of keyboard shortcuts for tools, menu functions, view and controls— and choose your own.

Rotate canvas

Rotate your canvas to view your artwork at a different angle—aiding brush work, focussing on fine details and tablet-assisted design.

Real-time embedded document editing

Embed other Affinity files in your current design and view results in real-time when editing embedded documents.

Instant undo history

Instantly scrub through thousands of undo steps with the history slider. Plus, save your history with your document to undo editing steps from any session.

Vector brushes

Draw editable strokes and apply stretching or repeating texture brushes to vector curves, along with pressure adjustments. A large library is supplied and you can easily create your own.

Design aids

Snap objects and curve nodes to placed ruler guides, multi-column guides or to any shape's geometry. Other aids include repositioning your spread origin, alignment guides to snap your selections to positions on the page.

GET THE MOST OUT OF THIS WORKBOOK

To use this workbook, you must have Affinity Designer installed on your PC or Mac. You can buy Affinity Designer from the Mac App Store or from affinity.serif.com

For full system requirements, please visit https://affin.co/designerfeatures

Be familiar with the Interface

The projects in this book assume that you have a working knowledge of the interface of Affinity Designer already, or that you have read and understood the Interface Tour (p. 13).

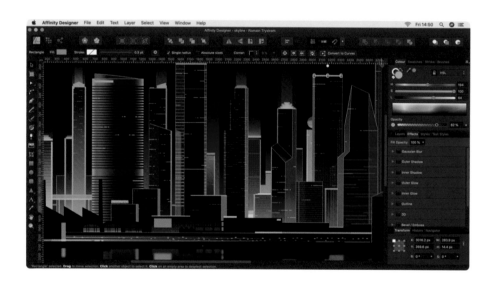

Master the Core Skills

The projects in this book also assume that you have mastered the core skills of Affinity Designer, or that you have understood the principles outlined in Core Skills (p. 73). At the beginning of each project, core skills that you'll need will be referenced.

Project Resources

At the beginning of each project you'll be provided with a link to download all the designer's resources for that project, e.g.

https://affin.co/panther

On later pages, you may see references to downloaded resources that you can use to follow along with the project.

Resource
example.afdesign sketch.jpg

Use the Defaults

The projects in this workbook assume that you are using the default settings of Affinity Designer. See Interface Tour (p. 13) to find out how to reset to the default workspace.

Keyboard Shortcuts

At the back of this book you can find some handy pull-out keyboard cheat sheets to help you learn the default keyboard shortcuts. The default keyboard shortcut for each tool is referenced whenever a tool is first mentioned in a project.

You can also learn about customising the keyboard shortcuts to your liking in the Interface Tour referenced above.

JOIN OUR COMMUNITY

Access our latest news and updates, plus get more resources

We are delighted to provide a wealth of help and support to our growing Affinity Community. Here's how to get involved...

Keep up to date and get support

Our **Twitter**, **Facebook** and **Instagram** pages are great places to get up to date news, exclusives and sneak peeks. Plus, you can sign up to our newsletter to get all the latest news, offers and competitions via email, and we promise to never send you spam, ever.

For in-depth questions and technical support, our **forums** are the best place to go. Our developers play an active role on our forums, so you can get help and updates straight from the source. This is also the place to take part in our free customer betas, so you can try out all our new features first.

Get inspired

Affinity Spotlight is a free, online resource created to share inspirational creative work we love, as well as important advice from professionals. From in-depth interviews with Affinity all-stars, to behind-the-scenes looks at projects created in Affinity to learning resources

such as tutorials and explanations of technical concepts, it's all in one place. Visit affinityspotlight.com to find out more.

Keep on learning

Affinity products are backed up by an impressive selection of video tutorials—all recorded in 4k. You can access them from the Welcome screen in the app by clicking **View Tutorials**. They'll help you to learn our software and develop your creative skill set and are intended for beginners and advanced users equally. We'll keep adding more tutorials as we develop more features.

Join our mailing list to get the latest Affinity news and updates at
affin.co/subscribe

 Learn how to use the Affinity suite with our comprehensive video tutorials at
vimeo.com/affinitybyserif and at affin.co/youtube

 Get news, updates, support and take part in our competitions by following us on Twitter
@affinitybyserif

 Get news, updates, support and take part in our competitions by liking us on Facebook
@affinitybyserif

 Share your work tagged with #madeinaffinity for a chance to be featured on our Instagram page
@affinitybyserif

 Get news, learning resources and inspiration from the award-winning Affinity team
affinityspotlight.com

 Take part in our free customer betas and get in-depth support from all our team—including our developers—on our forums at affin.co/forum

CHAPTER 1

Interface Tour

The interface of Affinity Designer combines industry standard concepts such as toolbars and Studio panels, as you'd expect, but also benefits from a context-driven workspace, where tools and tool options are presented as you need them.

In this chapter you will be introduced to the layout of the workspace of Affinity Designer and see how this well designed interface is both easy on the eye and efficient for your workflow.

AFFINITY DESIGNER

The Interface Explained

Toolbar
Use to switch Personas and access defaults, view modes, object control options and design aids (e.g., snapping).

Context Toolbar
Dynamically updates according to the selected tool or object so you only get the relevant options as you need them.

Tools Panel
Hosts all the tools relevant to the currently active Persona. The tool set will update when you switch Personas.

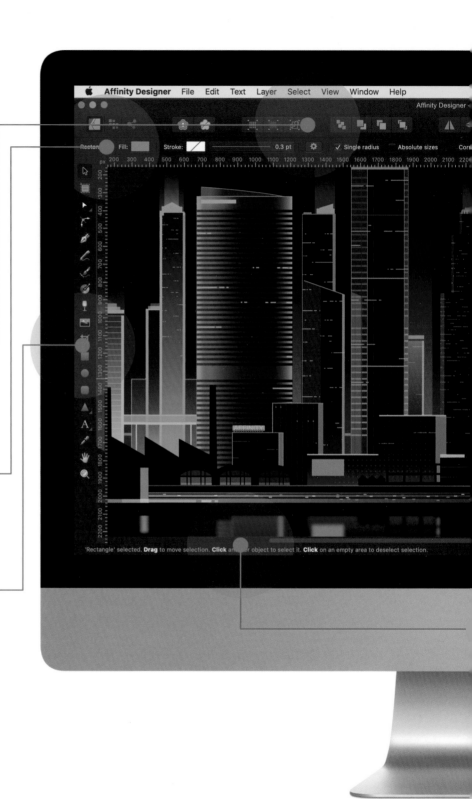

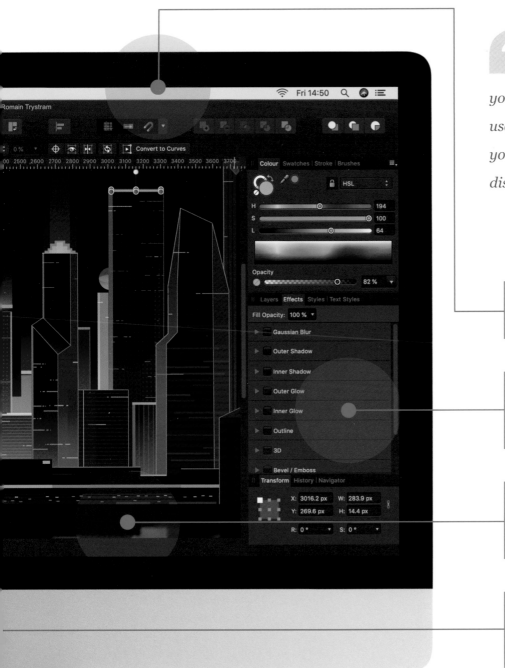

> *Go to **View Menu > Toggle UI** to toggle your interface on and off. This is useful when you want to look at your document without any distraction.*

Menu Bar
Provides commands and options via multiple menus.

Studio Panels
Let you change the properties of objects; other panels are provided to aid design.

Document View
This is your design 'real estate' shown as a single page or multiple artboards.

Status Bar
Provides handy tips and shortcuts in context with the tools and objects you're working with.

TOOLS PANEL

Available from the **Tools Panel**, some tools are grouped together and are accessible via a flyout menu. Grouped tools can be displayed by clicking the grey marker on an icon's bottom, right corner. Each time you select a new tool, the context toolbar shows the commands and options relevant to the selected tool.

> The tools on this page are so essential that they are available in each of the three personas in Affinity Designer.

Move Tool

This tool is so fundamental to vector design work that you'll probably use it subconsciously most of the time. It lets you move, rotate, resize, transform, copy and manipulate any selected object. In **Export Persona** the **Move Tool** becomes the **Slice Selection Tool**.
Keyboard shortcut: V

View Tool

This tool is used to move the visible portion of your document in the Document View. If you double-click on the View Tool's icon on the **Tools Panel**, the zoom will be set to 'Fit'.
Keyboard shortcut: H
Hot key panning: Spacebar

Zoom Tool

The **Zoom Tool** is used to change the zoom level of your page in the Document View. If you double-click on the Zoom Tool's icon on the **Tools Panel**, the zoom will be set to 100%.
Keyboard shortcut: Z

PERSONAS

Think of Personas as three different ways of working within your application:

 Designer Persona – for vector drawing

 Pixel Persona – for raster painting

 Export Persona – to output from your project

So if you want to work purely with vector tools you can design in the default **Designer Persona**; for additional raster textures and pixel brush stroke operations, the **Pixel Persona** is the choice for you. Finally, the **Export Persona** is ideal for exporting specific areas of your design as usable graphics (for web, print, etc.).

Each Persona comes with its own specific tools and Studio panels, whilst the top toolbar and menu bar update to show features and options appropriate to the Persona you are in.

Switching Personas

When you wish to swap disciplines, you simply select a different Persona from the **Toolbar** and continue working with a new tool set. Switching between Personas will result in the current workspace changing to display appropriate tools, toolbars, panels and menu options.

DESIGNER PERSONA TOOLS

Artboard Tool

This tool allows you to add, move and resize artboards within a document.

Node Tools

The **Node Tool** edits curves and shapes drawn with the **Pen** and **shape tools**. The

Point Transform Tool scales or rotates an object about a specific point in its geometry.
Keyboard shortcut: A (Node tool only).

Corner Tool

Rounds sharp corners on geometric shapes or on closed shapes drawn with the **Pen Tool**.
Keyboard shortcut: C

Pen Tool

The essential tool for vector design, allowing you to quickly create clean, crisp Bézier curves, whether you're a master or a novice. The Pen Tool is covered in-depth in the Core Skills chapter.
Keyboard shortcut: P

Pencil Tool

With the **Pencil Tool** you can create a hand-drawn look by drawing freehand, variable width lines as if you were drawing on paper. Use with a pressure sensitive tablet for a more natural line.
Keyboard shortcut: N

Vector Brush Tool

The **Vector Brush Tool** paints by scaling or repeating an image along a path (line). Brush types are applied using the **Brushes Panel**.
Keyboard shortcut: B

Fill Tool

Giving you the ability to apply highly customisable smooth gradients in real-time, this tool means you never have to compromise on perfect colour and shadows in your compositions.
Keyboard shortcut: G

Designer Persona is home to all your vector drawing tools and options. This is the first Persona you'll be presented with when you first launch Affinity Designer. It's the default Persona and likely to be the place you spend most of your time if your illustration or design is vector-based.

Designer Persona contains all your essential vector tools, including the **Pen**, **Fill**, **Transparency** and **Text** tools, as well as a variety of tools for creating geometric shapes.

Transparency Tool

The **Transparency Tool** allows you to apply and edit transparency gradients to vector and text objects.
Keyboard shortcut: Y

Place Image Tool

The **Place Image Tool** adds an image to your page at its default or custom dimensions by clicking or dragging, respectively.

Vector Crop Tool

The **Vector Crop Tool** allows you to remove portions of a selected object (or grouped objects) non-destructively. Images can also be cropped.

Colour Picker Tool

The **Colour Picker Tool** samples colours from your document and optionally applies it to the current selection. Sample sizes can be defined.
Keyboard shortcut: I

Shape tools

These tools allow you to add complicated geometric shapes to your designs with little effort. They are highly adaptable and editable and come in a variety of shapes including rectangles, stars, an ellipse and the multifaceted cog.
Keyboard shortcut: M *(cycles through the* **Rectangle Tool***,* **Ellipse Tool***, and* **Rounded Rectangle Tool***)*

Text tools

The **Artistic Text Tool** and **Frame Text Tool** allow you to add text to your design from single words to full page stories, but they also allow you to create and manipulate text on a path and text within a custom shape, respectively.
Keyboard shortcut: T *(cycles through* **Artistic Text Tool** *and* **Frame Text Tool***)*

PIXEL PERSONA TOOLS

Marquee Selection Tools

These tools allow you to select parts of your image using various shapes. There is also a **Freehand Selection Tool** to make a selection from a drawn outline.

Keyboard shortcut: M
*(cycles through **Rectangular**, **Elliptical**, **Column**, and **Row**). The **Freehand Selection Tool** uses L by default.*

Selection Brush Tool

The **Selection Brush** allows you to select a region of your image by painting. By simply dragging on your image, you can add or remove regions from a selection. The selection will grow or shrink depending on the brush settings.

Keyboard shortcut: W

Pixel Tool

The **Pixel Tool** draws pixel-aligned, hard-edged lines. This is in contrast to the **Paint Brush Tool** which gives softer brush strokes due to its antialiasing.

Keyboard shortcut: B *(cycles with the **Paint Brush Tool**)*

Paint Brush Tool

The **Paint Brush Tool** places coloured pixels onto a raster layer, allowing you to add raster elements to your design.

Keyboard shortcut: B *(cycles with the **Pixel Tool**)*

Erase Brush Tool

In contrast to the **Paint Brush Tool**, the **Erase Brush Tool** removes unwanted pixels as well as hiding painted areas of previously created vector layers.

Keyboard shortcut: E

Pixel Persona contains a range of raster-based tools, including painting and pixel selection tools, as well as **Dodge**, **Burn**, **Blur** and **Sharpen** brush tools.

If you're a digital artist, you might find yourself primarily working in this environment. However, if you're a vector illustrator and designer, this Persona is more likely to be used to add flair and finishing touches to your designs.

Flood Fill Tool

Allows you to fill in areas of your page, selection, or object with a single click. It works by replacing the colour of pixels on the current layer with the **Fill** colour set on the **Colour Panel**.
Keyboard shortcut: G

Dodge Brush Tool

With this tool you can precisely lighten areas of your image, and even limit the effect to just shadows, highlights or midtones. The effect is cumulative—the more you paint, the more pronounced the lightening effect will be.
Keyboard shortcut: O *(cycles with the **Burn Brush Tool**)*

Burn Brush Tool

In contrast to the **Dodge Brush Tool**, the **Burn Brush Tool** allows you to precisely darken areas of your image.
Keyboard shortcut: O *(cycles with the **Dodge Brush Tool**)*

Smudge Brush Tool

Produces an effect similar to dragging a brush or finger through wet paint by dragging colour around an image. It can be used to blend colours and create interesting brush effects.

Blur Brush Tool

Use the **Blur Brush Tool** to blur hard edges within an image. The effect is cumulative so the more you paint over an area, the more pronounced the blur effect will be. The blur is only applied to the currently selected layer. If a vector layer is selected, the layer will be automatically converted to a pixel layer by default.

Sharpen Brush Tool

Sharpening increases the contrast of neighbouring pixels. The **Sharpen Brush Tool** gives you full control over the areas that are sharpened and has a cumulative affect. You can easily apply clarity and unsharp mask sharpening selectively with a few strokes of a brush!

EXPORT PERSONA TOOLS

 ## Slice Tool

The **Slice Tool** allows you to create, move and resize areas of your design in readiness for exporting. Slices allow you export portions of your page design as individual graphics.
Keyboard shortcut: S

 ## Slice Selection Tool

The **Slice Selection Tool** lets you select objects, groups and layers so you can create slices from them.
Keyboard shortcut: L

Export Persona provides the perfect environment for exporting particular areas, selections, or layers of your design in isolation, at a variety of sizes. This Persona is ideal if you design web or app content, or you simply wish to export all your artboards in a single operation.

Export Persona hosts an exclusive tool used to create, position and resize areas for export: **the Slice Tool**.

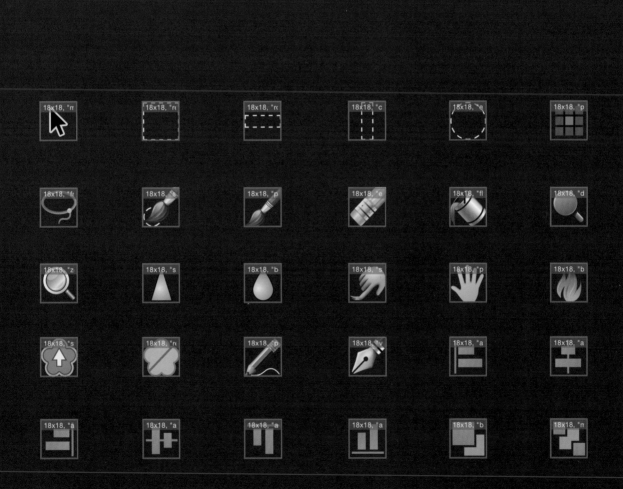

TOOLBAR

The three Persona icons precede a mix of icons that set object defaults, switch view modes, order, transform, align/distribute objects, set snapping criteria, create Boolean shapes and target layer placement (in icon groups from left to right).

We'll cover object control in more detail in the Core Skills chapter (see Objects on p. 80).

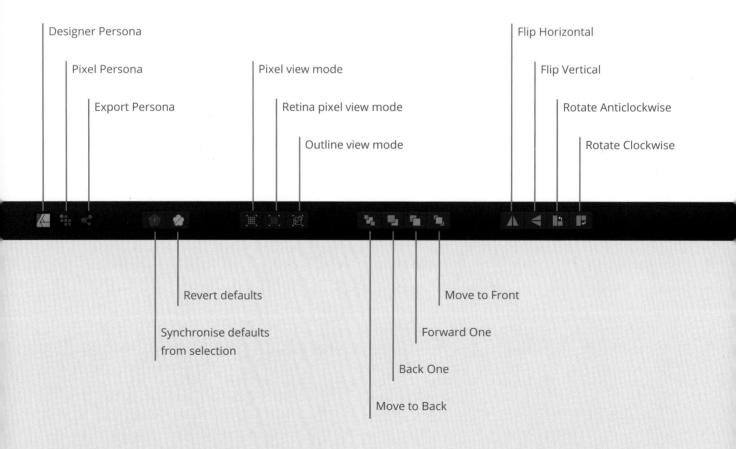

Designer Persona

Pixel Persona

Export Persona

Pixel view mode

Retina pixel view mode

Outline view mode

Flip Horizontal

Flip Vertical

Rotate Anticlockwise

Rotate Clockwise

Revert defaults

Synchronise defaults from selection

Move to Front

Forward One

Back One

Move to Back

Force Pixel Alignment

Move by Whole Pixels

Snapping

Insert behind the selection

Insert at the top of the layer

Insert inside the selection

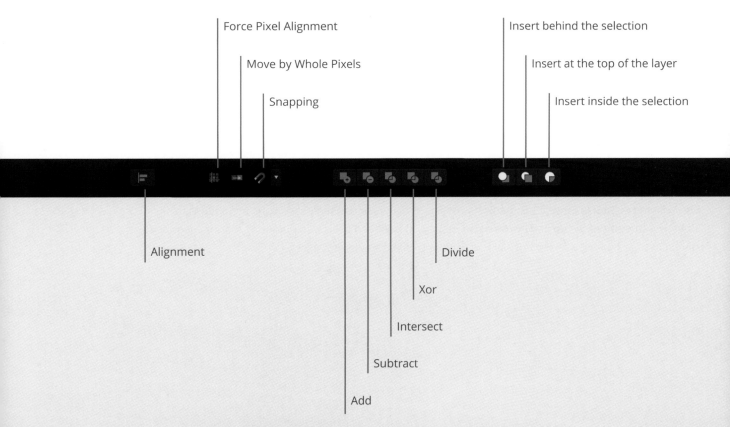

Alignment

Divide

Xor

Intersect

Subtract

Add

CONTEXT TOOLBAR

As the name implies, the options on the context toolbar will update depending on the selected tool. Regardless of the tool you switch to, you'll have quick access to appropriate options while you design.

For example, for the **Pen Tool** and **Artistic Text Tool**.

The context toolbar also provides editing options for selected objects, groups and layers. For example, for a curve selected with the **Move Tool**.

When the **Move Tool** is active, but no objects are selected, the context toolbar will present options to access the **Document Setup** and **Preferences** dialogs. The **Move Tool** is also unique in sharing many of its context toolbar options with the original tool used to create the selected object.

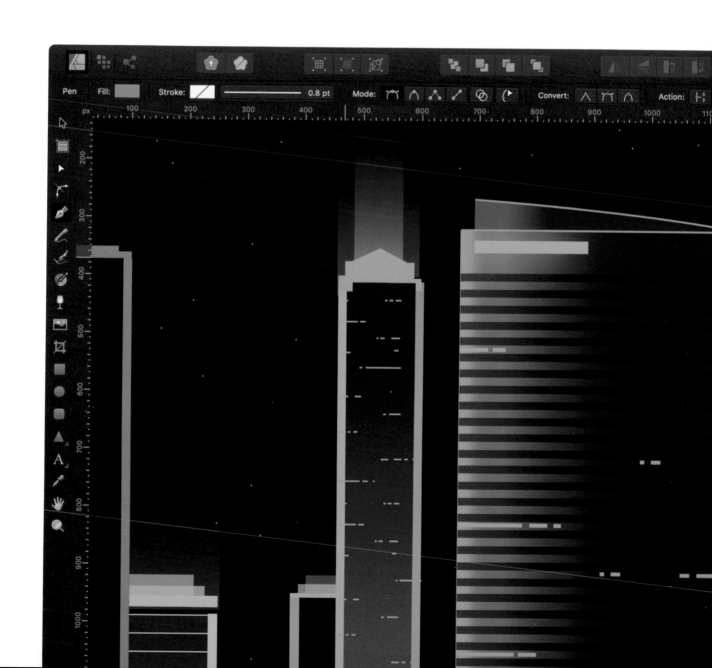

STUDIO PANELS

Once an object has been created and selected, it can be modified in a variety of ways using options which appear on the **Studio Panels**. Panels can also affect the functionality of selected tools.

Although the same named panels may appear in different **Personas**, they may have subtly different options and may function in a slightly different way. Which panels you use during the design process will vary depending on your style of working and the aim of the project. On the following pages you will find some information about the panels you'll encounter in Affinity Designer.

It's also worth knowing that not all panels are on by default, as some panels are for less common workflows. Go to **View Menu > Studio** to turn individual panels off and on and use **Reset Studio** to only show the default studio panels for the persona you are in.

Colour Panel

The **Colour Panel** is used to choose colour for various tools and selected objects. A pop-up version of the Colour Panel may appear when choosing colour from within other dialogs.

The Colour Panel can operate in several colour modes—HSL, RGB, CMYK and LAB—and has various ways of defining colour—colour wheel (HSL only), colour boxes and colour sliders. Colour tints can also be applied from within the panel.

The Colour Panel takes on different appearances depending on the active Persona and on the selected tool. For example, the **Fill Tool** and the **Vector Brush Tool** change the appearance of the Colour Panel.

In **Designer Persona**, objects have fill and stroke colour properties. The stroke colour is represented by the cutout (donut) colour selector. The fill is represented by the solid colour selector.

In **Pixel Persona**, the panel shows colours represented by two solid colour selectors indicating Colour 1 (Foreground) and Colour 2 (Background).

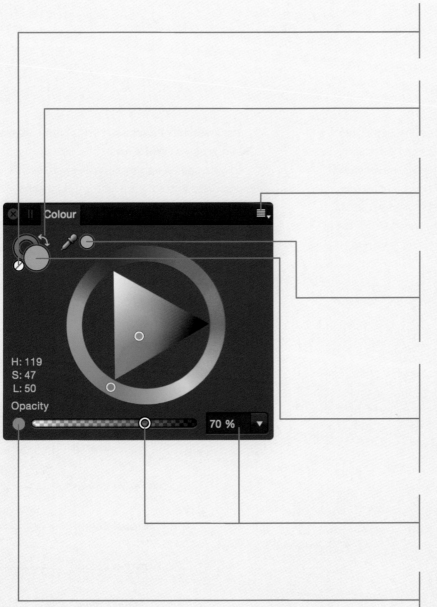

None
Removes colour from the active selector.

Swap
Switches the colours applied to the selectors.

Panel Preferences
Change colour selection preferences, models and modes.

Colour picker and **picked colour swatch**
Allows colour sampling from individual pixels and application to active selector.

Stroke/Fill or Colour 1/Colour 2
The active colour selector is shown at the front of the two colour selectors. Choosing a new colour will apply it to the active colour selector.

Opacity/Noise Controls
Sets the opacity and/or noise of the active colour.

Opacity/Noise
Click to switch between Opacity and Noise.

Swatches Panel

The **Swatches Panel** stores your recently used colours and lets you access a range of pre-defined palettes, each containing solid or gradient fill swatches. These can be selected for use with various tools and for applying directly to objects. You can also create and store your own swatches as custom colour palettes either for the document or application (system-wide for macOS version).

As well as accessing palettes, you can create global and spot colours, and make colours overprint. Your registration colour can also be customised.

Like the **Colour Panel**, the Swatches Panel has different states depending on the active Persona and on the selected tool. The large colour selectors indicate the currently selected colours.

The **Swatches Panel** also shows **None**, **Black**, **Mid-grey** and **White** swatches, recently used colours and an opacity control. Swatches are organised into colour palettes by category.

In contrast to the **Colour Panel**, use this panel if you'd rather select colours from a pre-defined palette. You can choose colours from a temporary (**Recent**) palette as well as from custom and pre-defined palettes such as **PANTONE®** colours.

Search ├───────────────────
Overprint Colour ├───────────────────
Global Colour ├───────────────────
Registration Colour ├───────────────────
Spot Colour ├───────────────────

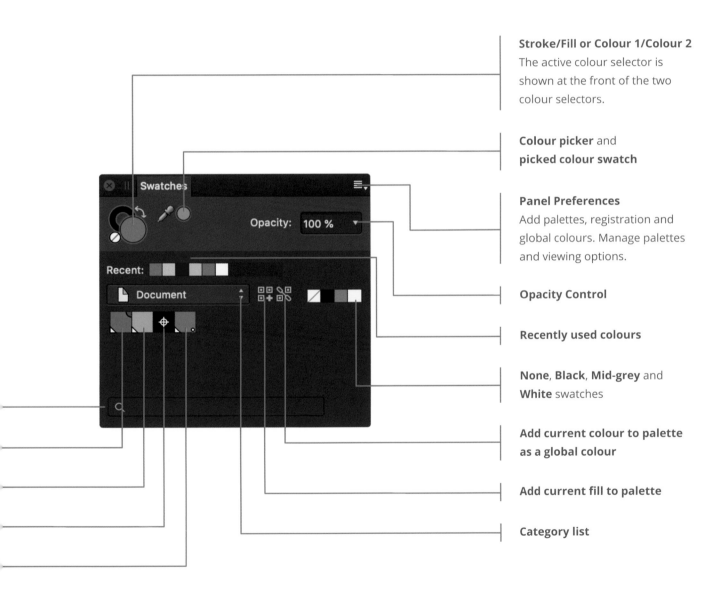

Stroke/Fill or Colour 1/Colour 2
The active colour selector is shown at the front of the two colour selectors.

Colour picker and
picked colour swatch

Panel Preferences
Add palettes, registration and global colours. Manage palettes and viewing options.

Opacity Control

Recently used colours

None, **Black**, **Mid-grey** and **White** swatches

Add current colour to palette as a global colour

Add current fill to palette

Category list

Stroke Panel

This panel allows you to customise the lines, curves and outlines of selected objects. You can use it to modify a stroke's thickness, how it scales, and where it's positioned relative to the object.

Taking things further, you can use this panel along with the **Appearance Panel** (p. 46) to create multi-stroke objects.

> When the Dash Line Style is selected, you will also get options to set the design and the phasing of the dash style.

Width
Drag to change the thickness of the selected line.

Cap
Round, **Butt**, or **Square** cap style to end the contour of a line.

Join
Use a **Round**, **Bevel**, or **Mitre** join style to determine the contour of the corner of the selected object.

Align
Select one of the align buttons to control where the stroke is placed in relation to the object edge.

Order
Draws the stroke either behind or in front of the object. For multi-stroke objects (p. 46), the active stroke can be reordered.

Arrowhead styles (Start and End)
Sets the style for each end of your arrow. Tail (fletching) styles are also available.

Properties
Click to edit the brush used as your **Texture Line Style** via a Brush dialog.

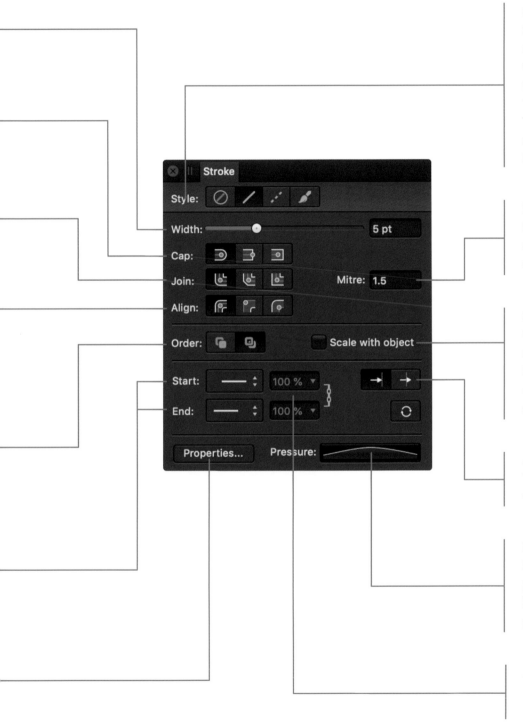

Style

Select a line style button to change how the line is drawn. Choose from **None**, **Solid Line Style**, **Dash Line Style**, and **Texture Line Style**, respectively. The last option applies the currently selected brush in the **Brushes Panel** to the stroke.

Mitre

Sets the length of the extension of **Mitre Joins** to create either sharp or flat corners.

Scale with object

Check to scale the width of the stroke when resizing an object. Uncheck to keep stoke width constant, regardless of object size changes.

Arrowhead positioning

The arrowhead can be placed within the line or extend the line.

Pressure

Displays the current pressure profile applied to a curve or brush stroke. Click to edit the profile and save it for future use.

Arrow scaling

Controls arrowhead scaling in relation to stroke width.

Brushes Panel

The **Brushes Panel** hosts a selection of brush presets which can be selected for use within your design. As well as the pre-designed brushes provided, any custom brushes you design can be saved to your own category. ABR brush files can be imported and will be available in their own separate categories.

Designer Persona and **Pixel Persona** have their own separate set of brushes.

Designer Persona offers stretching or repeating brushes which can be applied to strokes and curves using the **Vector Brush Tool** or **Stroke Panel**.

Switching to Pixel Persona offers you the chance to work with pixel brushes (e.g., spray), which can be used with any of the **Brush tools**, primarily the **Paint Brush Tool**.

Edit
Loads the selected brush in the Brush Editor, allowing it to be customised and saved as a new brush preset.

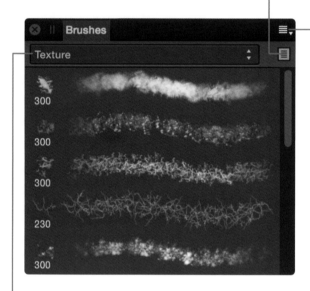

Category Menu
Select a category to load the brushes and thumbnails for that category.

Panel Preferences

Create, rename and delete categories. Import
brushes (including ABR format) and export brushes.

**For vector brushes
(Designer Persona only):**

- **New Solid Brush**
  Creates a basic, solid vector design.

- **New Textured Intensity Brush**
  Creates a design based on the opacity
  values of a raster image.

- **New Textured Image Brush**
  Creates a design based on the colour
  values of a raster image.

**For pixel brushes
(Pixel Persona only):**

- **New Intensity Brush**
  Creates a brush design based on the
  lightness (intensity) of a raster image.

- **New Round Brush**
  Creates a brush design with a soft,
  feathered edge.

- **New Square Brush**
  Creates a brush design with a hard,
  square edge.

- **New Image Brush**
  Creates a brush design based on an
  image.

Layers Panel

The **Layers Panel** controls the stacking order (Z-order) of objects on your page, organises your artboards, layers and objects, and controls layer visibility, locking, opacity and blending. It provides information about a layer, such as its type and whether it has effects applied. In **Export Persona**, this panel is used to create slices from layers and exclude layers from export.

Opacity
Adjusts the transparency of the selected items.

Expand/Collapse
Click to expand the item, revealing nested or grouped content. Click again to collapse.

Item
Created object showing a thumbnail of contents, item name, item type (in parenthesis) and if Layer Effect applied.

Symbol indicators
Coloured line connects a symbol and its contents.

Edit All Layers
Allows selection and editing of objects across all artboards and layers (rather than the current artboard or layer).

Mask Layer
Creates a layer mask to reveal a portion of the layer while the rest of the layer remains hidden.

Adjustments
Adds an adjustment layer to the current layer for tonal and colour correction.

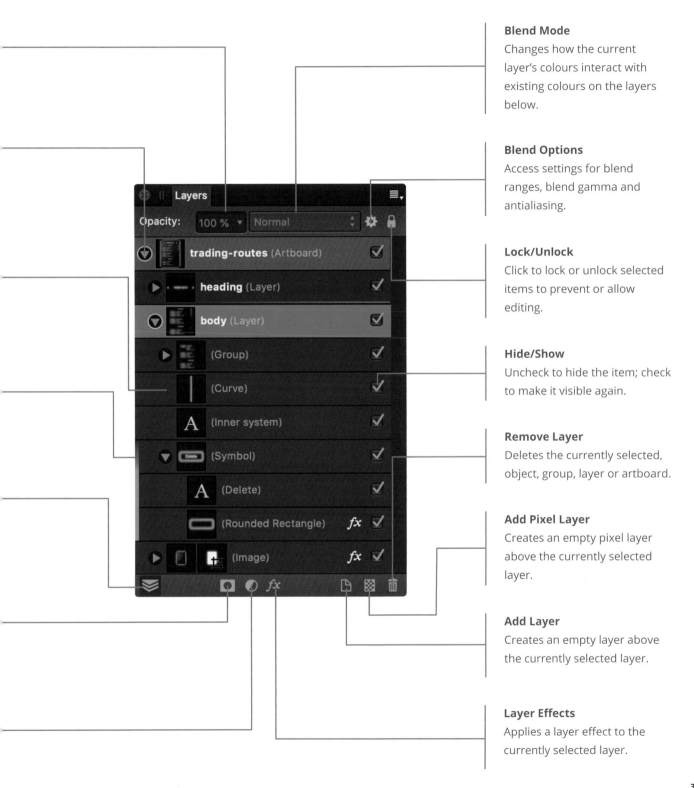

Blend Mode
Changes how the current layer's colours interact with existing colours on the layers below.

Blend Options
Access settings for blend ranges, blend gamma and antialiasing.

Lock/Unlock
Click to lock or unlock selected items to prevent or allow editing.

Hide/Show
Uncheck to hide the item; check to make it visible again.

Remove Layer
Deletes the currently selected, object, group, layer or artboard.

Add Pixel Layer
Creates an empty pixel layer above the currently selected layer.

Add Layer
Creates an empty layer above the currently selected layer.

Layer Effects
Applies a layer effect to the currently selected layer.

Layers

Opacity: 100 % ▼ Normal

trading-routes (Artboard)
heading (Layer)
body (Layer)
(Group)
(Curve)
(Inner system)
(Symbol)
(Delete)
(Rounded Rectangle)
(Image)

Effects Panel

The **Effects Panel** offers copious settings for applying and modifying object effects such as blurs, shadows, glows, and more.

Layer effects can be applied to the currently selected object or entire layer. These effects are also completely non-destructive so you can change them at any time.

Outer Shadow
Adds a shadow behind the object.

Outer Glow
Adds a colour glow that emanates from the outside edges.

Outline
Adds an outline to the object edge.

Bevel/Emboss
Adds various combinations of highlights and shadows.

Gradient Overlay
Applies a linear gradient to object.

Fill Opacity
Alters the stroke and fill opacity of the object, without altering the opacity of the applied layer effect(s).

Gaussian Blur
Blurs the object.

Inner Shadow
Adds a shadow inside the object edge.

Inner Glow
Adds a colour glow that emanates from the inside edges.

3D
Adds lighting to give a 3D appearance.

Colour Overlay
Applies a solid colour to the object.

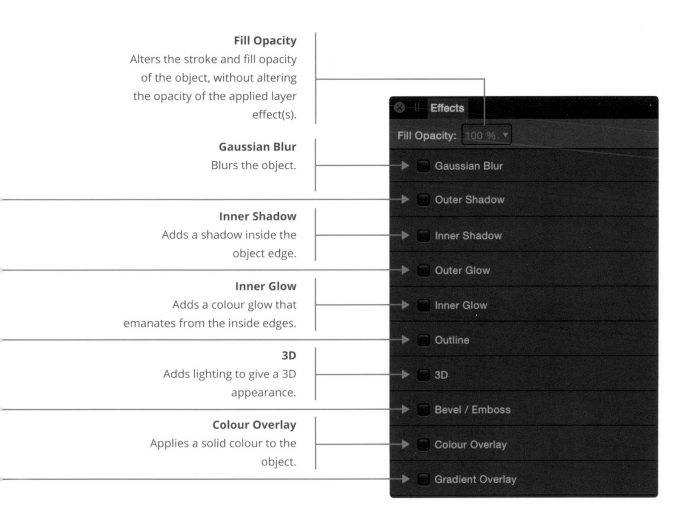

Styles Panel

The **Styles Panel** lets you apply pre-designed styles to your objects. Styles are made up of effects, stroke properties, or text attributes and combinations of these. The Styles Panel lets you apply these properties easily by drag-and-drop or selecting an object and clicking on a panel thumbnail. You can also save any object's style to the Styles Panel for future use.

Panel Preferences
Add, remove and rename style categories. Import and export styles. Save a new style to the category based on the current selection.

Category Menu

Search

Text Styles Panel

A text style is a set of one or more attributes which can be applied to text in bulk. Later, if you choose to modify a text style, any text which uses that style will update to conform to the changes you've made. The **Text Styles Panel** enables you to create, apply and manage text styles within your design.

Current Formatting
Displays the formatting applied to the current selection or caret position. Click arrow to show more details.

Text Style
Entry includes name, preview of its formatting, its predominant type and its shortcut keys.

Create
Launches the Edit Text Style dialog ready for creating a new paragraph, character or group text style, respectively, from scratch.

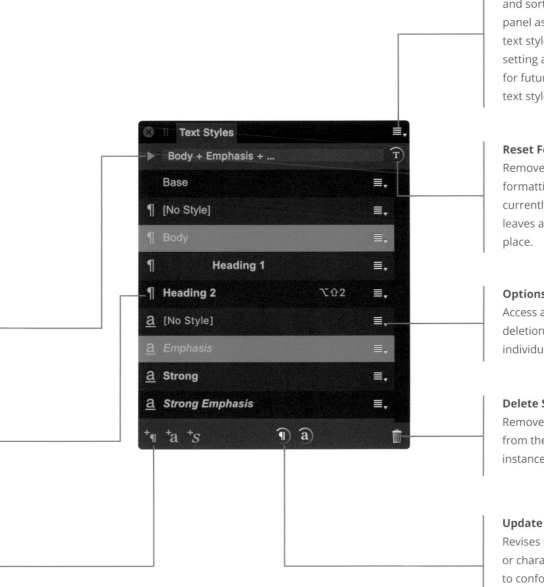

Panel Preferences
Gives you options for displaying and sorting the text styles in the panel as well as detaching all text styles then deleting them, setting a text style as a default for future text and importing text styles.

Reset Formatting
Removes overrides and local formatting applied to the currently selected text but leaves applied text styles in place.

Options menu
Access application, creation, deletion and editing options for individual text styles.

Delete Style
Removes the selected text style from the document and any instances of its application.

Update
Revises the current paragraph or character style, respectively, to conform to the local formatting of the selected text.

Transform Panel

The **Transform Panel** allows you to design with the utmost precision by controlling the horizontal (X) and vertical (Y) position of an object on your page or artboard, as well as its overall width (W) and height (H). Rotate and shear options complete the panel. All transforms are carried out in relation to a defined anchor point—corner, edge midpoint or centre.

X—Horizontal position:
Adjusts the horizontal position of the object (layer) in relation to the selected anchor point.

Y—Vertical position:
Adjusts the vertical position of the object (layer) in relation to the selected anchor point.

Anchor point selector:
Transforms are carried out from the selected anchor point. Click on an anchor point to select.

R—Rotation:
Rotates the object (layer) by a specified number of degrees in relation to the selected anchor point.

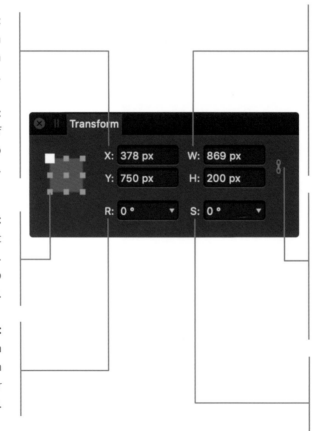

W—Width: Adjusts the object (layer) width in relation to the selected anchor point.

H—Height: Adjusts the object (layer) height in relation to the selected anchor point.

Link: When enabled, width and height are adjusted in proportion to each other, maintaining the current aspect ratio. When deselected, they can be adjusted independently.

S—Shear: Shears the object (layer) by a specified number of degrees in relation to the selected anchor point.

History Panel

The **History Panel** tracks changes and shows each state as a labelled entry in a list, allowing you to return to earlier points in time. The oldest state is the topmost in the list, and when edits are made, new states are added to the bottom of the list. If you click on an earlier state and then make a change, you can still reinstate later states.

A document's history can be saved along with the document too by enabling **Save History With Document** in the **File Menu**, so earlier edits can be returned to even if the document is closed and reopened.

> Unless you choose to save the document's history, the undo states listed in the **History Panel** are cleared when the document is closed.

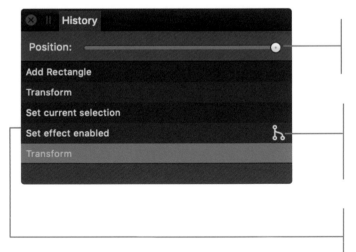

Position—Drag the slider left to undo a change, right to redo a change.

Cycle futures—Click to reinstate your 'lost' redo history after making an edit at a state in your undo history.

State—gives a brief description of the edit made to the document. Click a state to jump to that edit

Navigator Panel

This panel is unique as its use has no effect on your design at all. Instead, it allows you to pan and zoom around your Document View and set up specific **View Points** so you can jump, and zoom, to particular areas of your project in an instant.

Panel Preferences
Displays the **View Point Menu** and **Settings**.

Zoom
Use the slider, buttons or the percentage display to zoom in or out.

View Rectangle
Pan around your design by dragging the view rectangle around in the panel. The main view displays the areas enclosed in the rectangle.

View Point Menu
Select a named View Point to jump and zoom to its preset position in the Document View.

View Point Settings
Add, remove and rename view points.

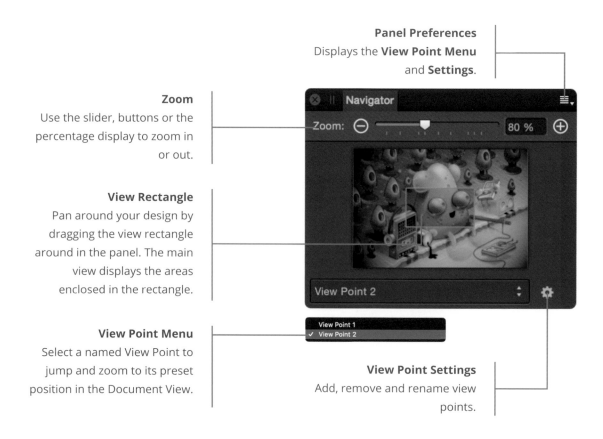

Symbols Panel

The **Symbols Panel** lets you create and store symbols from selected objects, groups or layers in your document.

Once symbols are created within the panel they can be dragged onto the page or an artboard multiple times. These placed symbol instances are linked and, due to synchronisation, any edit made to an individual symbol instance will be applied across all symbol instances automatically.

Detach
Converts selected symbol instances back into standard objects.

Create
Creates a new symbol based on the objects, groups and layers currently selected in the document.

Symbols
Displayed as a thumbnail with name. Symbols can be renamed and deleted by ctrl-clicking (Mac) or right-clicking (Win) a symbol thumbnail.

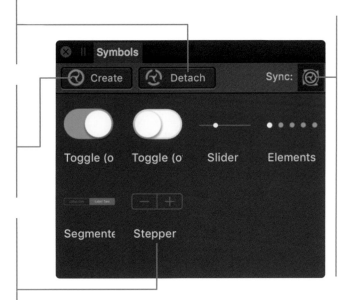

Sync
When activated, all symbol instances update to match a change made to one instance. When deactivated, symbol instances can be changed without affecting other symbol instances. If synchronisation is reactivated, attributes which were not changed during the unsynchronised period are still linked.

45

Appearance Panel

The **Appearance Panel** lets you apply multiple strokes and/or fills to any selected object. With drag-and-drop ordering and control of stroke widths and per stroke/fill blending, you can achieve striking creative effects.

Stroke
The stroke entry showing the stroke colour, width and blend mode.

Active stroke and fill
The spot indicates the stroke and fill that will be affected by Stroke and Colour Panel editing.

Fill
The fill entry showing the fill colour and blend mode.

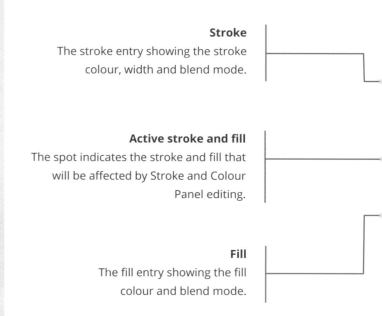

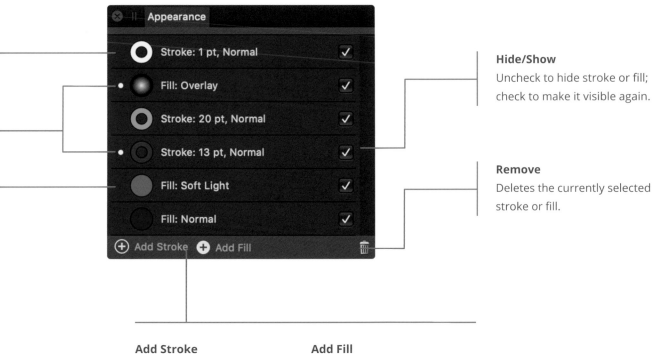

Hide/Show
Uncheck to hide stroke or fill; check to make it visible again.

Remove
Deletes the currently selected stroke or fill.

Add Stroke
Creates a new active stroke above the current active stroke.

Add Fill
Creates a new active fill above the current active fill.

Assets Panel

Assets are archived objects (or group of objects) which can be accessed from any open Affinity Designer document. They are conveniently stored in the **Assets Panel**.

Assets are created by selecting an object, group or layer (or multiples of these) and then from a subcategory's options menu, selecting **Add from Selection**.

Assets are added to a document by simply dragging it from the **Assets Panel** onto an artboard or page.

Asset categories and subcategories can be created at any time to help you organise your assets. They are then listed in the pop-up Category Menu at the top of the Assets Panel. Each category can accommodate an unlimited number of subcategories.

Assets in the panel can be displayed as thumbnails in a grid (default) or as a named list. Tooltips display the name of an asset.

Category Menu
Select a category to load assets within subcategories.

Subcategory
Click to expand to reveal hosted assets. Click again to collapse.

Search

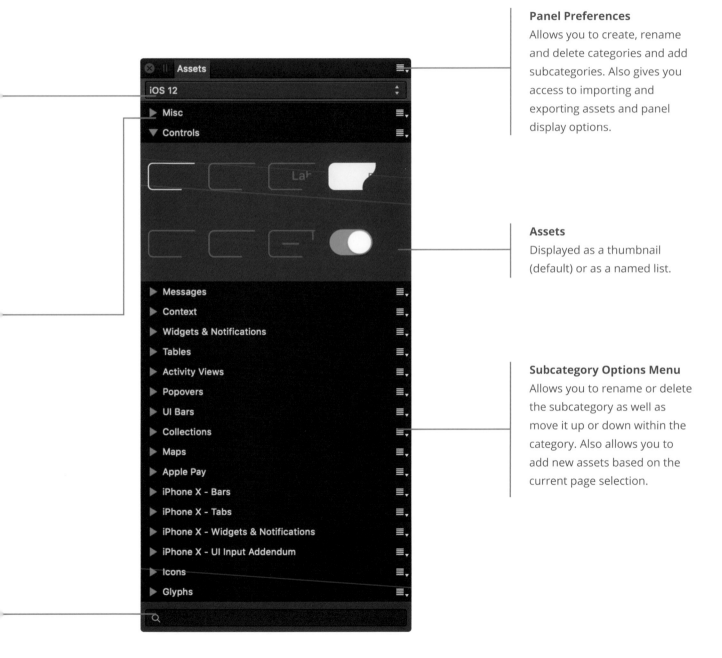

Panel Preferences
Allows you to create, rename and delete categories and add subcategories. Also gives you access to importing and exporting assets and panel display options.

Assets
Displayed as a thumbnail (default) or as a named list.

Subcategory Options Menu
Allows you to rename or delete the subcategory as well as move it up or down within the category. Also allows you to add new assets based on the current page selection.

Constraints Panel

The **Constraints Panel** enables you to anchor a child object to a particular position within its parent object as well as preventing a child object from being scaled when its parent is resized. Vertical and horizontal scaling can be controlled independently and anchoring can be applied to top, bottom, right or left of the child object.

Child objects can be scaled and anchored in different ways. This allows you to present designs in different layouts quickly and easily. The feature is perfect for designing UI and web mockups. By controlling selectively which objects will/won't be scaled and anchored, your design will always respond correctly to scaling.

Constraints only work in parent–child object relationships. The child object's scaling and anchoring is always in relation to the parent object (i.e. its container). Constraining is exclusively set by clicking to activate elements on the Constraints Panel.

Anchor
Controlled by the lines extending from the inner square to the outer square. When displayed as a grey dashed line, the object is not anchored in that direction. When displayed as a white solid line, the object is anchored in that direction.

Lock
Child objects scale as their parents resize. If the parent's aspect ratio changes, the object's aspect ratio is maintained but its scaling depends on the **Fit** setting.

Min Fit
When the parent object is resized disproportionately, the child object may scale so it always fits within its parent object (if unanchored).

Inner Square/Outer Square

The inner grey square represents the selected, child object. The outer square represents a parent layer (or container).

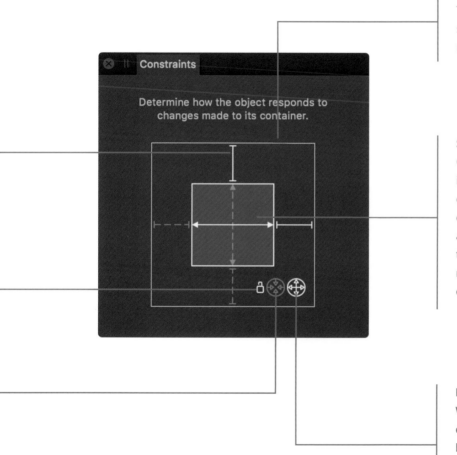

Scale

Controlled by the arrows contained within the inner square. When displayed as a grey dashed arrow, the object will not scale in that direction. When displayed as a white solid arrow, the object will scale in that direction. If the arrow displays as white and broken, this means the object is forced to scale in that direction because of anchoring.

Max Fit

When the parent object is resized disproportionately, the child object may scale but it will be allowed to be bigger than its scaled parent object, potentially clipping content from view.

Glyph Browser

The Glyph Browser lets you navigate glyphs or Unicode characters available with your currently installed fonts. By first choosing a font or using the Search option, you can apply a specific glyph to a selected character (or at an insertion point) by double-clicking.

Panel Preferences
Sorts glyphs by glyph or Unicode value, and sets glyph display size.

Lock Fonts and Traits
When unlocked, the font shown in the panel changes with the selected text's font; when locked, the font selected in the panel remains unchanged.

Character set
Select a glyph or Unicode character set, e.g. Cyrillic.

Search

Recent Glyphs

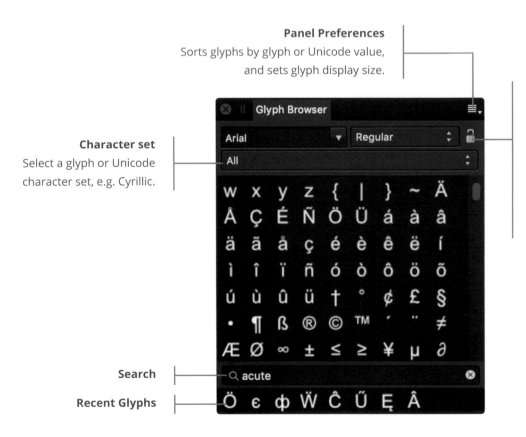

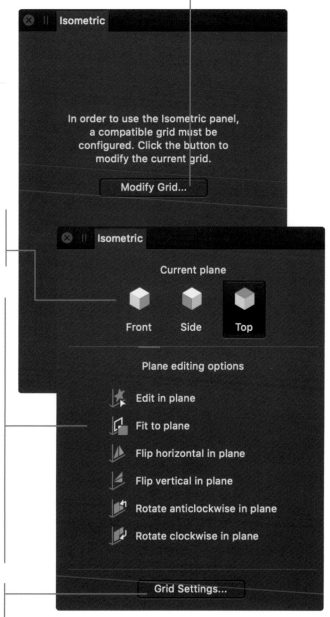

Modify Grid

Creates a new isometric grid or replaces any grid set up previously, then switches the panel to another view to allow plane switching and planar transformation of selected objects.

Isometric Panel

The panel configures a grid ready for isometric drawing onto any one of three planes—Front, Side and Top. With snapping enabled, objects can be transformed directly onto the active plane with precision and switched to other planes as needed.

Current plane
Select from **Front**, **Side** and **Top** to change the grid's plane.

Plane editing options—choose an option to transform an object onto or within a plane.

- **Edit in plane**—any object created is automatically fitted to the currently active plane.

- **Fit to plane**—fits either a selected two-dimensional object or object on another plane to the currently active plane.

- **Flip horizontal (vertical) in plane**—flips the selected object horizontally (or vertically) within the currently active plane.

- **Rotate anticlockwise (clockwise) in plane**—rotates the selected object 90° anticlockwise (or clockwise) within the currently active plane.

Grid Settings
Accesses the **Grid and Axis Manager** for set up of grid spacing and additional snapping/constraining axes.

Character Panel

The **Character Panel** allows you to apply local formatting to individual letters, words, sentences and paragraphs as well as entire stories.

Font
Sets the typeface for the selected text.

Font Style
Controls which typeface style is applied to the selected text.

Collection
Filters the list of available fonts in the **Font** pop-up menu.

Font Size
Controls the point size of characters.

Text Style
Allows a character text style to be applied to selected text.

Decorations
Applies underline, strikethrough or outline attributes with colour options.

Kerning
Controls the distance between two characters. **Auto** will give default kerning. Positive values give expanded kerning, negative values give condensed kerning.

Tracking
Controls the spacing between characters throughout a word.

Baseline
Controls the position of the bottom of text characters. Increasing the value lowers the baseline, decreasing the value raises the baseline.

Leading Override
Applies local override to selected text to increase the leading with regard to the paragraph's leading.

Font colour
Sets the colour of the text.

Background colour
Sets the colour applied behind the selected text (i.e., creating a highlight effect).

Shear
Controls the extent of text slant. Positive values will tilt text to the left, negative values will tilt text to the right.

Horizontal Scale
Stretches the characters and spacing with regard to point size.

Vertical Scale
Stretches the characters with regard to point size.

Super/Subscript
Applies either a superscript or subscript attribute.

Typography
Depending on your font, you can apply various typographic options to enhance your characters beyond their standard attributes. Access OpenType font features like ligatures, alternates, stylistic sets and more.

Language
Sets the languages for the dictionary (for spell checking), hyphenation and typography.

Optical Alignment
Controls the alignment of dashes, punctuation or any character you choose at the start of paragraphs.

Paragraph Panel

The **Paragraph Panel** gives you full control over paragraph-level formatting options. Paragraph formatting is applied to the entire paragraph in which selected text is located or to a paragraph in which the caret is located.

Alignment
Select from **Left**, **Centre**, **Right**, **Justify Left**, **Justify Centre**, **Justify Right** or **Justify All** (Force-Justified). The Justify options define what happens to the final sentence.

Text Style
Applies the selected paragraph text style.

First Line Indent
Controls the indent applied to the first line of the paragraph.

Paragraph Leading
Controls the distance between text baselines (vertical gap between lines) within the paragraph.

Space Above/Below Management
Controls how space above/below settings work together.

Tab Stops
Create, position and align paragraph tab stops.

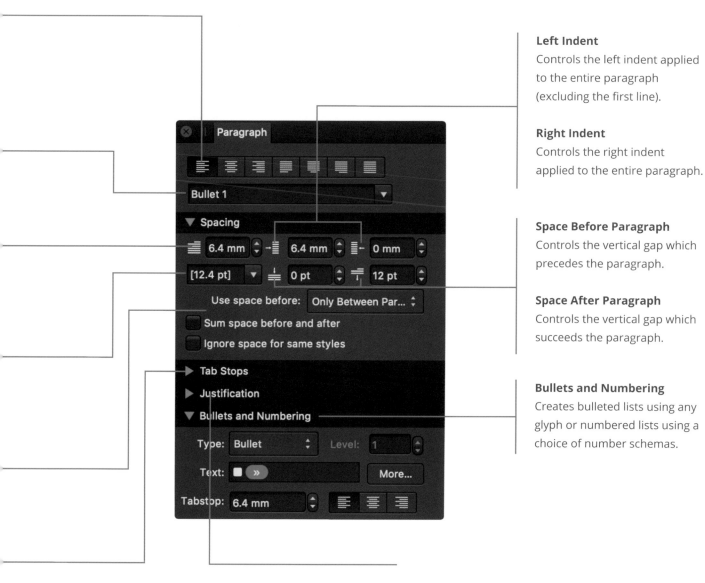

Left Indent
Controls the left indent applied to the entire paragraph (excluding the first line).

Right Indent
Controls the right indent applied to the entire paragraph.

Space Before Paragraph
Controls the vertical gap which precedes the paragraph.

Space After Paragraph
Controls the vertical gap which succeeds the paragraph.

Bullets and Numbering
Creates bulleted lists using any glyph or numbered lists using a choice of number schemas.

Justification
For justified paragraphs, you can control letter and word spacing.

Slices Panel

The **Slices Panel** gives you precise control over each export area (slice) in your document, defining where it will be exported and to what file format, or multiple formats, and what size(s). The Slices Panel works in combination with the Export Options Panel.

Batch builder
Applies a preset export setup to the selected slice(s), including **Builder** option.

Export preset
Applies a preset export setup to the selected slice(s).

Item
Indicates whether the slice is based on the document, a drawn slice or a layer as well as showing the slice export name and whether there are export issues to resolve.

Export Setup
Specifies the **Path** and **Builder** assigned to the formats to be exported. Allows you to add multiple file formats, each with multiple sizes. Use the plus icon to add a new format or size. Use the cross icon to delete the selected format or size.

Delete Selected Slice

Continuous
Slices are re-exported automatically to the previously 'exported to' folder, if the content within the slice changes.

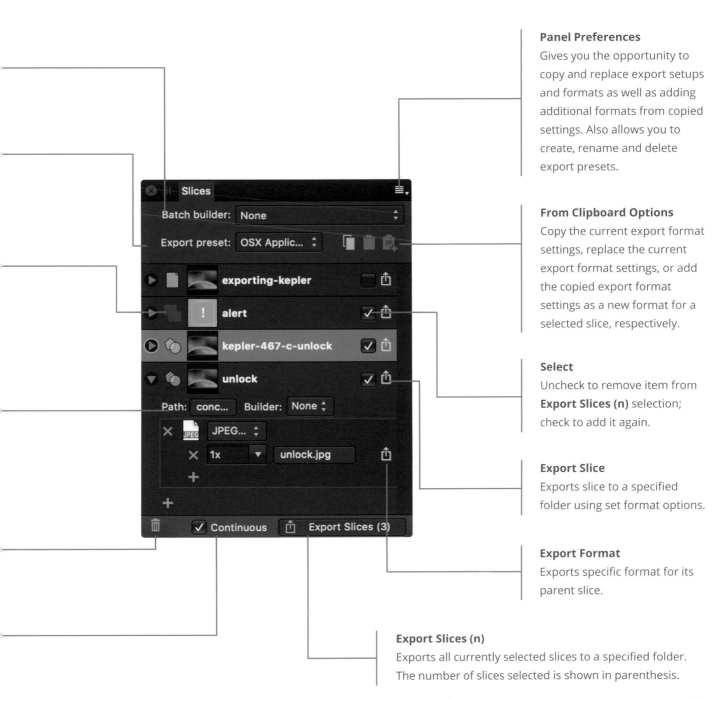

Panel Preferences
Gives you the opportunity to copy and replace export setups and formats as well as adding additional formats from copied settings. Also allows you to create, rename and delete export presets.

From Clipboard Options
Copy the current export format settings, replace the current export format settings, or add the copied export format settings as a new format for a selected slice, respectively.

Select
Uncheck to remove item from **Export Slices (n)** selection; check to add it again.

Export Slice
Exports slice to a specified folder using set format options.

Export Format
Exports specific format for its parent slice.

Export Slices (n)
Exports all currently selected slices to a specified folder. The number of slices selected is shown in parenthesis.

Export Options Panel

The **Export Options Panel** is used to define the settings for an exported file. These settings are unique to each file format and will update to match the **File format** selected.

Common export options:

- **Resampler**—select which resampling method is used when exporting a file at a different size to the design's original size.

- **Pixel format**—sets the colour mode for the exported image.

- **Matte**—sets the background colour for the exported image.

- **Quality**—sets the resulting quality of the exported image. Higher quality may result in significantly larger file sizes.

- **ICC Profile**—by default, this is set to the ICC profile of the document. However, the document's ICC profile can be overwritten for the exported file.

- **Rasterise**—select an option for rasterising design elements which are unsupported by the file format.

Selected PDF export options:

- **Include layers**—when selected, layer information is retained in the PDF output.

- **Include printer marks**—when selected, the PDF output will show printer marks around the page edge. All printer marks are added by default.

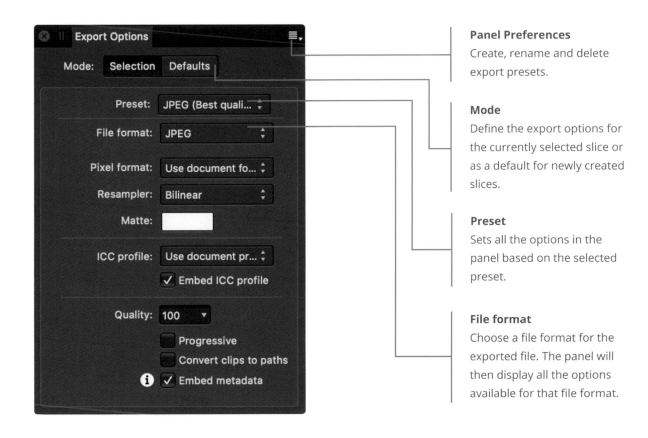

Panel Preferences
Create, rename and delete export presets.

Mode
Define the export options for the currently selected slice or as a default for newly created slices.

Preset
Sets all the options in the panel based on the selected preset.

File format
Choose a file format for the exported file. The panel will then display all the options available for that file format.

Snapshots Panel

Snapshots let you define a stage in your session from which you can restore. You might do this in advance of carrying out more complex operations where you might need to restore back to a previous point in time (if things don't go to plan!).

Once a snapshot has been created, it can become the starting point of a new document.

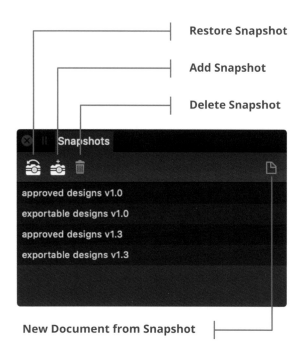

Restore Snapshot

Add Snapshot

Delete Snapshot

New Document from Snapshot

Export Status
A full, white icon indicates an item will be exported. A white and grey icon indicates a parent with a child which will be exported. If no icon appears, the item will not be exported.

Edit All Layers
Allows selection of objects across all artboards and layers (rather than the current layer).

Layers Panel (Export Persona)

Export Persona is used exclusively for exporting your design to industry-standard image file formats and therefore hosts a different version of the **Layers Panel**. This version allows you to create slices from document layers and hide specific layers from export. The Layers Panel works in combination with the Slices Panel.

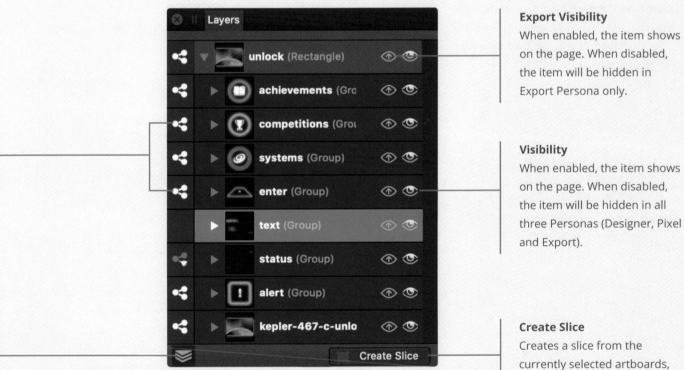

Export Visibility
When enabled, the item shows on the page. When disabled, the item will be hidden in Export Persona only.

Visibility
When enabled, the item shows on the page. When disabled, the item will be hidden in all three Personas (Designer, Pixel and Export).

Create Slice
Creates a slice from the currently selected artboards, layers, groups and objects.

CUSTOMISING YOUR WORKSPACE

Not everyone likes to work in the same way so with this in mind there are options in Affinity Designer that allow you to customise your workspace to best facilitate your workflow.

User Interface Preferences

Tweak the UI to your taste by updating your **Preferences**. Access via **Affinity Designer > Preferences** (Mac) or **Edit > Preferences** (Win) and choose **User Interface** to get the following customisable options:

- **Background Grey Level**—controls the greyscale level of the page background.

- **Artboard Background Grey Level**—controls the greyscale level of the pasteboard surrounding artboard(s).

- **UI Gamma**—adjusts the contrast of the user interface.

- **Font UI Size**—optionally increase the font size of UI text.

- **UI Style**—choose between a dark, light or the default OS user interface (Mac only).

- **Tooltip Delay**—set the length of time before a tooltip appears when hovering over a UI element.

- **Decimal Places for Unit Types**—controls the number of decimal places allowable for each document measurement unit and degree readouts.

- **Automatically lock background layer on import**—locks (or keeps unlocked) an imported image as a background layer.

- **Show Lines in points**—choose whether line width (thickness) displays in points or in the document's measurement units.

- **Show Text in points**—choose whether text is expressed in points or in the document's measurement units.

- **Show brush previews**—choose whether the brush cursor display a preview of pixels to be placed (Pixel Persona only).

- **Always show brush crosshair**—overlays a crosshair over the brush cursor for better targeting.

- **Monochromatic Iconography**—makes icons display in greyscale.

- **Auto-scroll to show Selection in Layers Panel**— As you select an object, the panel scrolls to show its layer entry.

- **Enable touch bar support** – Allows you to utilise the Touch bar on Apple MacBook Pro computers.

Workspace Modes (Mac only)

In the Mac version of Affinity, you can choose from two different workspace modes: **Normal** and **Separated** mode. You can change to either workspace mode from the **Window Menu**.

By default Affinity Designer will run in **Normal** (single window) mode. This means that all panels and view will be neatly docked together. **Separated mode** has no containing frame, the panels (or panel groups) and toolbars are floating, and each open document has its own view (although you can still create groups).

> When in full screen view, you cannot switch between workspace modes.

Customising your Studio panels

The way your **Studio panels** are set out will depend on what **Persona** you are working in. However, for each Persona you can still customise your workspace to fit your workflow.

If you wish to customise each Persona workspace, you can do so in the following ways:

To hide/show a panel:
- From the **View Menu**, click the panel name on the **Studio** flyout. To show again, click the panel name again.

To hide/show all panels:
- From the **View Menu**, click **Toggle UI** (Tab).

To collapse a panel group:
- Double-click on the active panel label.

To expand a panel group:
- Click on the label of the panel that you want to view.

To move a panel:
- Drag the panel label to its new position, either as a free floating panel or as an item in an existing panel group.

To resize a panel:
- Drag any corner of a panel.

To dock a panel:
- Drag the panel label to a panel group.
- Drag the panel label to an area of the studio. A highlight indicates where the panel can be docked.

To move a panel group:
- Drag the panel group to a new position, either as a free floating panel or as an item in an existing panel group.

To dock a panel group:
- Drag the panel group to another panel group.
- Drag the panel group to an area of the studio. A highlight indicates where the panel group can be docked.

To show/hide the left or right Studio (Mac only):
- From the **View** menu, click **Show Left Studio** or **Show Right Studio**.

To reset the Persona's workspace:
- Select the Persona that you want to reset the workspace for and from the **View Menu**, select **Studio > Reset Studio**.

Customising the Tools Panel

The **Tools Panel** can be docked or floating, or shown or hidden, depending on your preference. You can customise the panel to fit your individual way of working by removing tools and adding tools.

To dock/undock the Tools Panel:
- From the **View Menu**, select **Dock Tools**.

To show/hide the Tools Panel:
- From the **View Menu**, select **Show Tools**.

To remove or add a tool:
1. From the **View Menu**, select **Customise Tools**.
2. Drag a tool icon from the **Tools Panel** into the flyout, or vice versa.
3. Click **Close**.

To reset the Tools Panel:
- From the **View Menu**, select **Customise Tools**, then from the the flyout, click **Reset**.

To set the number of columns on the Tools Panel:
1. From the **View Menu**, select **Customise Tools**.
2. From the flyout, select from the **Number of Columns** pop-up menu.

Customising the Toolbar

The Toolbar organises some of the most commonly used commands and functions in each Persona to keep them at your fingertips. You can customise your Toolbar in the following ways:

To show/hide tool group labels on the Toolbar:
1. Choose **View > Customise Toolbar**.
2. From the dialog's **Show** pop-up menu, select **Icon Only** or **Icon and Text**.

To hide/show the Toolbar:
- Choose **View > Show Toolbar**.

To customise the Toolbar:
1. Choose **View > Customise Toolbar**.
2. Drag the items from the dialog to the **Toolbar**.
3. Remove items by dragging them off the **Toolbar** and onto your Document View.

To reset the Toolbar:
1. Choose **View > Customise Toolbar**.
2. Drag the default set item to the **Toolbar**. This will revert the Toolbar back to its original settings.

Your workspace customisation will be remembered between sessions.

KEYBOARD SHORTCUTS

You can quickly access common tools and commands using your keyboard. Many of the shortcuts are the same as those that you use in other apps.

You'll find many of the shortcuts listed next to menu items.

Customising keyboard shortcuts

Learning the keyboard shortcuts in Affinity Designer will speed up your productivity, but you may want to customise shortcuts on an application-wide or on a per-Persona basis. You can also save your customised shortcuts to a file that can be shared with other users or backed up for safe keeping. Go to **Affinity Designer > Preferences** (Mac) or **Edit > Preferences** (Win) and choose **Keyboard Shortcuts** to customise your shortcuts.

> Exported keyboard shortcut files can only be used on the same platform as they were created. A keyboard shortcut file exported from Affinity Designer on a Mac cannot be imported into Affinity Designer for Windows, and vice versa. The extension for the keyboard shortcut file is *.affshortcuts* on a Mac and *.afshort* on Windows.

Available settings are as follows:

- **Persona**—The pop-up menu sets the Persona for shortcut customisation.

- **UI Element**—The pop-up menu displays the menus, commands and operations for the currently selected Persona. A **Miscellaneous** category groups shortcuts for commonly performed operations and lets you switch on/off panels via shortcuts.

- **Apply to all**—If checked, the shortcut applied to a UI element is shared across every Persona. If unchecked, you can uniquely assign a custom shortcut to work just within the currently selected Persona in the initial Persona pop-up menu.

A warning triangle shows if a shortcut has already been assigned to another command. The tooltip will inform you which command.

An arrow symbol indicates that the shortcut is shared between several tools. Hover over the symbol to see the names of the other tools.

To delete a shortcut, click the cross icon at the end of the shortcut entry.

- **Ignore Modifier**—Lets you create shortcuts using a single letter designation instead of using keyboard modifiers.

- **Reset**—All customised shortcuts are reset back to default.

- **Clear All Shortcuts**—All default and customised shortcuts are removed.

- **Load**—Loads a previously saved shortcuts file. This will overwrite your current keyboard shortcut allocations.

- **Save**—Saves the current set of shortcuts to a file for sharing or backup.

RESETTING YOUR WORKSPACE

Now you have a good understanding of the Affinity Designer user interface it's important to ensure your workspace is reset to the default 'factory-supplied' layout before commencing the projects in this book.

It may be that you've inadvertently customised, repositioned or switched off toolbars or panels previously. By resetting, the project's written instructions will more closely match your own experience.

Reset the Toolbar

On the **View Menu**, select **Customise Toolbar**.
Drag the default set of tools at the bottom of the dialog over the Toolbar spanning the top of your workspace and release.

Reset the Tools Panel

On the **View Menu**, select **Customise Tools**.
Click **Reset** in the dialog.

Reset Studio Panels

On the **View Menu**, select **Studio > Reset Studio**.
This will need to be done for each Persona workspace.

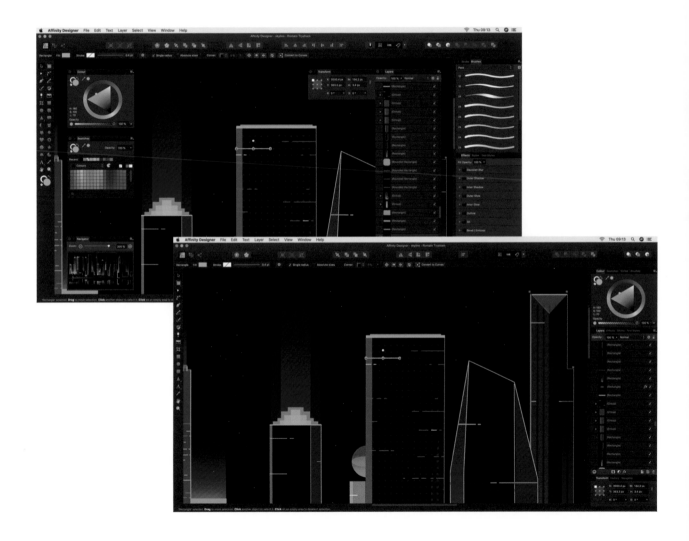

CHAPTER 2

Core Skills

This chapter teaches you the core skills you will need to get the very best out of the upcoming projects in chapters 3 and 4. Not all projects will use every core skill, but trying out each one in turn will give you a better grounding in Affinity Designer.

You can get all the resources you need for this chapter from **https://affin.co/coreskills**

ARTBOARDS

Artboards are design areas within which you can formulate your designs. You can set up separate documents for print, web or app design, each containing multiple artboards for various deliverables.

- For **print delivery** with hi-res professional CMYK printing in mind, deliverables would include: letterhead paper, envelopes, business cards, poster, leaflets, compliment slips.

- For **Web/social media delivery** for designing pixel-accurate web graphics, deliverables would include: web logo, web banners, toolbars, panels, icons, buttons.

- For **app delivery** for different physical mobile devices or tablets, deliverables would include: app icons, standard icons, buttons.

Key aspects

Here are some key aspects of artboards in Affinity Designer:

Create variations of a core design in different artboards

View all artboards at the same time

Use symbols across artboards for maximum productivity

Apply global colours across designs

Print and export individual or all artboards

Creating artboards

An initial artboard can be created at Document Setup, with additional artboards being added as required at any time.

1 Select **File > New**.

2 Choose your document **Type**, then a **Page Preset**.

3 Check **Create artboard**.

4 Click **OK**. Your artboard is placed centrally in your Document View.

5 Click the layer entry and rename it to be *Letterhead*.

Custom-sized artboards

- With the **Artboard Tool**, drag on the pasteboard to create an artboard of your chosen size

The artboard is added above your initial artboard in the Layers Panel.

On the **Layers Panel**, each artboard is created as its own layer; each artboard can be selected, renamed, hidden, or exported independently of other artboards.

> For UI design, a device-specific artboard can be chosen at Document Setup. Additional device artboards can be added via the Artboard tool's context toolbar.

Viewing artboards

Good viewing control is essential when working with numerous artboards.

- Zoom to selected artboard: **View > Zoom to Selection** or double-click on the artboard's layer thumbnail.

- Zoom to all artboards: **View > Zoom to Fit**.

Use **View > Zoom > Zoom to..** options for Windows.

Resizing artboards

- To resize, select the artboard and drag
  inwards or outwards from any handle.
  Resizing with the shift key (⇧) pressed,
  maintains the aspect ratio of the artboard.

Use Width (**W**) and Height (**H**) on the **Transform
Panel** afterwards to set the artboard size
precisely if needed.

> Artboard presets (if available) are always advisable as
> arbitrarily resized artboards may not reflect recognized
> document setups.

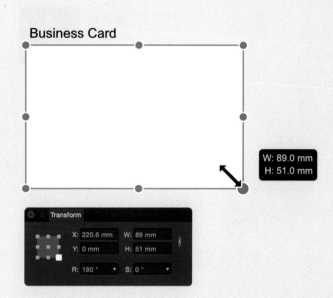

Repositioning artboards

Any artboard is treated like an object. This lets you
move a selected artboard around your Document
View and arrange artboards into groupings or a
sequential order.

Ordering may be important for artboards intended
for print artwork where a consecutive 'page' order
needs to be presented. Artboards can be reordered
by dragging in the **Layers Panel** into page number
order (lowest artboard in stack is the first page).
Exporting the document to PDF will then produce a
multi-page document.

Artboard example (Pro Print)

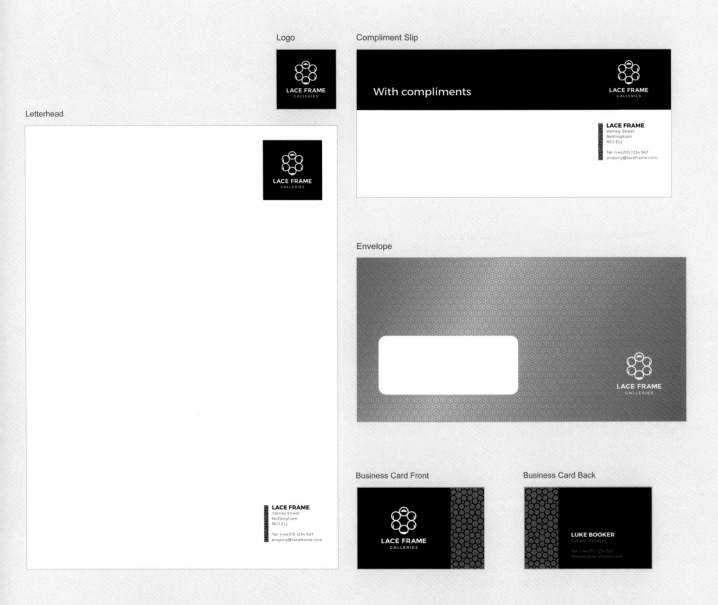

Logo

Compliment Slip

With compliments

LACE FRAME
Varney Street
Nottingham
NG1 ELL

Tel: (+44)115 1234 567
enquiry@laceframe.com

Letterhead

LACE FRAME
Varney Street
Nottingham
NG1 ELL

Tel: (+44)115 1234 567
enquiry@laceframe.com

Envelope

Business Card Front

Business Card Back

LUKE BOOKER
Gallery Manager

Tel: (+44)115 1234 567
lbooker@laceframe.com

Panel   Back   Front

Verso   Middle   Recto

OBJECTS

Opacity

As well as opacity being a property of colour, a drawn object can have opacity applied to it as well. When used in projects, opacity can be used to soften objects or subtly show underlying objects, often being used along with blur effects for diffuse shadowing.

The **Opacity** setting on the Colour Panel is the opacity of a chosen colour—either an object's Stroke or Fill. Whereas, the **Opacity** setting on the Layers Panel is that of the entire object. In fact, you can reduce the opacity of an object's Fill and Stroke separately and in addition to applying an overall opacity to the object.

Setting object opacity

- On the **Layers Panel**, expand the Objects - Opacity artboard, then the Head layer and change the **Opacity** values of head components.

Use the number keys on your keyboard to quickly set the overall opacity for your object (e.g., *4 = 40%* opacity, *4 and 3 = 43%* opacity).

Remember that layers and groups can also have their opacity adjusted.

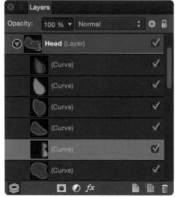

Opacity is the opposite of transparency, i.e. 100% opacity is the same as 0% transparency (and vice versa).

Multiply

Screen

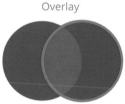

Overlay

Blend modes

Blend modes control how overlapping colours interact with each other to produce different and creative results. They are used in two ways—firstly, when applied to an object overlapping another, and secondly, when applied as part of an effect to an object.

Despite up to 30 blend modes being available, most designers typically only use several blend modes repeatedly, the rest being used on a much more infrequent basis. The most frequently used blend modes are **Multiply**, **Screen** and **Overlay**.

Multiply produces a darkening effect that is perfect for strengthening shadows, such as those as cast from our character's arm.

When the effect is applied to the shape under the arm, it realistically darkens the colour of the body shape underneath.

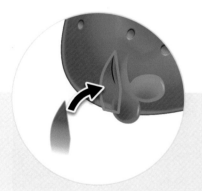

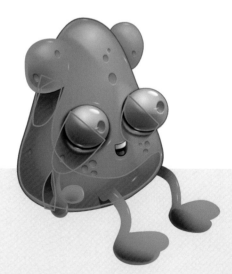

Let's experiment with Multiply and other blend modes.

Setting blend mode (on object)

1. On the **Layers Panel**, expand the Objects - Blend modes artboard, then the Fisherman layer and Body group and then select Arm Shadow.

2. Select *Multiply* or any other blend mode from the blend mode pop-up menu (originally listed as *Normal*).

Setting blend mode (as part of an effect)

1. On the **Layers Panel**, expand the Eyes group and Eye 1 group and then select Eyeball.

2. Click the **Layer Effects** icon on the Eyeball entry.

3. In the **Layer Effects** dialog, select **Inner Glow** and from the **Blend mode** pop-up menu, choose *Multiply*. Experiment with other blend modes as desired.

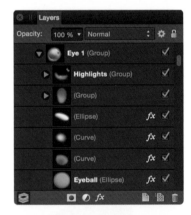

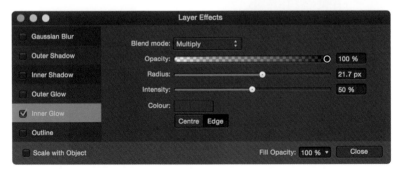

Arranging

Objects on the page occupy a set position in the document—the very front or back, or at a position in between. This isn't the object's position on the X or Y axis, but its position on the Z axis (called the z-order) in relation to all other objects. This z-order is dictated by how objects are positioned in the Layers Panel.

In the example, the blue object at the foreground is positioned at the top of the layer stack (Front), while the yellow object it the furthest back (Back).

> Ordering is important when your design uses overlapping objects!

Creating objects in front of others

1   On the **Layers Panel**, expand the Objects - Arranging artboard and select the Arranging layer.

2   With the **Triangle Tool** (**Tools Panel**), draw a triangle which overlaps the top, blue triangle. Expand the Arranging layer to see the new triangle has been placed at the top of the layer stack by default.

3   In the **Layers Panel**, select the yellow Back triangle and draw another overlapping triangle. This time it is drawn between the yellow and red triangles rather than at the top of the stack.

Changing object order

You may need to reorder an object as part of a redesign.
It can be placed behind or in front of an adjacent object,
or at the back or immediate front.

1 Select the turquoise triangle.

2 Do one of the following:

- On the **Toolbar**, click **Back One**, **Forward One**,
  Move to Back or **Move to Front**.

- Drag the triangle's layer entry in the **Layers
  Panel** up or down to a new position in the layer
  stack.

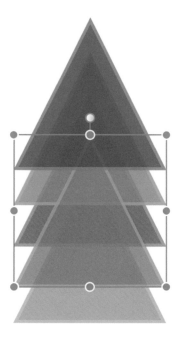

Targeting

Affinity Designer offers some alternative options to target where a new object is to be placed in your layer stack—below the object, always at the top of the layer stack or inside the selection (clipping), respectively.

Changing target order:

1   Expand the **Targeting** layer and select the red triangle.

2   On the **Toolbar**, select **Insert inside the selection**.

> The **Insert inside the selection** option is useful for ensuring new objects are always **clipped** inside (contained within) a parent object.

3   Draw an 'overlapping' circle using the **Ellipse Tool** (M).

4   Repeat the above steps but select either **Insert behind the selection** or **Insert at the top of the layer** to see the differing results.

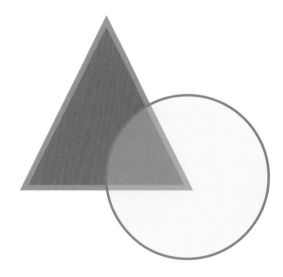

Aligning and distributing

Both of these operations work better when working
with multiple selections. You'll typically use these to
arrange more than one object in a single operation
which guarantees precise alignment. Compare this to
snapping (p. 118), which allows a single 'moving'
object to be aligned to other already placed objects.

You can align and distribute objects within their
selection bounds or in relation to the page spread.

Aligning

1 Select the icons by dragging over them.

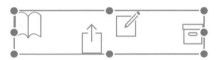

2 On the **Toolbar**, select **Alignment**, then click an
Align Vertically option. In this instance, **Align
Bottom** is perfect.

The icons are all aligned by their bottom edges.

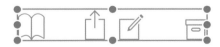

This looks better but the icons aren't evenly spread out.
You can fix this by distributing them.

Distributing

Distributing is a powerful way to space multiple objects evenly. **Space Horizontally** and **Space Vertically** options are available from the same pop-up panel as previously discussed, shared with align options.

1 Select the previously aligned set of icons.

2 From the same flyout, select the **Align Horizontally** option, called **Space Horizontally**.

The icons are now spaced evenly horizontally, as well as aligned.

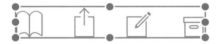

You can spread the icons out even further (rather than between outer selected objects) by unchecking **Auto Distribute** and specifying a 'buffer' physical measurement in the adjacent input box.

Resource

core_skills.afdesign (Artboard: Objects - Flipping and Rotating)

Flipping and rotating

Flipping mirrors an object about an invisible horizontal or vertical axis. This is useful when reworking your composition, e.g. when creating symmetrical shapes or for creating reflections.

Rotating is self-explanatory, but several methods can be used for both incremental or degree-specific rotation.

Flipping

1 Click to select the skyscraper in Flipping section.

2 Duplicate the skyscraper using **Edit > Duplicate**.

3 On the **Toolbar**, select **Flip Horizontal** or **Flip Vertical** and then reposition and add effects as necessary.

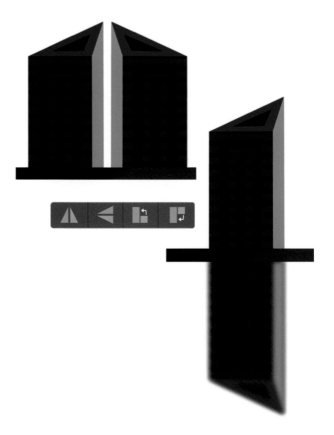

Rotating

For precise degree-specific rotation:

- With the **Move Tool** selected, select the green
  shape in the Rotating section, hover over the
  rotation handle above the selection and drag left
  or right.

For incremental 90° rotation:

- With the red shape selected, click **Rotate
  Clockwise** or **Rotate Anticlockwise** on the
  Toolbar.

For absolutely precise rotation, use the Rotate (**R**) option
on the **Transform Panel**. This also lets you rotate about
a chosen object handle using an anchor point.

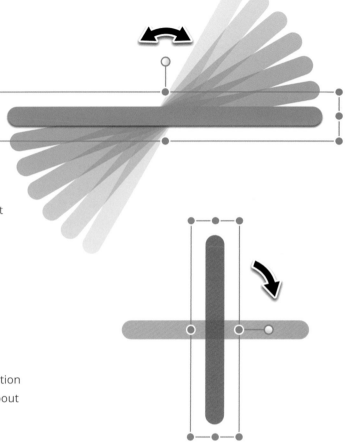

Hold down the shift key (⇧) while rotating to constrain the
rotation to 15° increments.

Clipping

A powerful feature of Affinity Designer is its **clipping** support. Clipping sounds technical and complicated but it simply means containing a 'child' object within the outline of another 'parent' object; the 'parent' object becomes the new boundaries for the 'child' object. Any areas of the child object which lie outside the parent's outline will be masked (hidden).

Vector clipping

With clipping, the original strokes or objects are always preserved (avoiding destructive Divide Boolean operations) and the operation is always reversible.

- On the **Layers Panel**, drag the darker ellipse (the object to be clipped) under the lighter orange ellipse, ensuring that the object is nested (i.e., indented).

To unclip a clipped object you simply drag the clipped object to its original position.

Raster clipping

The technique is identical to vector clipping but brushed raster textures created in **Pixel Persona** can be clipped to vector shapes.

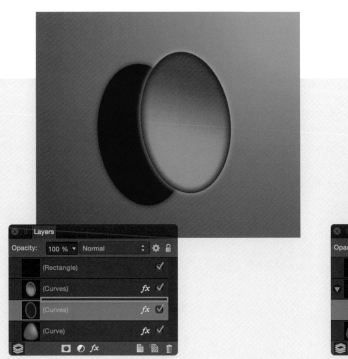

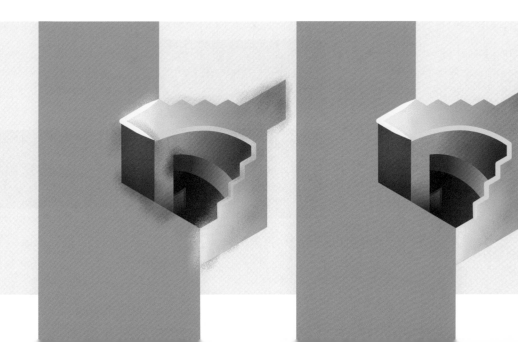

┌───┐
│ Resource   │
├───┤
│ core_skills.afdesign (Artboard: Layers and Groups) │
└───┘

LAYERS

So far we've looked at objects, and learnt that they are ordered by z-order (p. 84) and have their own properties including colour, stroke, opacity and blend modes. This suggests that all designs are made up of potentially hundreds of objects, each having to be controlled individually. In reality, most designers need more organizational control in their design, and use **layers** and **groups** to bring this control to hand.

Creating a vector layer

- On the **Layers Panel**, select the Layers and Groups artboard and click **Add Layer**.

If you want to introduce creative or retouch raster strokes you can either add an empty pixel layer by clicking the adjacent **Add Pixel Layer** icon or jump to **Pixel Persona** and begin painting. Select the artboard again before clicking the icon.

Layer naming

- Double-click on a layer name (e.g., *Layer1*) and type your new layer name, e.g. *Moon*.

By keeping objects organized within layers you'll find your design much easier to manage. Layers let you:

- Separate areas of your design logically and meaningfully into 'containers', e.g. background, trees, body.

- Isolate selection and editing to a specific 'active' layers.

- Apply both opacity and blend modes on the layer in addition to an individual object's opacity/blend mode properties.

- Change the order of multiple objects simultaneously by repositioning their 'containing' layer.

- Hide areas of your design temporarily for experimentation or to aid design.

- Protect (lock) completed areas of your design from accidental change.

Layer locking

Locking is useful for protecting your work or fixing the position of an imported sketch to prevent accidental movement, resizing, or other transforming operations.

- Select the Moon layer, then click **Lock/Unlock**. A lock symbol appears on your layer entry.

Hiding/showing layers

Once your design progresses, you may wish to temporarily hide one or more layers from display. When hidden, a layer is also excluded from being exported.

- On the **Layers Panel**, click the **Show/Hide Layer** check box on the pixel layer entry.

Groups

Groups are created to gather multiple objects together that logically belong together, perhaps in preparation for moving or resizing. For instance, individual rocket parts can be created, selected and then grouped together to make a **Rocket** group. Keeping the individual components grouped together like this is ideal.

Creating Groups

1 Expand the Example layer and select the seven unnamed shapes and curves using the shift key (⇧) or drag a marquee over rocket's objects.

2 On the context toolbar, click **Group**.

One key aspect of groups—a single click is all that's needed to select it, instead of having to reselect individual objects!

Once you've created a group, you can move it, resize it, flip it and rotate it, as if it's a single object.

Finding objects in the Layers Panel

Layer management is important, particularly with complex pieces. Finding objects and groups in the Layers Panel efficiently speeds up design and illustration work.

- Ctrl-click (Mac) or right-click (Win) the newly created Rocket group on the page and select **Find in Layers Panel**. If collapsed, the containing layer will expand to reveal the object's entry.

Resource

core_skills.afdesign (Artboard: Geometry Tools)

GEOMETRY TOOLS

Geometry (Boolean) tools can be used to 'combine' previously drawn, overlapping shapes. In Affinity Designer, these Boolean operations can be performed non-destructively and result in an object known as a **Compound**. A Compound can be deconstructed or revised at any future point.

> Compounds are a great way of creating a complex shape from simple components, especially when these are drawn using the Shape tools.

Using Compounds

1 With the four white shapes selected, hold down the option ⌥ key (Mac) or alt key (Win) and select **Add** on the **Toolbar**. The shapes will be added together and the new Compound will adopt the properties of the lowest shape.

> Rather than creating a Compound, you can create a standard shape by ignoring the modifier key. In this case, the process is destructive and only immediately reversible using the **Undo** command.

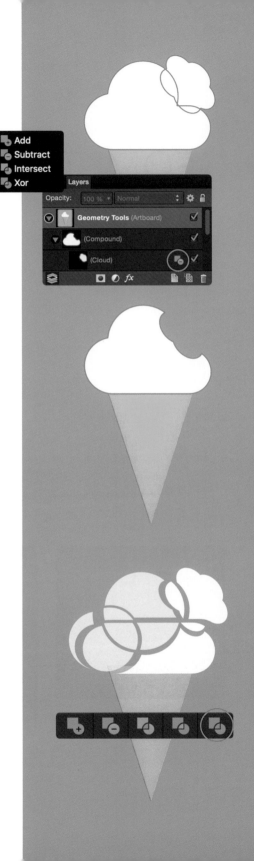

2 On the **Layers Panel**, expand the Compound layer by clicking the arrow to the left of the entry. To change the geometry operation, select an object's **Add** icon and select an alternative operation, for example, **Subtract**. Try the other options to see how the results differ.

Any layer within the Compound can possess a different geometry operation and can also be transformed (e.g., repositioned and resized) at any point. The resulting Compound will adjust to accommodate these changes.

A selected Compound can be broken up into its constituent parts by selecting **Release Compound** from the **Layer Menu** or you can use **Convert to Curves** on the context toolbar to fix the Compound as a single shape.

Divide operation

Divide is the only geometry operation which is inherently destructive and will never result in a Compound. This is because the outcome consists of multiple shapes with their boundaries defined by the overlapping edges of the original shapes.

PEN TOOL: CURVES & SHAPES

The foundation for most vector illustrations and designs are lines, curves and shapes. The Pen Tool allows you to draw these with precision and ease. Knowing how the tool works will dramatically improve the efficiency with which you create and design.

In Affinity Designer, a **curve** is a 'path' which connects distinct points called **nodes**. Nodes signify a change in the curve's direction, determined by the node's **control handles**. The section of the curve between two nodes is known as a **segment**.

If the two end nodes of a curve are connected together, this is known as a free-form **shape**. While a curve of only two nodes is commonly called a **line**.

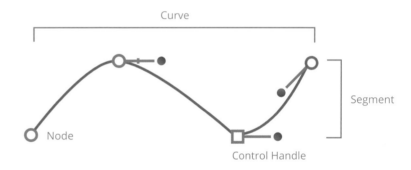

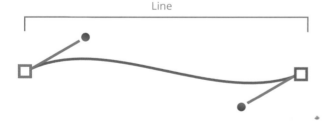

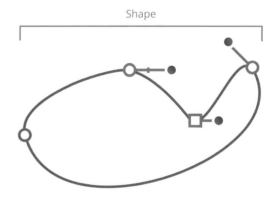

With these terms in mind, let's move onto how you can trace a guitar using the Pen Tool.

Curves, shapes and Pen Mode

Tracing a Guitar: Creating curves in Pen Mode

For best results, study the subject's outline and imagine where natural inflection points occur. These are the points on an outline at which a change in curve direction occurs and where you should be clicking.

1   On the **Tools Panel**, select the **Pen Tool** (P) and, on the context toolbar, set the **Mode** to **Pen Mode** to draw Bezier curves.

2   Click on the page at the guitar body's left end pin (strap button). This will place a Sharp node on the page (a).

3   Position the cursor at the first inflection point clockwise then drag upwards and outside the curve slightly and release. A curve is created that fits the outline as you adjust the leading control handle.

This will place a Smooth node (b) on the page and present you with a set of control handles (c).

4   Repeat at further inflection points, adding more smooth nodes until you get to the guitar neck.

The resource file shows inflection
points around the guitar outline as
square target markers where you
should click.

> " You should aim to get natural and accurate results
> without the need to edit the curve. The position and
> length of the solid blue control handles determine the curvature
> of the segments leading to and from any Smooth node.

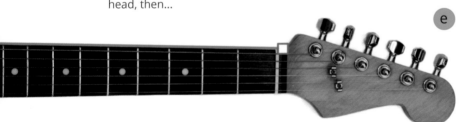

Introducing a sharp corner (cusp)

- Position the cursor at the intersection of body and neck (d) then, without releasing the mouse button, hold down the option ⌥ key (Mac) or alt key (Win) and drag the leading control handle along the guitar neck's outline to the guitar head, then...

- Click to create a straight line that follows the neck (e).

A sharp corner (cusp) is introduced at the intersection of body and neck (the modifier converts the Smooth node to a Sharp node).

You can redraw any smooth node on the curve by dragging from its
centre again.

More complex curves

- Continue drawing around the guitar's headstock introducing sharp corners as indicated.

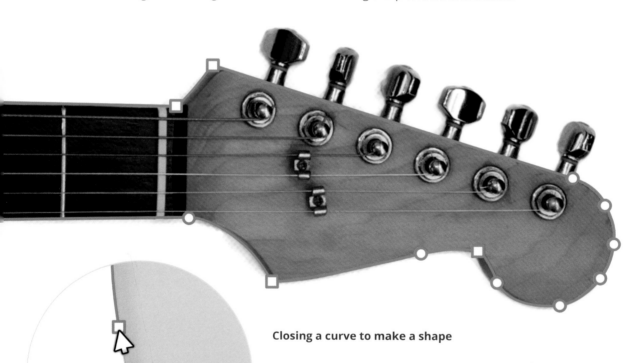

Closing a curve to make a shape

A drawn curve can be converted to a closed shape at any time.

1. Once you've drawn the rest of the neck, finish off the lower body but stop at the last smooth node so the curve can be closed.

2. With the last smooth node selected, click on the very first end node you created. Alternatively, with any node selected, on the context toolbar, click **Close Curve**.

Editing curves

The headstock is a more complex area than the guitar body so it's possible that your curves aren't as accurate as you'd like. Let's now take a look at how you can perform various types of curve editing to resolve this.

All curves can be edited as you draw with the **Pen Tool** by holding down the cmd ⌘ key (Mac) or ctrl key (Win). You can also adjust any curve on your page at any point in the future using the **Node Tool**.

Moving segments and nodes

Drag segments, nodes and control handles to reposition the curves to fine-tune the outline.

 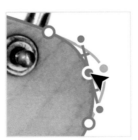

Adding nodes

Where more complexity is needed on an existing curve you can introduce new nodes. For example, the machine heads (guitar keys) can be introduced onto the curve afterwards.

- Click at both positions where the machine head meets the headstock, adding smooth nodes at each point.

Changing node type

It's possible that you may want to a convert a node to another type, perhaps to introduce a new sharp corner.

- Select each smooth node, then from the context toolbar, select **Sharp.**

Introducing new segments

Drag the segment upwards to form a curve, then add a further seven nodes around it.
These can be repositioned over the machine head's corners by dragging.

Asymmetric reshaping of curves

Up to now we've seen that nodes around the guitar's outline are smooth and
symmetric, giving precision Bézier curves. This is because the control handles at each
node are balanced by default and don't need adjustment. However, sometimes these
nodes can be edited, making them asymmetric, by simply moving a smooth node's
control handles. This may make a curve fit better to an outline.

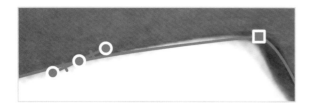

Notice how the left most control handle's length remains unchanged and its crossbars vanish
(because the handles are no longer the same length). This means the smooth node will no
longer be symmetrical. Both control handles can now be resized independently, though they
will always remain linear.

If we return back to our guitar key example, the added nodes are automatically symmetric on creation but, after repositioning, may need to be fine-tuned asymmetrically to fit the outline better.

Other Pen Tool Modes

Once it's fully mastered, the Pen Tool's **Pen Mode** is the most efficient way of drawing curves in Affinity Designer. However, the tool comes with alternative modes which may suit you better.

Guitar plectrum: Smart Mode

Smart Mode creates flowing curves by simply clicking on the page. In this mode, the Pen Tool creates Smart nodes, which link together using automatic 'line of best fit' segments.

1   With the **Pen Tool** enabled, select **Smart Mode** on the context toolbar.

2   To draw the plectrum, click three times to represent the corners of the plectrum. The Smart nodes automatically shape the curve as it transits each node.

3   Hover over and click on the first node to close the shape.

> The option ⌥ key (Mac) or alt key (Win) will create a Sharp node when in this mode.

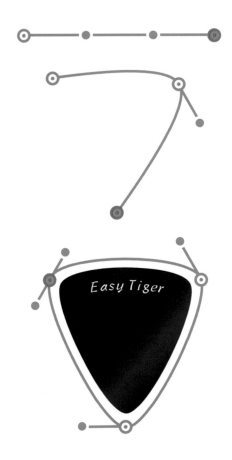

Guitar bridge: Polygon Mode

Polygon Mode connects Sharp nodes with straight segments by clicking repeatedly on the page.

1 Select **Polygon Mode** on the Pen Tool's context toolbar.

2 Click around the guitar's bridge (where the guitar strings enter the guitar body).

3 Close the shape by clicking on its initial node.

4 (Optional) Use the **Corner Tool** (C) to round off selected Sharp corners.

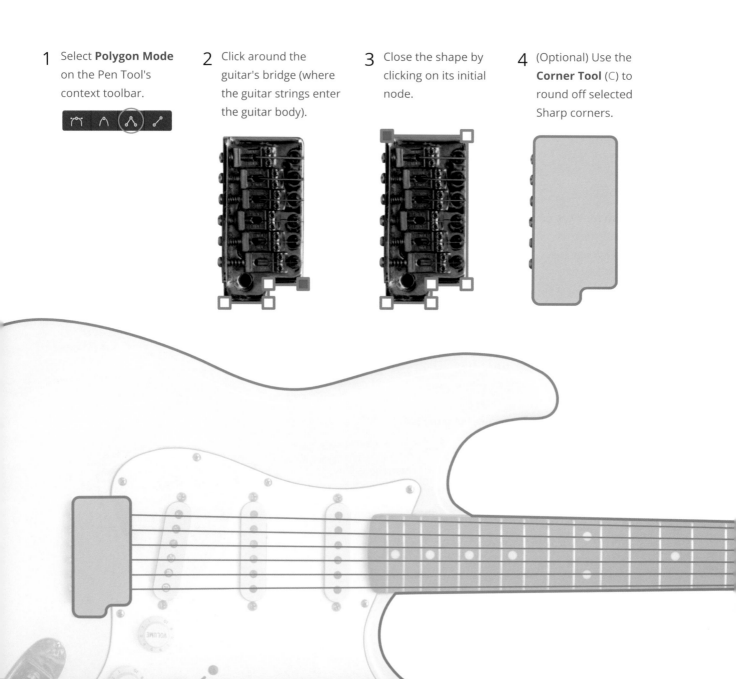

Guitar strings: Line Mode

Line Mode will give you a straight line which terminates when releasing the mouse button. The mode is perfect for drawing repeating straight lines quickly.

1   Select **Line Mode** on the Pen Tool's context toolbar.

2   Drag across the page several times over each guitar string one by one.

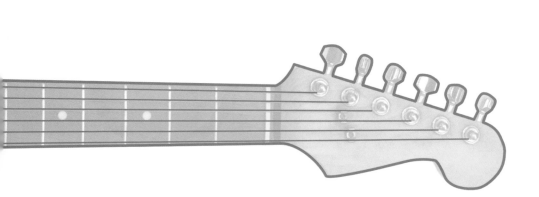

COLOURS & GRADIENTS

Affinity Designer provides a multitude of options for setting the fill and stroke (outline) of objects with solid colours or seamless gradients.

The three main areas of the interface where you'll find options for applying and updating colour are the Colour Panel, Swatches Panel and context toolbar. On the context toolbar, Fill and Stroke colour properties are split into distinctly labelled selectors, while on the panels you will see the Fill represented as a solid circular selector and the Stroke represented as a donut selector.

In Pixel Persona, the panels display two solid circular selectors which simply represent two separate selected colour options which can be efficiently switched between using the x key.

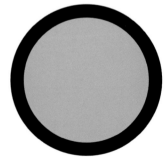

Colour Panel

The Colour Panel contains options for mixing your own colours. By default, you're presented with the HSL colour wheel for this purpose, but other modes are also available.

1 Select the circle on the artboard and then, on the **Colour Panel**, click on the solid circular selector (a) and then click anywhere on the outer ring of the HSL wheel to set the Hue of the object's fill (b). Then click on the inner triangle to set the Saturation and Lightness value (c).

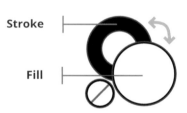

2 Click the panel's donut selector and it will now display in front of the solid circular selector. The foremost selector is the currently active selector. From panel preferences, select *Sliders* to change the panel layout to sliders and then select a colour mode from the pop-up menu. Use the sliders to set the colour of the object's stroke.

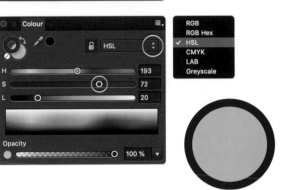

Swatches Panel

The Swatches Panel hosts preset and custom palettes which contain pre-defined colours. By default, you're presented with the Greys palette, but other palettes are also accessible along with the option to create your own.

- On the **Swatches Panel**, with the stroke (donut) selector still active, select *Colours* from the pop-up menu, and then click a swatch from the palette to apply the colour to the object's stroke.

The context toolbar's separate **Fill** and **Stroke** selectors will present you with a pop-up panel which gives you access to most of the features of the Colour and Swatches panels.

Before we move on, let's examine some of the common features of the Colour and Swatches panels:

Switch

None

- The white swatch with a red line through it is known as **None** and will remove all colour attributes from the current object's fill or stroke. Alternatively, use the **/** key.

- The double-headed arrow will switch the colours set on the object's fill and stroke, i.e. a white circle with a black outline will become a black circle with a white outline. Alternatively, use the keyboard shortcut **shift (⇧)+x**.

- The **colour picker** allows you to select any colour on your screen and store it in the swatch just to the right of the pipette icon. Drag the icon from the panel to the pixel you want to sample and then apply that colour to your object's fill or stroke by selecting the pipette's swatch.

- The **Opacity** setting allows you to apply solid transparency to your object's fill and stroke colour independently.

Gradient control

In addition to solid colours, Affinity Designer gives you the ability to apply colour gradients to the fill and stroke of objects.

1 With the circle selected, from the **Tools Panel**, select the **Fill Tool** (G). On the context toolbar, set the **Type** to *Linear* to apply a default gradient or drag across your object to set a custom path for the gradient.

2 Drag across the artboard to change the length and direction of the gradient path and drag the midpoint marker to change the midpoint of the transition between the current stops.

3 Position the cursor along the path and it will change to display a plus symbol. Click to add a new stop, which can then be moved anywhere along the gradient path.

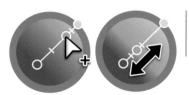

A selected stop can be deleted using the **delete** key.

Once you have a gradient in place, each stop possesses its own unique colour and opacity properties. Colour is applied to a stop in the same way a solid fill is applied to a Fill or Stroke of an object.

4 With the circle selected and the **Fill Tool** active, click any stop on the gradient to select it. Then on the **Colour** or **Swatches Panel**, apply a colour to the selected stop and/or reduce the stop's **Opacity**.

> Notice, when using the Fill Tool, the panels update to show only one colour selector. This is because the selector now applies to the currently selected stop on the gradient. To switch between Fill and Stroke attributes, use the **Context** option on the context toolbar.

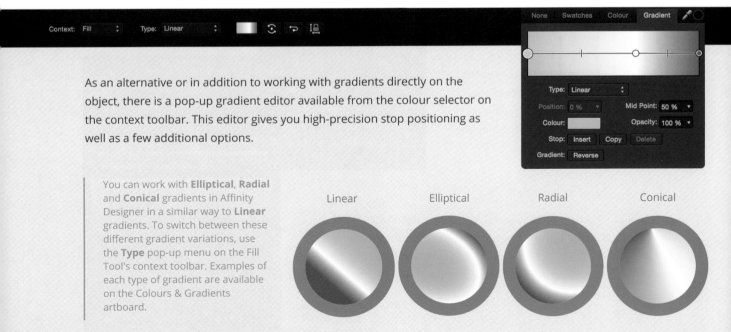

As an alternative or in addition to working with gradients directly on the object, there is a pop-up gradient editor available from the colour selector on the context toolbar. This editor gives you high-precision stop positioning as well as a few additional options.

> You can work with **Elliptical**, **Radial** and **Conical** gradients in Affinity Designer in a similar way to **Linear** gradients. To switch between these different gradient variations, use the **Type** pop-up menu on the Fill Tool's context toolbar. Examples of each type of gradient are available on the Colours & Gradients artboard.

Linear   Elliptical   Radial   Conical

Colour with noise

Visual noise is a creative type of 'interference' which can be applied to break up smooth colours. It works by randomly introducing tiny darker or lighter areas. Visual noise within a selected colour is controlled on the Colour Panel.

Global colours

Global colours are linked colours which are defined in a custom palette within the Swatches Panel. They are applied to objects in the same way as standard, fixed colours. However, if a global colour is modified in the future, every instance of that colour within your document will update to match.

1 From panel preferences on the **Swatches Panel**, select **Add Global Colour**. In the dialog, set the colour's **Name** and mix a colour using any mode available from the pop-up menu. Then click **Add** to create the global colour and add it to an automatically generated custom palette.

- With the circle selected, and the appropriate fill, stroke or stop selector active, click the **Switch to noise** circular icon to the left of the **Opacity** slider. This will change the slider to a **Noise** slider. Drag the slider to the right to add noise to the colour.

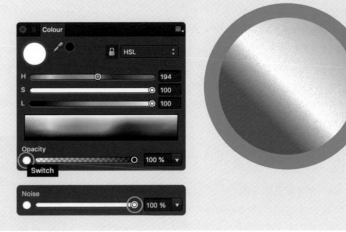

2   Once your custom palette has been created, you can quickly add new global colours by repeating step 1 or selecting the **Add current colour to palette as a global colour** icon on the **Swatches Panel** to add the colour in the colour selector to the palette as a global colour. To modify a global colour at any time, ctrl-click (Mac) or right-click (Win) on the global colour swatch and select **Edit Fill.**

 Global colours are distinguishable from standard colours by the appearance of a small triangle indicator in the bottom left corner.

Resource

core_skills.afdesign (Artboard: Effects & Adjustments)

EFFECTS & ADJUSTMENTS

Affinity Designer gives you the ability to add a range of powerful effects as well as apply photographic adjustments, without the need to use an external app. These effects and adjustments can be set for individual objects as well as be applied to groups, layers or the entire design. You'll find a myriad of effects and adjustments used throughout the projects in this Workbook. The way you apply an effect to a layer is the same for all effects, and the same goes for adjustments. Let's look at some common examples so you can get a feel for it.

Gaussian Blur effect

Gaussian Blur softens all the lines in the current selection and applies feather to edges. It is a great way of imitating the 'falling off' of highlights and shadows.

1   On the **Layers Panel**, select the nested ellipse layer on the Effects & Adjustments artboard.

2   Switch to the **Effects Panel** and click the arrow next to the **Gaussian Blur** effect to expose its basic settings. Adjust the settings as desired.

3   Repeat for the lowest, dark ellipse layer.

When a Gaussian Blur effect is applied to layers and groups, rather than individual objects, it can be used to give the illusion of depth of field.

The fx icon which appears on the object's entry on the Layers Panel, indicates that an effect is currently applied to that object. Clicking this fx icon will display the Layer Effects dialog.

Shadow effects

In Affinity Designer, Shadow effects come in two varieties: Outer and Inner. Outer creates a drop shadow outside the boundaries of the object to 'lift' it from the page. Inner, which we'll cover here, adds depth to an object by adding shadows inside the object.

- Select the red ellipse layer on the **Layers Panel** and then switch to the **Effects Panel**. Click the arrow next to the **Inner Shadow** effect to expose its basic settings. Adjust the settings as desired. Although the sliders have an upper limit, the **Radius** and **Offset** settings can be further increased by typing in values in their input boxes.

The **Angle** control determines the direction of the light source and therefore the position of the shadow. The Angle can be adjusted directly on the Effects Panel, where the small line on the dial indicates the light's position, or you can select **Offset Tool** to drag on the page to determine the direction of the light and the shadow's offset.

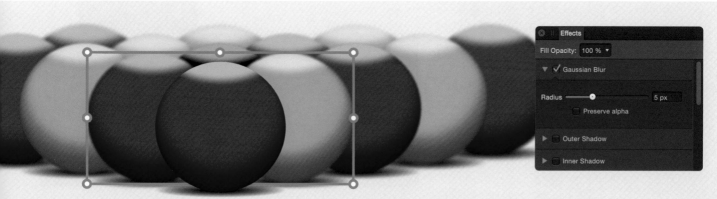

Glow effects

Like the Shadow effects, Glow effects also come in two varieties: Outer and Inner. Outer creates a halo around the edges of the selected object. Inner places the halo on the inside of the object's edge or originating from the centre. We'll add an Inner Glow here and expose you to all the option's available settings.

1 With the red ellipse still selected, on the **Layers Panel**, click its fx icon (or the fx icon at the bottom of the panel). This will expose the **Layer Effects** dialog, which gives you access to all the available layer effects and all their settings.

2 Select **Inner Glow** from the list on the left and then adjust the settings on the right.

Glow effects are initially presented as a lightening effect because their default settings are a **Blend mode** of **Screen** and a white colour. Conversely, Shadow effects have default settings of a black colour with a **Multiply** blend. However, Affinity Designer gives you the flexibility of modifying both these settings. As an example, the **Inner Glow** effect can be used to create a subtle, uniform shadow around the inner edge of an object by setting the **Blend mode** to *Multiply* and the **Colour** to *HSL 0,0,60*.

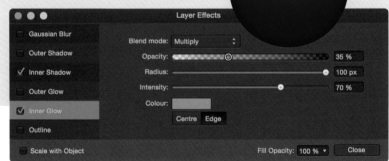

Brightness and Contrast adjustment

A Brightness and Contrast adjustment is particularly useful for altering the overall colours, shadows and highlights of a composition near the end of a project. It can save a great deal of time by circumventing the need to go back and tweak colour values en masse.

1 On the **Layers Panel**, select the artboard and then click the **Adjustments** icon and select **Brightness and Contrast**. A Brightness/Contrast Adjustment layer is added to the Layers Panel.

If the adjustment layer is clipped (nested) within a layer, drag it to the top of the layer stack to ensure it affects everything in your document. For more information, see p. 83.

2 In the dialog, set a new **Brightness** and **Contrast** using the available sliders.

Other tonal adjustments, such as Levels and Curves, are also available for correcting your design or illustration.

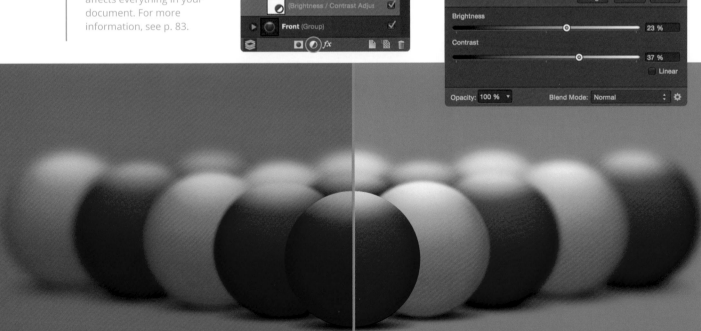

Recolour adjustment

The Recolour adjustment is an instant way of converting an illustration to monochrome.

- On the **Layers Panel**, select the artboard and then click the **Adjustments** icon and select **Recolour**. In the dialog, set the **Hue** and **Saturation** of the monochrome design using the available sliders.

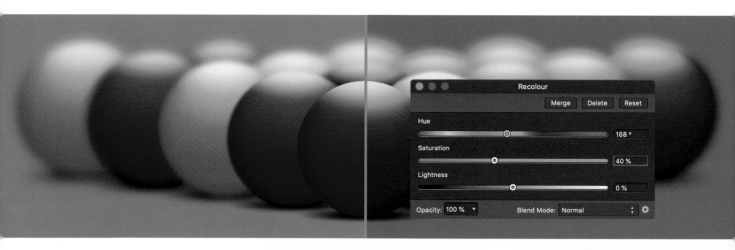

Rather than converting the design to monochrome, an alternative is to modify the illustration's colours by blending the Recolour adjustment with the document. This can be done by changing the **Blend Mode** directly in the Recolour dialog or on the entry in the Layers Panel.

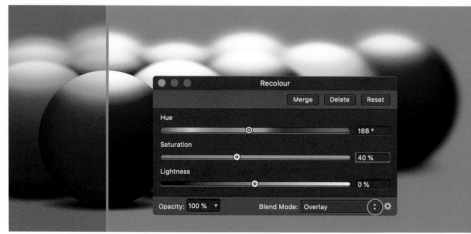

Soft Proof adjustment

The Soft Proof adjustment allows you to change the colours in your illustration to match a range of colour profiles, without having to physically convert your document.

- On the **Layers Panel**, select the artboard and then click the **Adjustments** icon and then **Soft Proof**. In the dialog, select the **Proof Profile** you wish to emulate. You can then toggle the adjustment layer's visibility to see how changes to your document will display in the alternative colour profile. Switch off the layer after proofing.

If you're designing to output on different platforms, you might wish to set up multiple Soft Proof adjustment layers with different profiles set on each to replicate each media.

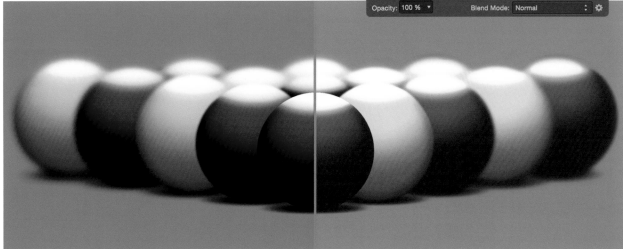

DESIGN AIDS

Knowing what design aids to call upon, and when, is a skill that will allow you to work with absolute precision and will make layout so much easier. As core design aids, we'll look at snapping and then visual alignment tools such as grids and guides.

These design aids can be enabled or disabled at any time, so they can be used exactly when needed.

Snapping

This feature allows 'moving' images, brush strokes, lines, shapes, and selection areas to align precisely to already placed objects or document elements. As its name suggests, an object will try to 'snap to' another as if magnetized to it. Alignment is to object bounding boxes, key points on shapes, and to an object's geometry, even if objects don't touch. Ruler guides and grids can also be aligned to.

Snapping to an object

1 On the **Toolbar**, click **Snapping** to enable the feature.

2 Drag one object to another object. In close proximity, the moving object will try to align with the other object's bounding box in different ways depending on the moving object's position.

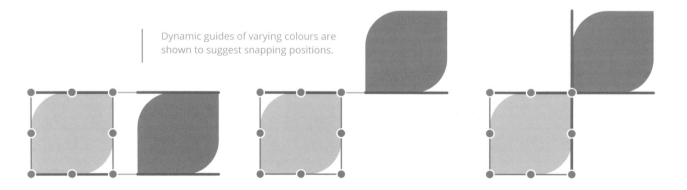

Dynamic guides of varying colours are shown to suggest snapping positions.

Choose a snapping preset

The default snapping settings are ideal for page layout and object manipulation, but you can swap to another preset more suited to your way of working.

1 Click the **Snapping** option's arrow.

2 From the **Preset** pop-up menu, select a preset. For example, *UI Design* is an ideal snapping preset when designing apps.

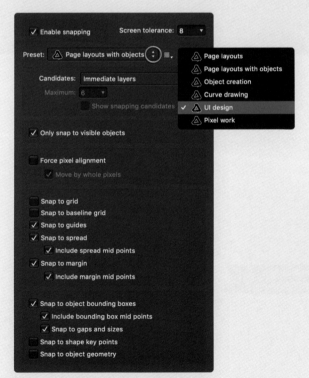

Customising a snapping preset

- With a preset chosen, check individual options on/off to override the current settings.

Grids and Guides

Grids and guides are great when working with more regular layouts such as in icon design, plans, etc. Using these means the frustrations of manually positioning objects 'by eye' are eliminated, as positioning is guaranteed by aligning to a visible grid or a layout of previously positioned guides. Grids and guides have added value when used in conjunction with snapping. When enabled, objects snap to grid or guide with absolute precision.

Let's switch on a grid, adjust its spacing, and make objects snap to it.

Switching on the grid

- On the **View** menu, select **Show Grid**.

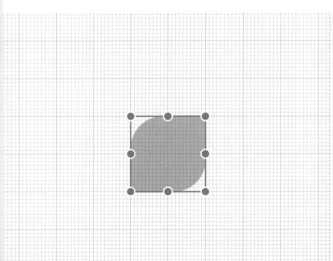

Changing grid type

By default, you'll get an automatic grid that changes grid intervals with zoom level, but you can create a fixed grid unaffected by zooming if needed.

1 On the **View** menu, select **Grid and Axis Manager**.

2 Uncheck **Use automatic grid**, and set up your fixed grid settings.

Enabling snapping to grid

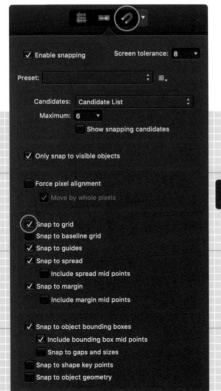

- On the **Toolbar**, click the **Snapping** option's arrow, then check **Snap to Grid**.

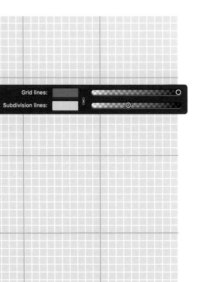

Changing grid colour and opacity

If your grid isn't easily seen on a darker page/artboard background, you can adjust the grid colour and/or opacity to make the grid more visible.

1 On the **View** menu, select **Grid and Axis Manager**.

2 Change **Grid line colour** or **Grid line opacity** by clicking the swatch or adjacent slider, respectively.

Guides

Guides are non-printable non-exportable coloured lines that come in two forms—dynamic guides and ruler guides. Their purpose is to precisely align objects to either each other or to fixed positions on the page.

Dynamic guides are available as soon as snapping is enabled (p. 118) and show as red or green lines when a moved object approaches another 'target' object. The lines are displayed only when needed, and let you 'lock onto' an object's edge or centre.

Hiding guides

From the **View** menu, select **Show Guides**. A checkmark is displayed next to the menu item when the guides are visible.

Fixed guides

Fixed guides are created manually and show permanently, although you can hide all guides temporarily if needed.

Adding guides

Do one of the following:

- Drag from either the horizontal or vertical ruler which can be switched on via the **View** menu.

- From the **View** menu, select **Guides Manager**. Click the **Add new guide** icon for either horizontal or vertical guides.

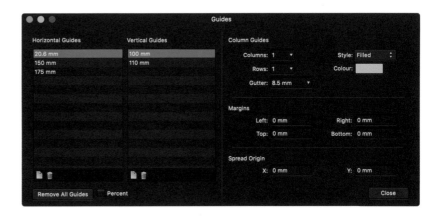

Resource

core_skills.afdesign (Artboard: Symbols)

SYMBOLS

Symbols are linked objects where a change to one object will immediately propagate to the other instances.

They can be created from any object, group or layer on the page and are ideal for controlling identical content across multiple artboards and creating and maintaining complex patterns, where slight variations in design may be envisaged.

Creating a symbol

1 Switch on the **Symbols Panel** via **View > Studio**.

2 On the **Layers Panel**, select the Logo group then, on the **Symbols Panel**, click **Create**.

> If you have multiple objects selected, a symbol will be created for each object. If you want multiple objects added as a single symbol, they must first be grouped (as in the example).

Although a new item appears in the Symbols Panel, nothing appears to have changed on the page.

We get a better impression of the presence of symbols if we glance at the Layers Panel.

The **(Group)** entry has been updated to read **(Symbol)** and there is a coloured graduated line on the entry's left. This indicates that the entry is the symbol's **container**.

All nested entries are the symbol's **contents** and are indicated by a solid coloured line to the left.

The distinction between a symbol's container and its contents is extremely important. We'll discuss this later.

Creating another instance of a symbol

- From the **Symbols Panel**, drag the symbol's thumbnail onto the artboard under the original design.

Any standard process of copying an object can be used to make a copy of a symbol, provided the symbol's **container** is selected. If a symbol's **contents** are copied, this will duplicate them **inside** every instance of that symbol.

Making changes to a symbol: container versus contents

Any changes you make to the **contents** of a symbol will be mirrored in all other instances of a symbol, including the version in the Symbols Panel. However, changes made to the symbol's **container** may only affect that instance, depending on the modification.

For example, repositioning, resizing, or rotating a symbol's container will only affect that instance, whereas colour modifications to a container (hue, opacity, blend mode, etc.) will update all other instances.

To see this in action:

- In the **Layers Panel**, select the symbol's container entry for the second instance and resize it.

Now, let's see the consequences of transforming the **contents** of a symbol:

1 In the **Layers Panel**, expand the original symbol's container by clicking the arrow on the left, and then select the Curves object.

2 On the **Toolbar**, select the **Flip Vertical** icon and temporarily recolour the object magenta.

The duplicate symbol updates to match the changes to the original, as does the thumbnail in the Symbols Panel.

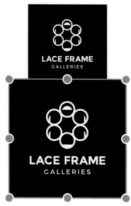

Implementing variations

There may be times when you want an object which possesses most of the features of a symbol, but not all of them. In other words, you want a slight variation on a symbol. By default, all instances of a symbol are linked together. However, you can remove this link to make changes to one instance without it affecting other instances.

1 On the **Symbols Panel**, select the **Sync** icon to disable synchronisation.

2 Make any changes to any symbols. For example, remove the words and increase the size of the Curves object.

The **Layers Panel** will list any changed contents of a symbol with a dashed coloured line to the left. This indicates that some attributes of that object are no longer linked with the symbol in the **Symbols Panel**.

Importantly, when synchronisation is off, only the attributes you specifically alter will break link. Anything you leave untouched will remain connected when you reactivate synchronisation.

3 On the **Symbols Panel**, enable the **Sync** icon again.

Changes you make now will be updated across all versions, such as changing the rectangle's corners.

If you want to convert a single instance of a symbol back to a standard object, i.e. remove all its connections from other instances, simply select the instance and select **Detach** on the **Symbols Panel**. To convert all instances of a symbol back to unlinked, standard objects, ctrl-click (Mac) or right-click (Win) a symbol's thumbnail on the **Symbols Panel** and select **Delete Symbol**.

CHAPTER 3

Illustration Projects

In this chapter you will learn how to create different styles of illustrations in Affinity Designer from a host of illustration gurus.

Learn how to illustrate your own characters and worlds using both vector and raster techniques, plus learn all about using colour and opacity and how to create your own brushes.

1

The Panther

Flat vector character design by *Ben the Illustrator*

Follow Ben's instructions to create a panther with simple vectors, plus find out how to use opacity to add fluidity and movement.

My 'Fluid Animals' series is about capturing movement with simple vector shapes and using transparencies to add depth.

BEFORE YOU GET STARTED

Resources

 You can get all the resources that are referenced in this project from:
https://affin.co/panther

Knowledge of Affinity Designer

To get the most from undertaking this project, you will need to:

- Know how to use the **Pen Tool** in Affinity Designer. Master the **Pen Tool** by completing Pen Tool: Curves & Shapes on p. 97.

- Be familiar with the interface of Affinity Designer. You can learn more about the interface in the Interface Tour chapter, starting on p. 13.

- Have good core skills. See the skills table below to see which additional aspects of Affinity Designer you need to be confident with to complete this project:

Objects	p. 80
Layers	p. 92
Geometry Tools	p. 95
Colour & Gradients	p. 106

CREATING
THE CONCEPT

This project uses the Pen Tool, transparency and gradients to capture the natural fluidity of animals.

As with all artwork, consider composition from the outset. My Fluid Animals illustrations are usually for products (like calendars, cards or art prints), so tell a story.

If you're illustrating an animal, choose your resources wisely. Drawing real life is best but can be tricky.

Personally, I draw from film. Nature documentaries are perfect: well-shot, close-up, capturing an animal's true movements. Aim to replicate this in your sketch. Photos, or other illustrations, should be a last resort.

If the photo is sourced online, chances are someone else will have already illustrated it, and your originality instantly vanishes!

When sketching, I break the animal into simple shapes, often teardrops. I also extend lines into other areas and continue some lines outwards to emphasise the movement of the character and create a basic background.

DOCUMENT SETUP

Set up the document to place the scanned sketch.

1 Scan your sketch (or photograph it with a camera or smartphone) and save it to your computer.

2 In Affinity Designer, select **New** from the **File Menu** and create a Print (Press Ready), A3 document. Set this to *landscape* by switching off the **Portrait** option.

Importing the sketch

1 From the **File Menu**, select **Place**. Then select your scanned sketch (or panther_sketch.jpg) and click **Open**.

2 Drag across the document, ensuring the sketch fills the entire page and then lock the layer by clicking the **Lock/Unlock** icon on the **Layers Panel**.

3 On the **Layers Panel**, select the **Add Layer** icon, and then click on the new layer's name to rename it *background*.

4 Save your document using the option on the **File Menu**. The first time you do this, you'll be asked to name the file and select a folder to place it in. Subsequent saving will overwrite the previously saved file.

Resource

panther_02_backgroundlines.afdesign

PEN DRAWING

We'll start by defining the lines extending from our subject into the background. These will form part of the background design. We'll use the Pen Tool to do this. If you're new to using the Pen Tool and Bézier curves, then do give yourself time to get used to it. It's a wonderful illustration skill once you're able to work naturally with it.

Background lines

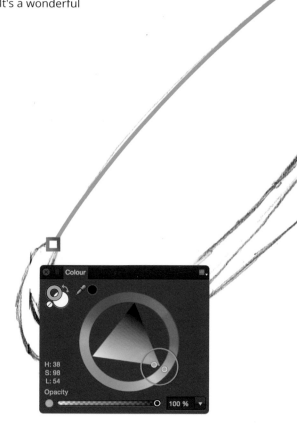

1 On the **Tools Panel**, select the **Pen Tool** (P). The tool is set to **Pen Mode** by default but can be changed on the context toolbar.

2 On the **Colour Panel**, select the **Stroke** colour selector (the donut icon in the top left corner). Click on the outer ring of the HSL wheel and then click in the inner triangle to set the stroke colour to bright orange (*HSL 38,98,54*). This will help us see the lines as we trace.

3 On the **Stroke Panel**, increase the **Width**, using the slider, to *3 pt*.

4 With the background layer selected on the **Layers Panel**, click once near the tail's tip.

5 Then position the cursor on the pasteboard above the page and drag to the right to add another node and bend the segment (which now connects the two nodes) to match the line on the sketch.

6 Release when you are happy with the curvature of the segment and then press the esc key to cease drawing that particular line.

7 Repeat steps 4–6 to trace the remaining background lines which extend from the body of the panther sketch.

If you need to adjust a curve at any time, you can temporarily switch to the **Node Tool** by holding down the cmd ⌘ key (Mac) or ctrl key (Win) when the **Pen Tool** is active. You can then reposition nodes and node handles to change the curve.

Resource

panther_03_inkingsubject.afdesign

If you're tracing a pencil drawing I find it helps to use a bright colour for the line work at this point (not black or grey) so it is always clear and stands out on top of your pencil drawing.

Inking the subject

We're going to use the Pen Tool again to define the shapes which make up our subject. To help us stay organized, we'll draw these new lines on a new layer.

1 On the **Layers Panel**, add a new layer and label it *subject*. Hide the background layer by clicking its check box. With the **Pen Tool** selected, and **Pen Mode** enabled on the context toolbar, click to place the first node on the front paw (1).

2 Further along the paw's outline, click-drag downwards (2); this defines the curve connecting the nodes. Then, where the paw curves under, hold down the option ⌥ key (Mac), or alt key (Win), and click to create a sharp node (3).

3 Further along the paw's outline, click-drag upwards (4) to define the curve then click once back on the original node to make it a shape. Use the **Node Tool** (A) to tidy up the segments, by repositioning nodes and handles, so the shape closely follows the sketch.

At this stage you can continue to ink in the remaining shapes in the sketch using the Pen Tool. Alternatively, in some cases, you can use geometric shapes. We'll discuss this is the next section.

GEOMETRIC SHAPES

Resource

panther_04_geometricshapes.afdesign

In addition to the Pen Tool, you can use the geometric shapes available from the Tools Panel. These shapes can be morphed using adjustable settings and can be converted to curves and manipulated just like pen drawn lines.

1 Select the **Tear Tool** from the pop-up shape menu on the **Tools Panel** and drag on the page to create a tear drop shape the same width and height as the panther's ear.

2 On the **Colour Panel**, select the **Fill** colour selector (the solid circle icon in the top left corner) and then click the small white circle with the red line through it (just left of the colour selectors) to set the fill of the shape to *None*.

3 Drag the red handles to adjust the shape until it closely matches the shape of the ear and then click **Convert to Curves** on the context toolbar.

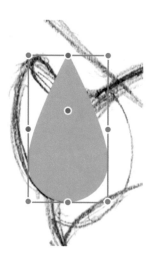

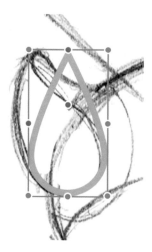

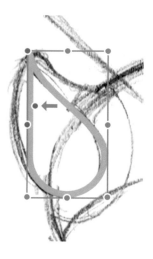

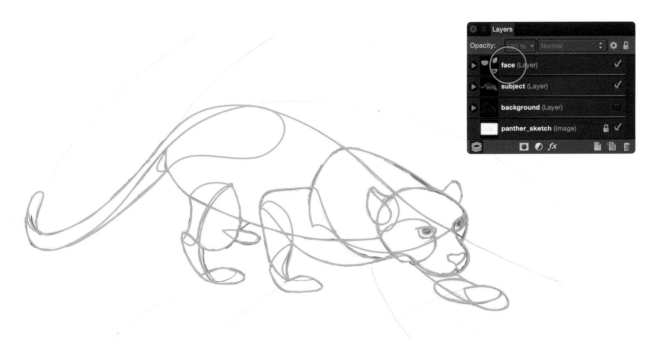

4 With the **Node Tool**, adjust the shape to match the lines in the sketch.

Use the techniques covered so far to ink the remaining sketch lines. Aim to complete shapes with as few nodes as possible. Use a new layer for defining the face of the subject, i.e. the eyes and nose. Name the layer to be *face*.

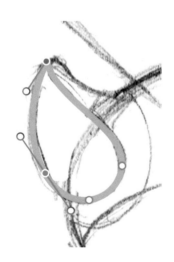

CHAPTER 3: ILLUSTRATION PROJECTS | THE PANTHER

Perfect shapes

We'll be taking our design beyond the sketch to add life to the eyes of our subject.

1 On the **Layers Panel**, hide the panther_sketch layer and select the face layer. Zoom into the eyes and select the **Ellipse Tool** (M) directly from the **Tools Panel**.

2 Drag on the page to create an ellipse in the eye on the left. Hold down the shift key (⇧) as you drag to confine the shape to a perfect circle. On the **Stroke Panel**, set the **Width** to *1 pt*. Repeat this to create a total of three circles in each eye. The lower circle in each eye will become a halo highlight. This can be created by converting the circle into a donut.

3 Select the lower circle in one eye and, on the context toolbar, click **Convert to Donut**. Repeat with the lower circle in the second eye.

> Donuts can be created directly using the Donut Tool available from the shapes pop-up menu.

Finishing off our shapes, a rectangle can be added as a background.

4 Select the *background* layer and make it visible once more, then select the **Rectangle Tool** (M) directly from the **Tools Panel**. Switch on **Snapping**, using the icon on the **Toolbar**, and then drag out a rectangle which fills the entire page. Move this shape to the bottom of the z-order by clicking the **Move to Back** icon on the **Toolbar**.

COLOUR

With the line work complete, the process of colouring involves taking the shapes we have just inked and adding a fill.

1 With the background rectangle selected, on the **Colour Panel**, select the two-headed arrow to the top right of the colour selectors. This will switch the Fill and Stroke colours, making the rectangle's stroke invisible and its fill orange.

It might appear that all your lines have disappeared. Don't panic! They are still there. They're just the same colour as the background rectangle.

2 With the **Fill** colour selector active (i.e. displayed in front of the Stroke, donut selector), drag in the HSL colour wheel's inner triangle to set the colour to a rich black (*HSL 38,100,0*).

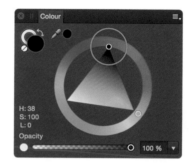

3 Lock this background layer to prevent further editing.

When using rich blacks in an illustration, it's worth defining the black colour using your print shop's preferred CMYK rich black formula.

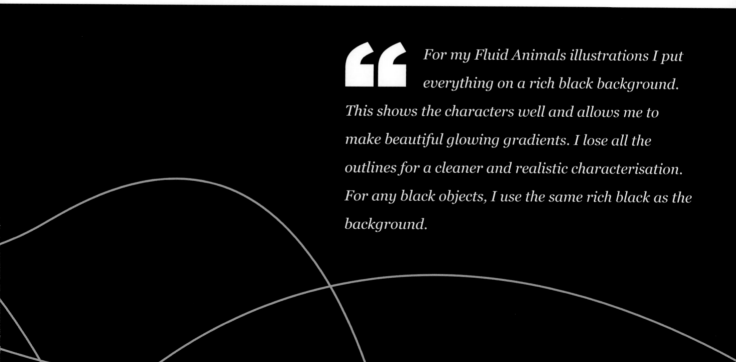

" *For my Fluid Animals illustrations I put everything on a rich black background. This shows the characters well and allows me to make beautiful glowing gradients. I lose all the outlines for a cleaner and realistic characterisation. For any black objects, I use the same rich black as the background.*

4 Select each object in the face layer and repeat steps
1 and 2 to remove their strokes and colour them
black, *white* or *red-orange* (see below).

- To quickly select white for the highlights, switch
to the **Swatches Panel**, and select the quick
access *white* swatch listed alongside the *none*,
black and *mid-grey* swatches.

- For the red-oranges: select the iris shapes and,
on the **Swatches Panel**, click on the pop-up
menu which reads *Greys* by default. This is
where preset and custom palettes are stored.
Select **PANTONE+ Solid Coated-V2** and in the
search facility at the bottom of the panel, type
1655. Select the displayed PANTONE *1655 C*
swatch. Then clear the search term.

If the names of colours do not appear in the Swatches
Panel, from panel preferences, select Show As List from
the Appearance pop-up menu.

Any Pantone colours you apply to your objects will be
added to a custom Document palette as a Global Spot
colour for easy access.

5 Lock the face layer and then repeat the colouring
process for every shape on the subject layer, picking
colours from the Swatches or Colour Panels.
I coloured most of my shapes using *CMYK 31,93,81,62*
with splashes of *PANTONE 1655 C*, *PANTONE 1815 C*
and *PANTONE 4975 C*.

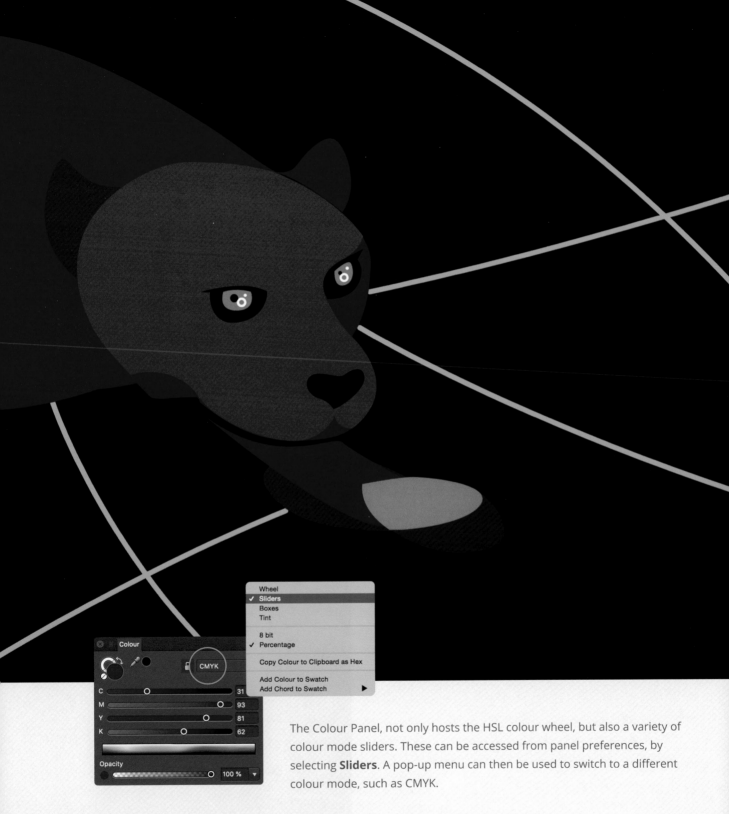

The following menu items appear in the pop-up:

- Wheel
- ✓ Sliders
- Boxes
- Tint
- 8 bit
- ✓ Percentage
- Copy Colour to Clipboard as Hex
- Add Colour to Swatch
- Add Chord to Swatch ▶

Colour panel values:

- CMYK
- C 31
- M 93
- Y 81
- K 62
- Opacity 100 %

The Colour Panel, not only hosts the HSL colour wheel, but also a variety of colour mode sliders. These can be accessed from panel preferences, by selecting **Sliders**. A pop-up menu can then be used to switch to a different colour mode, such as CMYK.

Resource

panther_06_opacity.afdesign

OPACITY

With the removal of all the strokes, our subject has lost its definition. We'll use the interaction of layer opacities to help the shapes that make up the subject re-emerge and start to bring a magical essence to the illustration.

> By default, Edit All Layers is active, which means you can select and modify any object, regardless of which layer it resides on (with the exception of locked layers). If Edit All Layers is deactivated, you can only interact with objects within the current layer.

1   On the **Layers Panel**, click the **Edit All Layers** icon to switch off the functionality. Select the subject layer and the **Move Tool**, then from the **Select Menu**, click **Select All**.

2   Using the option at the top of the **Layers Panel**, drop the **Opacity** of all the objects to *75%*.

3   Examine how each object interacts with the objects underneath. Use your creative judgement to change the stacking order (z-order) of objects. Do this by dragging entries up or down in the **Layers Panel** (being careful not to nest them), using the **Alignment** icons on the **Toolbar**, or using the options from **Layer > Arrange**. Feel free to change any object's colour.

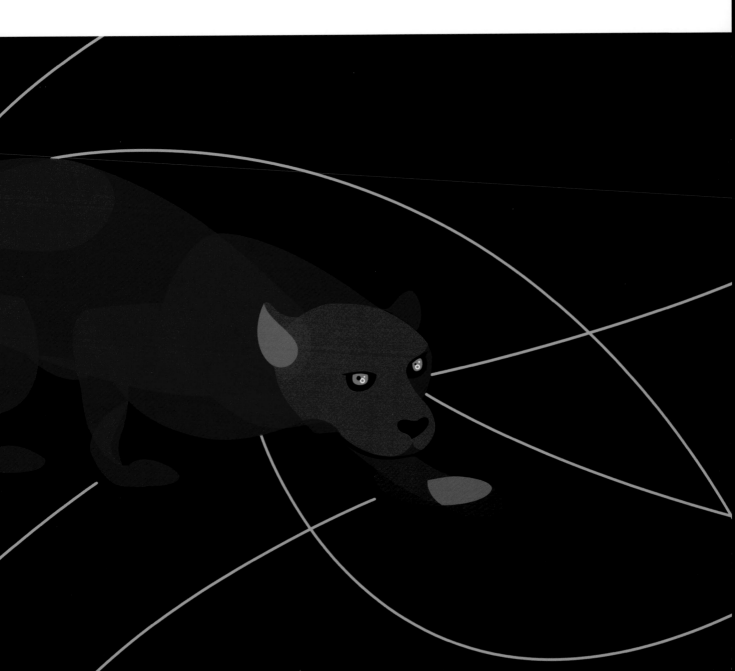

Resource

panther_07_gradients.afdesign

LIGHTING WITH GRADIENTS

Now we're going to add rich gradients to bring an ethereal quality to the piece.

1 Select the shape which defines the inside of the ear. From the **Edit Menu**, select **Duplicate** to create an identical shape immediately on top of the original.

2 Select the **Fill Tool** (G) on the **Tools Panel**, and from the context toolbar, ensure the **Context** is set to *Fill* and the **Type** is set to *Linear*. A horizontal gradient is immediately applied to the shape using the original solid colour as a starting point.

3 Click to select the stop on the right of the gradient path and then select a new colour (I chose *CMYK 0,92,77,73*) from the Colour Panel or a pre-existing colour from the Swatches Panel. Click the stop on the left and apply the exact same colour as you did to the right stop. Then, on the Colour or Swatches Panel, reduce the **Opacity** to *0%*. The results give a shaded appearance to the inner part of the ear.

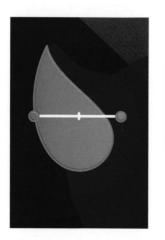

Notice how the Colour and Swatches Panels have updated to only display a single colour selector. This is because, when using the Fill Tool, you can only adjust one attribute at a time, either Fill or Stroke.

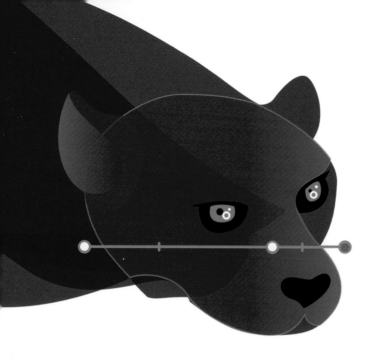

When working on this type of illustration, I prefer to apply gradients to a second, identical layer placed above the object with a solid fill. I then set the gradient with one end at 0% opacity. This allows the gradient to blend beautifully with the colours underneath.

4   Repeat the above process for the main head shape except use a lighter colour in the gradient. Then click on the gradient path just to the right of the eye to add an intermediate stop. This stop will automatically adopt the properties of the gradient directly below it. Adjust the opacity of this stop to 0% to create a smooth transition for the right side only.

The above process should be repeated across the remainder of the subject but shouldn't be applied indiscriminately. Some shapes will not need overlaying with a new gradient object while, at other times, a more complex set of graduated objects (as described below) might be preferable.

5   Select the two shapes which represent the body-tail and shoulder-neck sections of the subject. Duplicate these and, with the duplicates selected, select the **Divide** option on the **Toolbar**. This will split the selection into three distinct shapes based on overlapping content. Individual layer opacities and/or gradients can then be applied to these shapes.

See the Geometry Tools (p. 95) for more information on this functionality.

Grouping

The subject layer is getting crowded, so let's group elements together.

1   On the **Layers Panel**, select all the objects which correspond to the head of the subject and then, with the **Move Tool** (V) selected, click **Group** on the context toolbar. Name the group to be *head*, as you would any layer.

2   Group the remaining objects together to create a body group.

Gradients on Strokes

Gradients can be applied to an object's stroke as well as its fill. We'll convert all the curves on the background layer to gradients.

1   Select any background curve (select the *background* layer first, if you still have *Edit All Layers* deactivated) and then select the **Fill Tool**. On the context toolbar, set the **Context** to **Stroke** and the **Type** to **Linear**.

2   Set the two stops to the same colour but set the **Opacity** to *0%* for the stop closest to the subject. The colour of the curve will now gradually become more transparent as it moves from the edge of the page.

To temporarily hide the gradient path, hold down the spacebar.

Final touches

3 Add additional stops along the path, by clicking on the path, to adjust the opacity at intermediate points. You can drag directly on the page to define a new length and direction for the path.

Hold down the shift key (⇧) while dragging out the new path to constrain it to *45°* angles.

4 Once you have applied the gradient to one curve you can copy it to the other curves by using the **Copy** and **Paste Style** options from the **Edit Menu**. If this results in the gradient running the wrong way, select the **Reverse gradient** option on the context toolbar.

While working on the curves on the background layer I felt the two lines at the bottom left added nothing to the illustration, so I removed them.

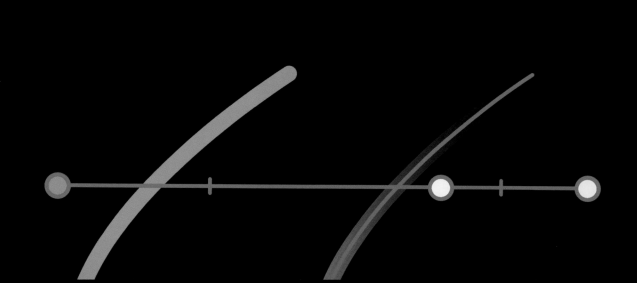

2

Reflected Skyline

Illustrating dramatic light and reflections by *Romain Trystram*

Join Romain as he creates a sumptuous illustration of a rain-drenched city skyline at night, with a focus on colour, light and creating reflections.

BEFORE YOU
GET STARTED

Resources

 You can get all the resources that are referenced in this project from:
https://affin.co/skyline

Knowledge of Affinity Designer

To get the most from undertaking this project, you will need to:

- Be familiar with the interface of Affinity Designer. You can learn more about the interface in the Interface Tour chapter, starting on p. 13.

- Have good core skills. See the skills table below to see which additional aspects of Affinity Designer you need to be confident with to complete this project:

Objects	p. 80
Layers	p. 92
Colours & Gradients	p. 106

CREATING THE CONCEPT

The design I wanted to create had to be visually stunning with a richness in lighting effects and vibrant beautiful colours across the skyscrapers. I coupled this with dark building silhouettes in the foreground along with a reflection which sets off the piece.

I don't start out with photos, references, or even a sketch when I create my illustrations. Instead, I start with a blank canvas and use my imagination to illustrate the scene I have in my mind.

I create the background main shapes first, then the background sky, then the middle shapes and finally the foreground. I think my technique is like the technique used in paper cutting in this way. I then do the 'in-betweens' with shapes and colours as I add more and more details.

I choose my colour palette as I progress with the illustration. It is really based on how I feel and I use the knowledge I have gained from illustrations I have made before. My goal is to always have good harmony between colours.

Resource

skyline_01_documentsetup.afdesign

DOCUMENT SETUP

1 Select **File > New**.

2 Set up the document using recommended settings, ensuring the **Page Width** and **Page Height** is set to *5120x2880 px*.

3 Ensure your **Document Units** are set to *Pixels*.

4 To aid alignment, draw a ruler guide via **View > Guides Manager**, and set a Horizontal Guide at *1938 px*. This will help to align shapes to this 'baseline' guide to maintain my composition.

BACKGROUND

The skyscrapers created in the background are tall rectangles which will provide a backdrop to the overall scene.

For the moment, the rectangles once created will need to be 'blocked in' with temporary solid fills. These fills will eventually be changed to gradient fills which will take on most of the colour vibrancy in the design and strongly suggest directional lighting.

Blocking in

1 On the **Layers Panel**, click **Add Layer**.

2 Click the layer name and type a new layer name called *Background scrapers*.

3 On the **Colour Panel**, select a solid Fill (*HSL 255,82,15*) and no stroke colour.

4 Using the **Rectangle Tool** (M) on the **Tools Panel**, draw rectangles of different heights to represent skyscrapers. Allow rectangles to overlap to form interesting skyscraper outlines where needed.

At this point you can optionally make use of Outline view mode on the Toolbar to see how skyscrapers are arranged and overlap.

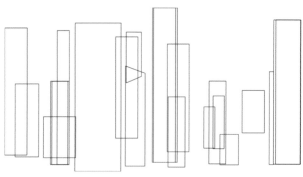

NIGHT SKY

I now want to introduce a background made up of the dark blue night sky and a soft pink glow that radiates from the city. The latter has transparency applied to blend nicely into the sky.

1   On the **Layers Panel**, click **Add Layer**.

2   Click the layer name and type *Night sky*. Drag the layer below the Background scrapers layer.

For the night sky:

3   With the **Rectangle Tool**, drag a rectangle over the page from top-left corner to bottom-right corner.

4   With the **Fill Tool** (G), apply a linear gradient by dragging upwards on the rectangle. Set the gradient from *HSL 245,63,9* (top) to *245,63,19* (bottom).

For a pink glow which blends with the dark sky:

5   Draw another rectangle that is offset on the page by setting dimensions in the **Transform Panel** (opposite).

6   Apply another linear gradient by dragging upwards, then using the **Colour Panel**, make the bottom end stop red (*HSL 0,100,59*) and the top end stop *0%* **Opacity**.

7   On the **Layers Panel**, give the rectangle an **Opacity** value of *42%*.

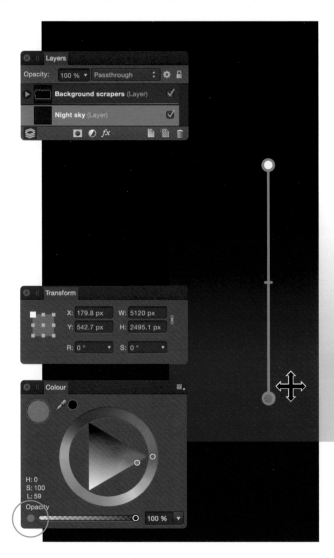

Resource

skyline_03_nightsky.afdesign

MIDGROUND

By introducing a midground layer we can draw in more buildings, predominantly skyscrapers, in front of the background scrapers. Again, these can initially be blocked in with a solid fill.

In a later stage of design, I'll introduce very subtle linear gradients and strong highlighted edges suggesting directional lighting. Compared to the background scrapers, fairly subdued gradients will be used.

Blocking in

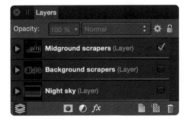

1   On the **Layers Panel**, select the Background scrapers layer, then click **Add Layer**. Name the layer *Midground scrapers*, then switch off the Background scrapers layer.

2   On the **Colour Panel**, select a dark blue solid Fill (*HSL 240,73,12*).

3   Draw skyscraper rectangles of different heights using the guide as the water's edge. Allow rectangles to overlap to form interesting skyscraper outlines where needed. I've also added a dark 'baseline' shape across the page, and changed the fill to *HSL 247,100,3* for some shapes.

If you're having trouble differentiating midground and background scrapers (they use a similar blue block fill), try hiding the Background scrapers and Night sky layers if needed!

Alternatively, for polygon shapes, use the **Pen Tool** (P) using the shift key (⇧) to constrain to horizontal or vertical as needed.

Resource
skyline_05_foregroundbuildings.afdesign

FOREGROUND

The next task is to introduce the darker buildings and structures in the foreground of the city. This area, around the water's edge, needs to be naturally backlit so the object fills are exclusively black.

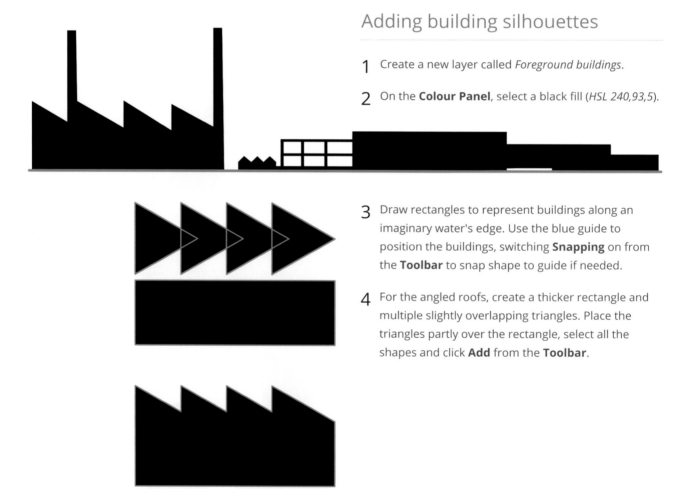

Adding building silhouettes

1 Create a new layer called *Foreground buildings*.

2 On the **Colour Panel**, select a black fill (*HSL 240,93,5*).

3 Draw rectangles to represent buildings along an imaginary water's edge. Use the blue guide to position the buildings, switching **Snapping** on from the **Toolbar** to snap shape to guide if needed.

4 For the angled roofs, create a thicker rectangle and multiple slightly overlapping triangles. Place the triangles partly over the rectangle, select all the shapes and click **Add** from the **Toolbar**.

Use this principle to create an angled-roof building that sits in the 'water' in readiness for later. The foreground is more or less complete except for any minor adjustments I might want to make later.

This is a great time for a recap. You should have a blocked-in design separated into a background, midground and foreground, which is set against a night sky.

The solid blue colours chosen for the skyscrapers appear dark and similar but these are a perfect starting colour from which to now develop lighting and detail. Although your design may not look spectacular at the moment, be assured that the basic design is on track!

Resource

skyline_06_midgroundlighting.afdesign

skyline01.afpalette

LIGHTING

I am always looking for ways to express lighting in my work and I try to make something different from what I have seen elsewhere.

In this design I wanted to add lighting to both the midground and background skyscrapers. For the former, the buildings are front lit with a very subtle blue or purple light, perhaps suggesting street lighting. The latter, more vibrantly coloured buildings emanate warmth with oranges and reds and contribute greatly to the overall piece. The colours used are chosen as the design progresses but choice is always considered and dependent on light source.

Lighting for midground skyscrapers

We'll concentrate on specific areas of the design where the lighting technique can be applied then easily copied to other similar buildings. Two areas are of interest—the left most block of four buildings, and the tallest skyscraper and surrounding buildings right of centre.

Applying gradients to short buildings (lit in blue):

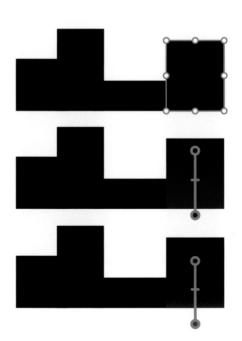

1   Select the midground layer.

2   From the block of buildings at the left, select the right-most building.

3   Using the **Fill Tool**, drag downwards across the shape to create the gradient.

4   On the **Colour Panel**, recolour the selected lower end stop to be *HSL 218,57,40,* then reposition either end stop (by dragging) to fine-tune the gradient path if needed. We'll copy this style to the other short buildings later.

> For these buildings, only the colour towards the light source needed to be set. This is why the solid colour was originally chosen with care, as it is consistent and harmonious with other buildings.

Applying gradients to skyscrapers (lit in purple/orange):

The same technique is needed but with more gradient manipulation. With buildings of differing height and varying colour requirements, the paths need to be of different length with both end stops being recoloured (rather than one).

1 Use the **Fill Tool** to apply a gradient to the middle building.

2 Change the gradient's end stop colours (*HSL 245,100,15 > 5,95,64*) and reposition the path by dragging end stops.

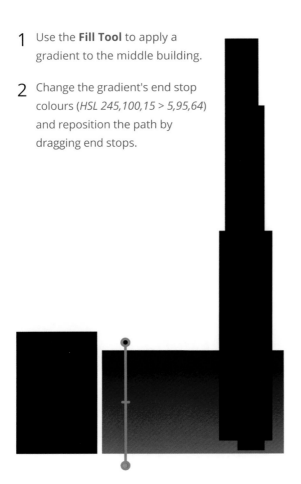

3 Repeat for the left and right buildings using different gradients (*HSL 245,100,15 > 328,65,23* and *HSL 253,82,16 > 328,65,23*), respectively.

Gradient paths can begin and end outside the object's outline.

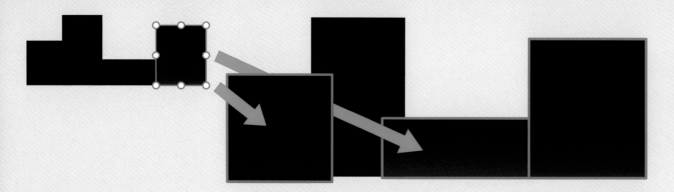

Copying styles

Some of the gradients can be shared between skyscrapers by copying styles—this is a quick and easy way to apply the same gradient between shapes simultaneously.

1 Select the 'source' shape.

2 From the **Edit Menu**, select **Copy**.

3 Select all other 'target' skyscrapers you want the gradient applied to.

4 From the **Edit Menu**, select **Paste Style**.

5 Fine tune the gradient paths on each skyscraper to make the gradient longer or shorter.

Side lighting

To finish this layer, I placed offset blue rectangles behind a few buildings to suggest side lighting from a strong blue light.

Lighting for background skyscrapers

The lighting for the background skyscrapers brings much more colour and vibrancy to the piece. These skyscrapers are exclusively illuminated using multi-coloured lights from street level. At this stage I need to consider light position, light direction and colour use.

Importing a document palette

- From panel preferences on the **Swatches Panel**, select **Import Palette > As Document Palette**. Navigate to, then select the file skyline01.afpalette, and click **Open**.

From the displayed palette you can use the swatches to apply colour to gradients.

> " *My choice of colour is driven by both inspiration and experience. To help you experiment with colour choice for the background skyscrapers, my choices are available in a downloadable document palette. By importing the palette, you can choose from these colours to get reproducible results.*

Resource

skyline_07_backgroundlighting.afdesign
skyline01.afpalette

Applying gradients to background skyscrapers

1 Select the background scrapers layer.

2 Use the **Fill Tool** to select a skyscraper, then drag downwards to set a default gradient.

3 Change the gradient's end stop colours, using colours available in the skyline01 document palette in the **Swatches Panel**.

4 Repeat for other skyscrapers.

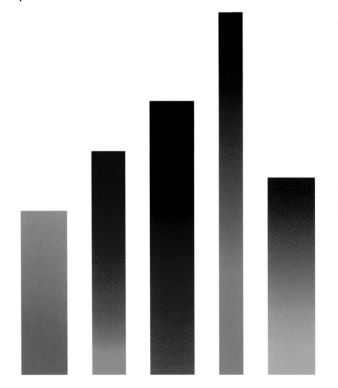

As soon as I apply the gradient, I like to give the already selected gradient end stop a lighter colour that matches my imagined source colour. I can then select the other end of the gradient and pick a complementary darker colour.

> *My lighting ideas in this project were based on several coloured light sources, i.e. light green, turquoise, brown, orange, and red.*

One variation on this approach was the cylindrical building to the left of the scene which needs to be lit from both sides. Here the gradient is drawn horizontally across the building, additional stops are added (by clicking) along the path, then all stops are recoloured from the **Swatches Panel**. The result is a rounded appearance because colours are lightened at the left and right building edges. Be sure to check Colours & Gradients on p. 106 for more details.

The completed Background scrapers layer should be rich in gradients and warm colours. The project should now be coming along nicely so let's take a sneak peek.

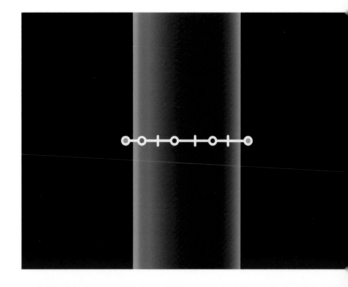

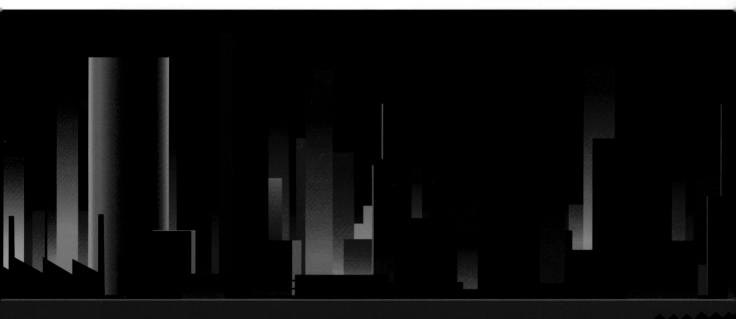

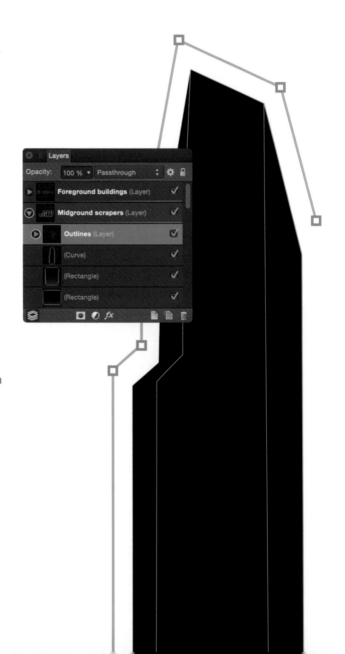

Resource

skyline_08_highlighting.afdesign

Highlighting edges

Now the shapes and colours are in place, the aim is to introduce further highlighting on selected skyscrapers. By adding brightly lit thin outlines, variable-width edges, and highlighted building faces the overall effect helps to 'pull' the skyscrapers out from the night sky and add depth.

Outlines

1 Create a new layer called *Outlines*, and place it within and at the top of the Midground scrapers layer.

2 On the **Colour** and **Stroke Panels**, set a turquoise stroke colour (*HSL 187,100,54*) and line **Width** of *0.6 pt*, respectively.

3 With the new layer selected, use the **Pen Tool** to click around the outline of selected skyscrapers to create a surrounding 'open' line made up of straight segments.

4 Repeat the process for the background scrapers too.

You can fine-tune colours to suit the lighting but keeping the edges bright is important.

> When drawing. keep the shift key (⇧) pressed to constrain the line to vertical, horizontal or a *45°* angle to match the skyscraper edges.

Variable width edges

Some skyscrapers need to be given a sense of depth by using strong side-lighting and a little top-lighting (this also helps contrast).

1 Select a building in the Midground scrapers layer.

2 Draw a thin rectangle that follows the horizontal or vertical outline of the skyscraper.

3 To suggest multi-coloured lighting, apply blues, greens, and purples as shown in the exploded view. These should suggest the colour of the nearby light source.

4 Repeat the process across more buildings and to the Background scrapers layer.

Alternatively, duplicate whole skyscrapers and offset the copy behind the 'parent' skyscraper. Only a faint edge needs to show. The advantage here is that you can reposition the rectangle at a later date.

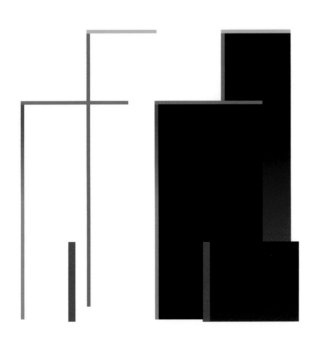

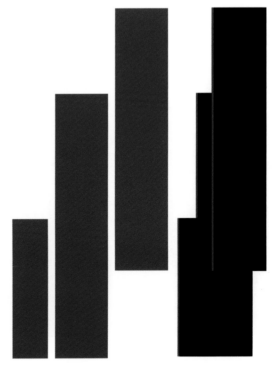

Highlighting building faces

Broader areas of highlighting can now be added to a few building faces.

1 Create a new layer called *Highlighted faces* and drag it under the Outlines layer.

2 With the **Pen Tool**, draw a polygon to fit within the skyscraper. Choosing a different colour which can be a solid or gradient fill.

Lighting will have made a big impact on the design. Let's take a look at both layers separately (Midground scrapers and Background scrapers) and preview some results. ▶

When both layers are switched on, results are even more impressive. ▶

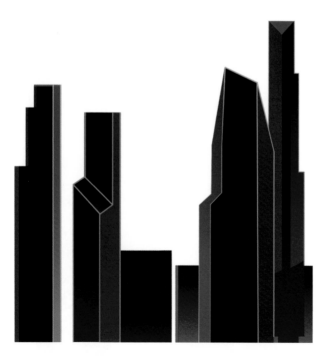

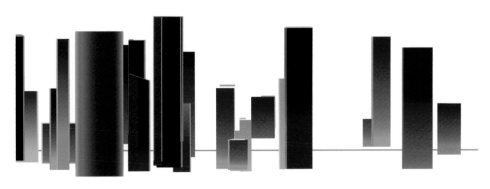

Background

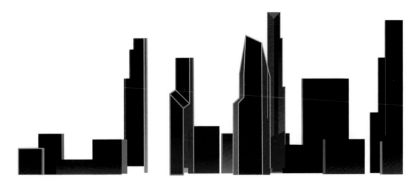

Midground

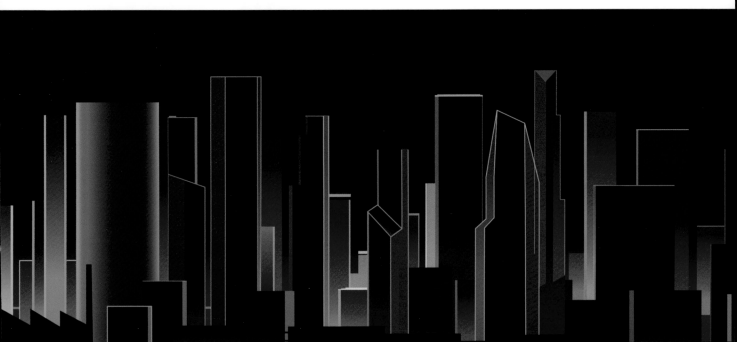

DETAIL

Adding details such as floors and windows make shapes transform into skyscrapers. Most of the detail can be created quickly by duplicating individual or grouped shapes to make patterns that represent floors and windows.

To break up uniformity, less regular patterns can be introduced to building frontage with just a few simple tricks. There's so much detail in this design that I'll just show a few examples exclusively—the floors and windows—because the basic design techniques I use are the same.

Skyscraper floors

Floors can be drawn as simple thin shapes that repeat regularly down the length of the skyscraper. To keep the floors within the building shape, **clipping** can be used. This stops me worrying about having to align the floors exactly to the building edges.

The spacing is important so be sure that you're happy with your initial placement.

1   Locate and select the blue skyscraper in the Background scraper layer. This is at the left of the scene and has a gradient.

2   With the **Rectangle Tool**, draw a thin rectangle close to the top of the blue skyscraper, which extends horizontally beyond the building sides. Apply a gradient (*HSL 200,54,41 > 251,71,10*).

3   Duplicate the rectangle using **Edit > Duplicate** and, with the shift key (⇧) pressed, drag the copy below the top rectangle. The key constrains the movement to vertical.

4   To **power duplicate**, keep pressing cmd ⌘ + J (Mac) or ctrl + J (Win) to create duplicates (I created 32 rectangles in the top floor section).

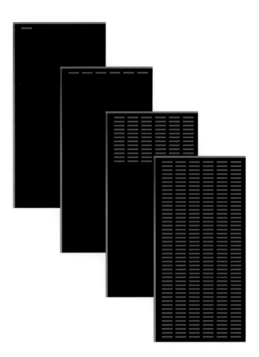

Use the same approach for skyscrapers with 'dotted' windows or those showing vertical features.

5 Select all thin rectangles, click **Group** from the context toolbar, and ctrl-click (Mac) or right-click (Win) to select **Find in Layers Panel**.

6 On the **Layers Panel**, drag the selected group inside the skyscraper rectangle. This clips the floors to the building outline.

7 Copy and paste the group, moving the copy down to fill the lower half of the scraper.

Skyscraper windows

As above, the window designs use a lot of duplicating. I'll want to copy the windows across and down the skyscraper by duplicating and grouping. All the windows should be uniformly spaced.

1 Locate and select the medium height skyscraper in the Midground scraper layer.

2 Draw a small rectangle (*HSL 211,78,45*) in the top left of the skyscraper and power duplicate it horizontally five times.

3 Group the windows, then power duplicate the group downwards 15 times as for the skyscraper levels above. Group these groups.

4 Power duplicate this group downwards twice and group all three groups.

You'll finish with a single group, containing three groups each containing 16 groups. These 16 groups all contain six windows each.

Applying a lighting gradient

At the moment the windows look very flat and uniform. By introducing a gradient across the group, the impression of upward light being reflected on window glass up the entire length of the skyscraper is possible.

1 Select the windows group.

2 With the **Fill Tool**, apply a linear gradient by dragging downwards across the skyscraper. Set the selected lower end stop colour to *HSL 244,49,13*.

Lighting windows selectively

As a final touch to the window design I'll recolour some windows sparingly. Maybe this suggests that some windows are slightly open and catch the light differently to the predominantly closed windows.

1 Click a chosen window with the cmd ⌘ key (Mac) or ctrl key (Win) pressed. Continue selecting more windows by also pressing the shift key (⇧) before further clicking.

2 Apply a solid fill to the windows, e.g., *HSL 192,78,45*. Selectively darken windows the lower their position on the skyscraper if needed.

With multi-level groups it's potentially tricky to select a grouped object. The modifiers use above 'drill' down into the group and target the object without any fuss.

More skyscraper windows

Up to now the floors and windows have been of a regular pattern. On a different skyscraper, let's create a more random and scattered arrangement of windows using dashes.

1 Locate and select the skyscraper with setbacks in the Midground scraper layer.

2 Draw thin rectangles (*HSL 140,95,61*) down and along the skyscraper. Give them different widths but keep the height to around *10 px*.

3 To create more interest, I applied a blue colour (*HSL 216,95,61*) to selected windows.

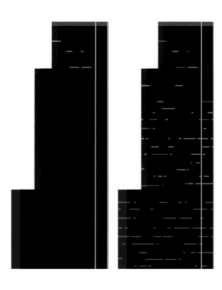

More detail

We've worked on three examples of different floor or window 'styles' across both Midground and Background scraper layers. The remaining windows and floors can be filled in for these layers, making sure that power duplicates and natural looking gradients are used.

I've also taken this opportunity to tidy up a few areas and fine tune my design by adding more detail above these two main layers.

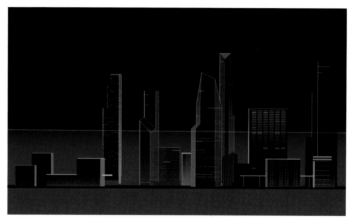

Midground layer in full detail

Foreground, Midground and Background layers viewed with extra details

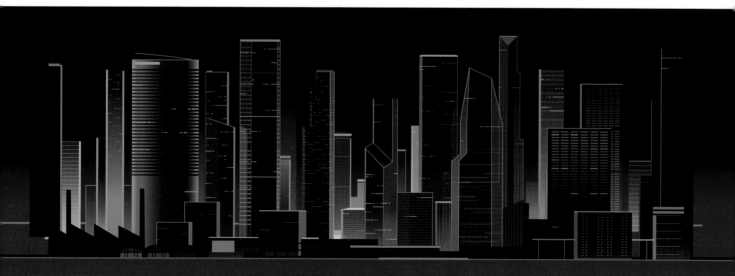

Resource
skyline_10_nicetouches.afdesign

NICE TOUCHES

The design possesses most of the detail now, but I'm keen to include some interesting additions before going any further.

Uplighting

I wanted to add multi-coloured uplighting above most of the skyscrapers. This gives the buildings a more contemporary look and really creates an impact in the overall scene. In terms of design, gradients are used which tail off into the night sky.

1   Draw a rectangle above a skyscraper, allowing it to extend to the top of the page.

2   Using the **Fill Tool**, drag upwards along the rectangle's length, and set the gradient to *HSL 212,69,21 > 360,100,67*.

3   Duplicate the rectangle, then make the rectangle at the back wider by dragging out from the side handle with the cmd ⌘ key (Mac) or ctrl key (Win) pressed. This resizes from object centre.

4   On the **Colour Panel**, drop the **Opacity** of the top and bottom rectangles to *20%* and *32%*, respectively.

Once all the uplights are created, group them together in an Uplights group and place at the bottom of the Background scrapers layer.

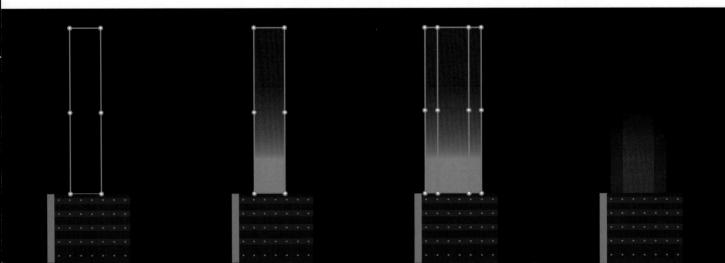

Rooftops

Some roofs can be added to a few skyscrapers using simple overlapping shapes.

A selected few can also be given various levels of opacity, giving them a glass-like appearance. These can be grouped for tidiness—I named my group *Scraper roofs* in the Background scrapers layer; other roofs were added to skyscrapers in the Midground scrapers layer.

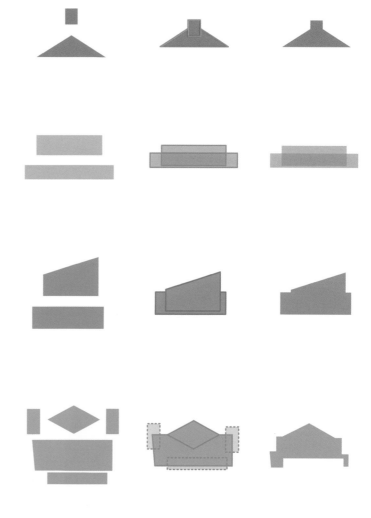

Adding stars

Although a subtle effect, a sprinkling of stars across the night sky are an absolute must have.

1 Select the Night sky layer.

2 Jump to **Pixel Persona** on the **Toolbar**.

3 Select the **Paint Brush Tool** (B) and set the **Width** and **Hardness** brush properties on the context toolbar.

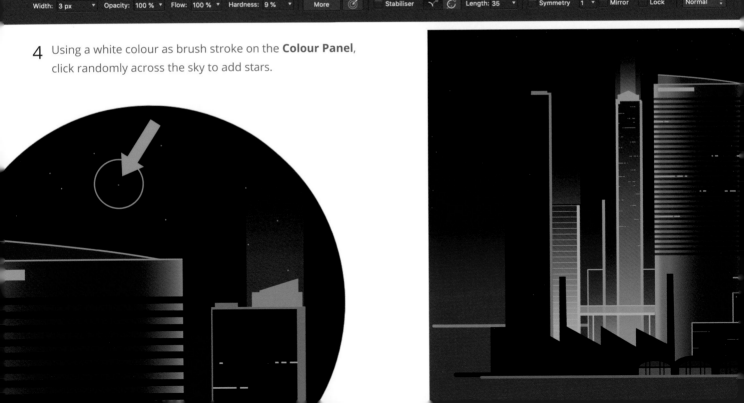

Width: 3 px ▾ Opacity: 100 % ▾ Flow: 100 % ▾ Hardness: 9 % ▾   More   Stabiliser   Length: 35 ▾   Symmetry 1 ▾ Mirror Lock   Normal ▴▾

4 Using a white colour as brush stroke on the **Colour Panel**, click randomly across the sky to add stars.

Waterside building

I'll add a foreground building using the same principles as before. This should be the last building and I'll place it in its own layer, called *Front building*, above the Foreground building layer.

REFLECTION

I love water reflections and these appear in many of my designs. For the Reflected Skyline design, the entire skyscraper scene is reflected onto the foreground water. It looks like a lot of work at this stage but a single transform operation achieves the look I want.

Reflection Base

First I want to add a dark base so the purple foreground is hidden. I'll then be able to put the reflection on top of this.

- On the **Layers Panel**, create a new layer called *Reflection base* above the top-level Roof highlight layer. For a dark foreground base, draw a black rectangle (*HSL 255,95,5*) covering the whole lower half of the page, with its top edge just touching the bottom of the foreground buildings.

Making the reflection

1 On the **Layers Panel**, select the following layers, keeping the cmd ⌘ key (Mac) or ctrl key (Win) pressed:

- Front building
- Foreground scrapers
- Midground scrapers
- Background scrapers

2 Duplicate the selection (**Edit > Duplicate)** then group it.

3 On the **Toolbar**, select **Flip Vertical**, then drag the group down so a reflection is formed. Use the shift key (⇧) while dragging to constrain vertically.

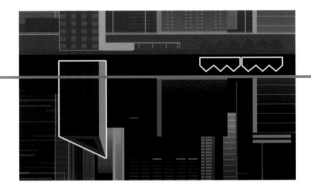

4 Create a new layer called *Reflection* above the Front building layer and drag the group into it.

At the moment, the reflection isn't as tight to the scene as I'd like. This is because the Front building extends into the foreground.

5 In the reflection group, select the Front Building layer and drag downwards to align with the bases of the other reflected shapes.

I chose to remove some detail from several reflected buildings at this stage. For example, the front building now has a solid fill without detail.

6 The entire reflection group can then be moved up to be closer to the main scene.

7 To give the reflection a realistic diffuse look, use the **Effects Panel** to apply a **Gaussian Blur** of *7.8 px* to the group. For the reflection tail off, draw a dark rectangle across the lower half of the reflection and apply a gradient from *HSL 230,81,4* to *0%* **Opacity**.

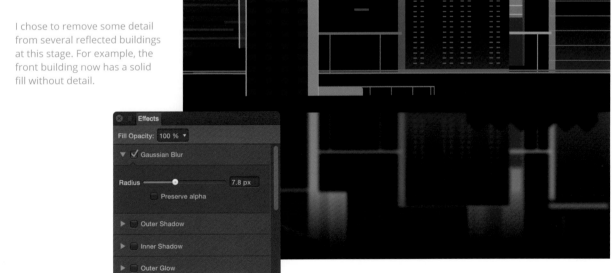

STREET

After adding the water reflection, the division between the city and the water needs defining. This was done by introducing an illuminated waterside city street that runs along the water's edge.

1 Select the Reflection base layer.

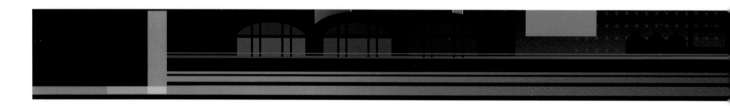

2 For the illuminated street lanes, draw three very thin rectangles (*6.8 px, 14.7 px, 23.9 px*) of full page width which are placed with increasing thickness towards the foreground. Give one a gradient of *HSL 0,85,64 > 217,75,19*, and copy its style from one to the others (using **Edit > Copy**, and **Edit > Paste Style**).

> *This project should have offered you an exciting and rewarding challenge. I hope you've enjoyed it and learnt something about my way of working and Affinity Designer.*

3 No city street is realistic without cars! Along the lanes, draw small rectangles, changing colours randomly as you draw.

3

The Whittler

Hybrid vector and raster painting by *Paolo Limoncelli*

In this project, Paolo explores creating a sci-fi illustration using both vector/raster techniques and shows you how to create your own brushes in Affinity Designer.

This illustration tells the story of a robot that lost his leg and tries to fix it using a branch from a tree he found in the forest...

BEFORE YOU GET STARTED

Resources

 You can get all the resources that are referenced in this project from:
https://affin.co/whittler

Knowledge of Affinity Designer

To get the most from undertaking this project, you will need to:

- Know how to use the **Pen Tool** in Affinity Designer. Master the **Pen Tool** by completing Pen Tool: Curves & Shapes on p. 97.

- Be familiar with the interface of Affinity Designer. You can learn more about the interface in the Interface Tour chapter, starting on p. 13.

- Have good core skills. See the skills table below to see which additional aspects of Affinity Designer you need to be confident with to complete this project:

Objects	p. 80	Colours & Gradients	p. 106
Layers	p. 92	Effects & Adjustments	p. 112
Geometry Tools	p. 95	Design Aids	p. 118

VECTOR VS. RASTER

Before we begin, let's explore why you would use vector or raster.

Vector and raster are two different kinds of digital graphics that are made, manipulated, and stored in different ways. To the eye their difference could be described in basic terms like the difference between a drawing (vector) and a photo (raster). They are both suited to different purposes and are based on very different technologies.

Not everyone who illustrates works in pure vector. Many prefer using raster programs over vector programs or other tools for vector work, creating very large bitmaps and scaling them down to final sizes to retain as much quality as possible. Others start with vectors in vector design software and then finish artwork elsewhere.

Affinity Designer, however, offers vector and raster design together in one app. One button switches the toolset—the document doesn't skip a beat, remaining scalable, native, and in one file format. This gives you the scalability of vector graphics with texture you can only get with raster.

Primarily, the benefits of having raster capabilities in a vector program are the ability to use raster brushes, let's look at an overview of why that is...

ABOUT VECTOR
AND RASTER BRUSHES

Vector brushes

A vector brush is composed of either a stretched bitmap or repeating bitmaps along the brush's path, along with an optional head and/or tail section. This makes them ideal for very expressive strokes. Brush size and opacity can be varied in response to pressure (from graphics tablet or mouse velocity).

Key characteristics of vector brushes:

- Fast vector performance.

- Brush strokes remain editable on page (colour, width, opacity, path direction).

- Perfect appearance at any export resolution.

- Great for blocking larger areas (e.g., watercolour washes).

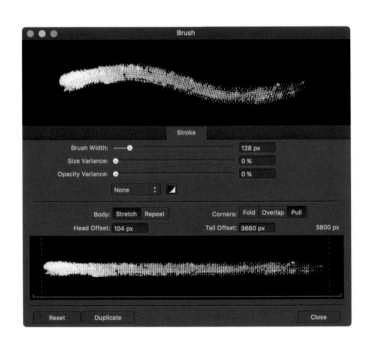

Raster brushes

Raster brushes are comprised of one or more brush nozzles (tips or nibs) that are laid down repeatedly along the brush stroke; these nozzles are loaded in the Brush Settings dialog. Nozzle spacing and rotation is controllable; a wide selection of jitter settings will respond to various brush controllers.

Key characteristics of raster brushes:

- Emulates natural media brushwork beautifully.

- Perfect for precision work and refinement.

- Scope for complex customisation (to utilize graphics tablet features).

- Organic results with controllable colour blending.

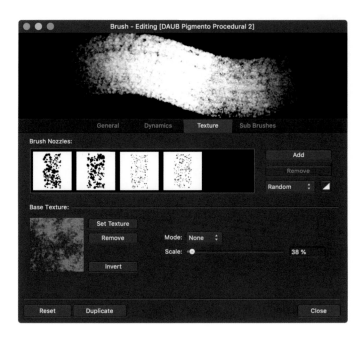

CREATING RASTER BRUSHES

Resource

nib_01.png

nib_02.png

paper_dark_seamless.png

In this project, we'll be creating a small set of digital media brushes which are perfect for both vector and raster work and will enable us to complete The Whittler illustration later on. However, if you want skip this section and get on with creating the illustration, go to p. 212. You will be able to download and import the brushes I have provided at the appropriate point.

First, let's look at creating raster brushes in Affinity Designer and for this you must be in **Pixel Persona**. I have created nozzle images for you to use to complete this section, but you can find out how to make your own nozzles on p. 202.

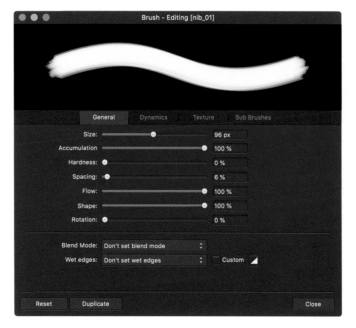

1   Switch to **Pixel Persona** and go to the **Brushes Panel**.

2   From panel preferences, select **Create New Category**. Rename the category to *DAUB Workbench* using panel preferences.

3   From panel preferences, select **New Intensity Brush**.

4   In the dialog, navigate to, select and open nib_01.png. You'll have now created a new brush, previewed and available from the **Brushes Panel**.

5   Double-click the brush to display the **Brush - Editing** dialog. In the **General tab**, use the settings shown to the left, but experiment with **Spacing** to control the distance between the repeating nozzles. A value of between *4%* and *6%* is ideal, with *6%* being perfect for making the texture show realistically.

Dynamics (pressure-sensitive flow)

The **Brush - Editing** dialog offers a **Dynamics tab** to control how the brush responds to pressure from a drawing device such as a tablet. Let's make brush flow in response to pressure by setting a **Flow Jitter** value of *100%* and enabling the *Pressure* controller.

For a non-linear pressure response, click the **Ramp** icon then select the third standard profile (concave parabolic). Delete one of the intermediate nodes, then reposition the remaining node as shown, shaping the curve.

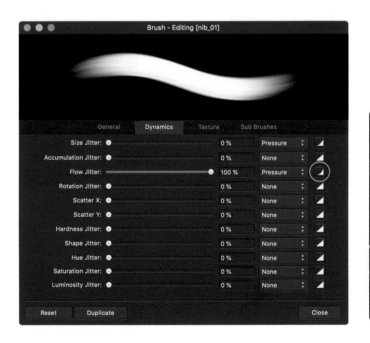
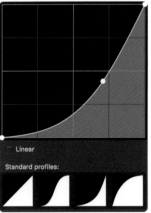

Dynamics (nozzle rotation with stroke direction)

Repeat the process for **Rotation Jitter**, increasing it to *100%* but change the controller to *Direction*. This allows the nozzles to rotate so they follow the stroke's current direction while keeping the stroke size constant.

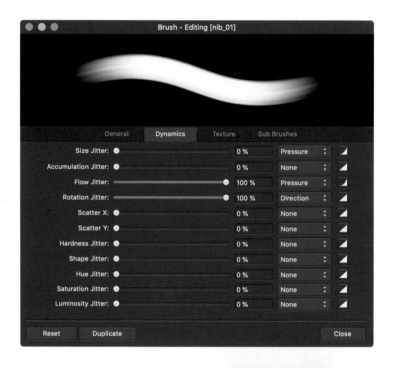

Colour blending

Let's make the brush blend colours as strokes are built up. From the dialog's **General tab**, set the **Blend Mode** to *Average*. Now an intermediate colour results when the current brush colour is applied over an already underlying stroke on the page.

Multiple nozzles

The brush is almost complete, but an extra nozzle can be added for a more natural look.

1   From the dialog, select the **Texture tab**.

2   Click **Add** and navigate to, select and open the second nozzle, called nib_02.png.

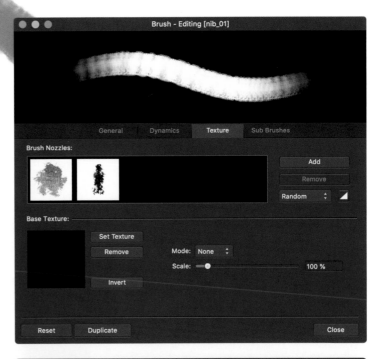

Adding texture

Finally, a base texture can be added for a deeper effect. The texture is sourced from a seamless greyscale dark pattern taken from a scanned piece of paper.

1   From the dialog's **Texture tab**, click **Set Texture**.

2   Navigate to, select and open paper_dark_seamless.png.

3   Set the accompanying settings: **Mode** to *Nozzle* and **Scale** to *200%*. The former applies the texture to every nozzle for a more organic look.

Naming your brush

It's a great idea to uniquely name your brushes to keep track of them. A hover over of the brush in the **Brushes Panel** will report the brush name as a tooltip.

- On the **Brushes Panel**, ctrl-click (Mac) or right-click (Win) the brush, and rename it *Main Stroke*.

CREATING A
DETAIL BRUSH

We'll create another brush for more detailed brush work. It will be initially based on the previously created brush.

1   From the **Brush - Editing** dialog, click **Duplicate** to make a copy of the *Main Stroke* brush you have just created.

2   Double-click the duplicated brush in the **Brushes Panel** to make it active.

3   On the **Texture tab**, delete the first nozzle (nib_01.png) by selecting its thumbnail and clicking **Remove**. Also delete the **Base Texture** by clicking **Remove**.

4   Change brush settings in the **General tab** to those shown to the right. This gives a flat bristle brush which is perfect for our needs.

5   Ctrl-click (Mac) or right-click (Win) the brush in the **Brushes Panel** and rename it as *Details*.

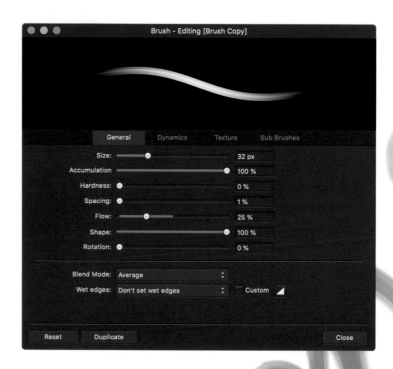

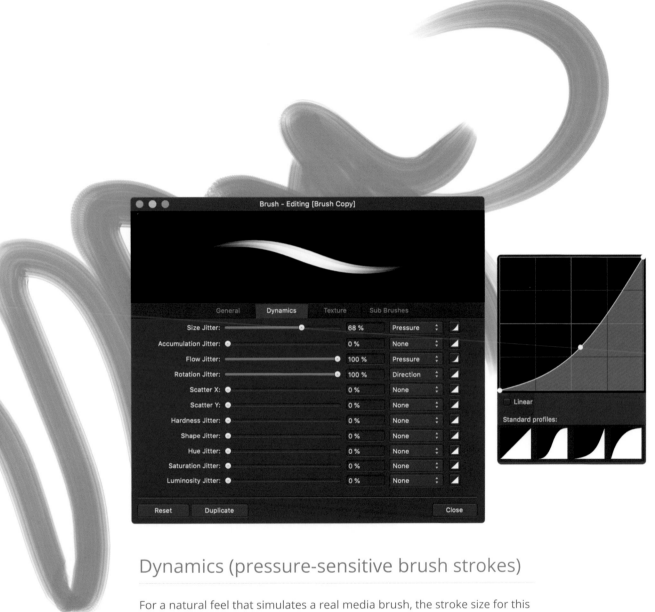

Dynamics (pressure-sensitive brush strokes)

For a natural feel that simulates a real media brush, the stroke size for this brush needs to respond to pressure.

1 In the **Dynamics tab**, ensure the brush's **Size Jitter** value is set to respond to *Pressure* with a jitter value of *68%*.

2 Choose a custom non-linear ramp for **Size Jitter** too.

If needed, vary these settings to fit your style and way of painting.

Resource

fractal_texture.png

CREATING A TEXTURE BRUSH

Our penultimate raster brush is a texture brush based on the previously created brush.

1 From the *Detail* brush's dialog, click **Duplicate** to make a copy, then double-click the duplicated brush in the **Brushes Panel** to make it active.

2 In the **Texture tab**, click **Set Texture**, then navigate to, select and open fractal_texture.png.

3 Set **Mode** to *Nozzle* and **Scale** to *40%* to shrink the pattern on the stroke.

4 Ctrl-click (Mac) or right-click (Win) the brush in the **Brushes Panel** and rename it to be *Details Textured*.

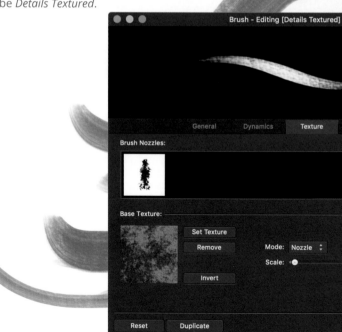

CREATING A SHADING BRUSH

Finally, a raster brush is needed for general support such as shading and erasing.

You'll need to create a new brush from scratch but use the **New Round Brush** option instead of the **New Intensity Brush** option. This brush will not be formed from a texture or nozzle image.

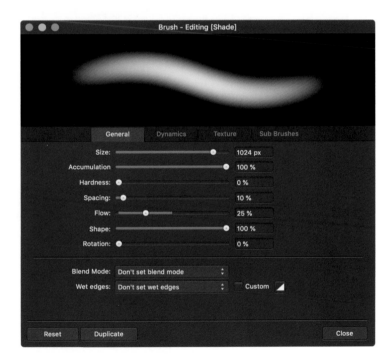

1 From the **Brush Panel,** click panel preferences and select **New Round Brush**. Rename the brush *Shade* and apply the above settings in the **General tab** of the **Brush - Editing** dialog.

2 In the **Dynamics tab**, set the **Flow Jitter** to *100%* and enable the *Pressure* controller.

CREATING VECTOR BRUSHES

Resource

stroke_01.png

Now let's create our watercolour vector brush in its own created custom category. To complete this section you need to be in the **Designer Persona** of Affinity Designer, as the **Brushes Panel** in this Persona is where we access and create vector brushes.

1 Ensure **Designer Persona** is enabled, then select the **Brushes Panel**.

2 From panel preferences, select **Create New Category** then rename the category *DAUB Vector Workbench*.

3 From panel preferences, choose **New Textured Intensity Brush**.

4 From the dialog, navigate to, select and open stroke_01.png. You'll have created a new brush, previewed and available from the **Brushes Panel**.

5 Double-click the brush to display the **Brush - Editing** dialog. In the **Stroke tab**, use the settings shown (above-right) to set up the brush. The *Pressure* controller should be enabled and should use a non-linear curve similar to that used for raster brushes.

6 In the **Brushes Panel**, rename the brush to be *DAUB Watercolour*.

> The **Brush - Editing** dialog in the **Designer Persona** is more simplistic than that for a raster brush. Basic and pressure variance settings are unified in a single tab.

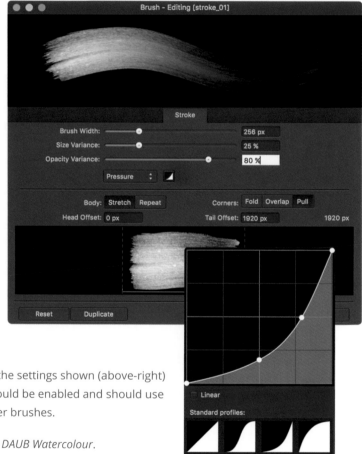

Vector brush texture control

As the brush is to be intended for short brush strokes, the brush's texture can be set to stretch along the length of the stroke.

For more grainy textures, the **Repeat** option is more suitable as the individual grains need to be preserved and should not be stretched.

1 Ensure **Body** and **Corners** are set to *Stretch* and *Pull*, respectively.

2 In the lower preview window, drag the red dashed lines at the head and tail inwards to trim the stroke. This cuts out the transparent space at the start and end of the brush stroke.

> For other textures, it's possible to 'freeze' the head and tail in order to prevent them from being stretched or repeated. In this project we won't do this, as we're emulating watercolours which would need further work to make the body section seamless—even the most perfect stroke would result in an unnatural look. For dry media strokes (such as chalks), spend time fine-tuning the head/tail offset positions too.

CREATE YOUR OWN RASTER NOZZLES

Resource

sketch_01_documentsetup.afdesign
nibs_01_documentsetup.afdesign

It is important to have a clear idea of the style you want to reach in your final piece. So, as we do with real media, we start choosing our brushes right at the beginning.

For the coming illustration, we created five brushes: four acrylic/oil raster brushes to add details to the image and a single watercolour vector brush for texture and an analog look.

This section details how I originally created the resources we've just used to create the five brushes.

> *Brush design is an inherently complex task and may require experimentation to get things just how you like them. When you're warming up or doodling ideas, don't be afraid to change settings; if you find something interesting, store the settings as a duplicated brush.*

Creating a sketch board

Let's initially create a sketch board where we can doodle and tune-up vector and raster brushes. You can use this at any time through the project.

1 Select **File > New**.

2 Set up the new document as shown to the right.

3 Save the file as sketch.afdesign.

About raster brush nozzles

Raster brushes require one or more brush nozzles to be defined. These are sourced from scans of real media brush dabs applied to paper.

Let's set up a base nozzle document to place our scanned nozzle images.

1 Select **File > New**.

2 Set the **Page Width** and **Page Height** to be *512 px* each. A **DPI** value of *72* is fine.

3 Select the **Rectangular Tool** (M) from the **Tools Panel** and draw a square which fills the page. Recolour the square's **Fill** to *white*.

4 Save the file as nibs.afdesign.

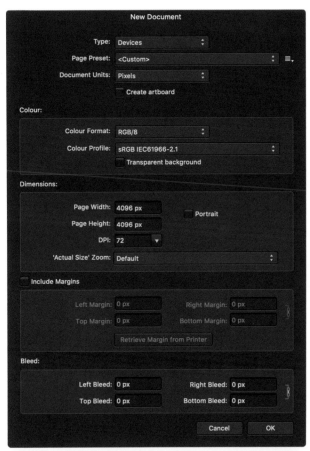

For any nozzle, a size of 512x512 px will be enough as brush sizes will typically be limited to <200 px for detailed work.

Resource
nibs_source.tiff

Scanning

Now get your brushes out and get creative!

1 Dab your chosen brush onto the paper for each nozzle you want to create. A larger rounded profile and a smaller thinner one is perfect for our two nozzles.

2 Once dried, scan the paper at *600 DPI greyscale*.

Alternatively, you can also photograph the nib sources using a digital camera or smart phone.

Opening the scanned image

1 Select **File > Open**.

2 Navigate to and select the nibs_source.tiff file.

3 Click **Open**.

Creating raster brush nozzles

The sources now have to be separated from each other
to make two unique brush nozzle images.

1 Jump to **Pixel Persona**.

2 Select the **Rectangular Marquee Tool** (M) from the
Tools Panel and drag a square marquee over the
larger source while keeping the shift key (⇧) pressed.

3 Select **Edit > Copy**.

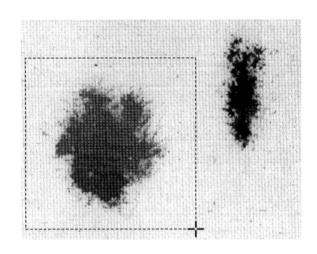

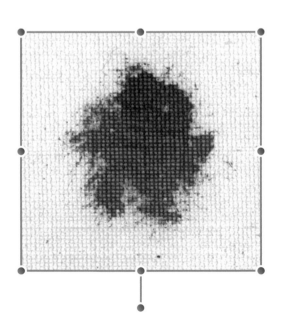

4 Jump to the already open nibs document and select
Edit > Paste. A new layer is created, which can be
named *nib_01*.

5 Reposition and resize the image so it fits the page.
Switch snapping on so the image snaps to the page
edges.

6 The image needs to be rotated 180 degrees. Use the
Rotate option on the **Transform Panel** and enter
180.

The nozzle image now just needs a clean up.

7 Do the same for the other nozzle, naming the layer
nib_02. Click the check box to hide this layer for the
moment.

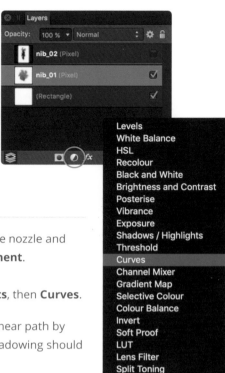

Resource
nibs_03_cleanup.afdesign

Cleaning up nozzle images

By manipulating tones in the nozzle image you can increase contrast in the nozzle and clean up canvas shadowing easily. We can do this using a **Curves adjustment**.

1 From the **Layers Panel**, select the nib_01 layer, then click **Adjustments**, then **Curves**.

2 Increase highlights in the **Curves** dialog by adding two nodes on the linear path by clicking, then drag nodes into position as shown below. The canvas shadowing should be reduced.

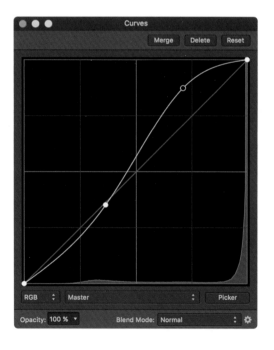

Instead of a Curves adjustment you could apply a Levels adjustment instead. This lets you set black and white points from which pixels outside these points are considered pure black or white, therefore avoiding halos.

Exporting the nib files

1 Export the file as a PNG using **File > Export**, naming the file nib_01.png.

2 From the **Layers Panel**, uncheck the nib_01 layer, check the second nozzle layer and repeat the procedure described above, creating nib_02.png.

nib_01.png

To clean up any peripheral speckles or dust, paint in white using the **Paint Brush Tool** on the **Tools Panel** in **Pixel Persona**.

nib_02.png

To transform your nozzles into raster brushes, go to section Creating raster brushes on p. 192.

To learn how to make nozzles for vector brushes, proceed to the next section.

CREATE YOUR OWN VECTOR NOZZLES

The process to create nozzles for vector brushes is similar to that for creating raster brushes. We'll start with real media—water diluted black pigment, a real brush, a sheet of paper and a scanner.

Scanning

After painting strokes of varying thickness and strength onto paper, scan the dry paper. If you're using a scanner, a resolution between 600 to 800dpi is acceptable.

For vector brush creation, scanning is preferred to photography as it gives more uniform illumination and a more natural constant tone. Resolution is also important, because we'll use them to fill large areas so they have to look as crisp as possible.

Let's create a document into which we'll place our scanned image.

1   Select **File > New**.

2   Set the **Page Width** and **Page Height** to be *1920x1080 px*, and *96 DPI*.

3   Add a black rectangle the size of the page and save the file as strokes.afdesign.

For the pigment, black hi-diluted India ink or acrylic is recommended as it displays well on screen once scanned. Alternatively, you can use watercolours or gouaches, or even coffee or wine, but in this case I suggest cheap ones!

Resource
strokes_source.tiff
strokes_02_scan.afdesign

Opening the scanned image

1 Select **File > Open**.

2 Navigate to and select strokes_source.tiff.

3 Click **Open** to display the image.

4 Repeat the steps you followed for Creating raster brush nozzles (p. 205) involving copying a stroke as a selection from the strokes_source.tiff into strokes.afdesign. Manipulate the pasted image to fit nicely on the page.

  We'll choose the stroke at the top right of the image to base our vector brush on.

5 As for raster brushes, apply a **Curves** adjustment to the image layer to increase contrast.

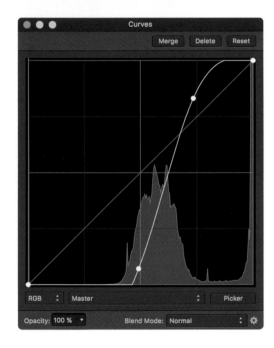

Resource

strokes_03_invert.afdesign

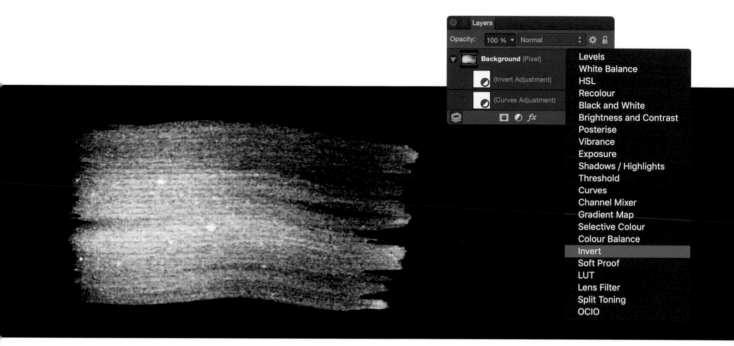

Inverting the stroke image

As Affinity Designer's vector engine interprets dark areas of the image as transparent and white areas as opaque, it's essential to invert the image layer. This is made easy by applying an adjustment.

- From the **Layers Panel**, select the image layer, then click **Adjustments**, then **Invert**.

Exporting the stroke file

- Export the image layer as a PNG using **File > Export,** naming the file stroke_01.png.

The sources are now ready to be used to create brushes. See Creating vector brushes on p. 200.

THE WHITTLER

In this section we will create The Whittler illustration. This illustration tells the story of a robot that lost his leg and tries to fix it using a branch from a tree he found in the forest.

1 To begin, create a *6000x4000 px* document in *RGB/8* **Colour Format**. Specify the **Document Units** as *Pixels*.

The final illustration will be cropped to 5120x2880 pixels, but start off with extra room in order to have enough space to fix any composition issues that may come up.

2 To give focus on the eventual actual size, use the **Rectangle Tool** (M) to create a rectangle that is *5120x2880 px* in size, and centre it on the page using the **Alignment** pop-up panel on the **Toolbar**.

3 Then, using the rectangle as a guide, use the **Guides Manager** to create a rule of thirds grid to help you with the composition even in the early concept stage.

4 Once the grid is complete, delete the rectangle.

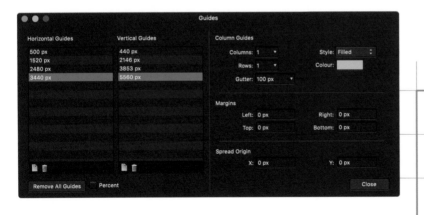

Resource
whittler_02_sketch.afdesign

SKETCHING THE CONCEPT

To create the concept sketch, switch to the **Pixel Persona** to sketch with a basic pixel (raster) brush to make rough lines. Sketch this scene using a photographic approach. Introduce perspective distortion and scale the image slightly as you move through to the background.

This is my concept sketch so I'm not looking for precision at this stage, but you can see how I use layers and colours to separate planes and perspectives.

Sketching steps

1 On the **Layers Panel**, click the **Add Layer** icon and rename the layer *sketch*.

2 Now create a new pixel layer called *foreground* using the **Add Pixel Layer** icon on the **Layers Panel**. This pixel layer will appear as a sub-layer of the sketch layer.

3 Jump to **Pixel Persona**, select the **Paint Brush Tool** (B) and select a *Basic* brush from the **Brushes Panel**. Use a purple colour to sketch trees and grass around the edges of your canvas.

4 When the foreground sketch is complete, sketch the robot and then two other planes (mid-ground and background), making a new pixel layer each time. Use a different colour for each perspective plane to help you with composition.

Checking composition

Create a frame to see what the illustration will look like when cropped to the final dimensions.

1 Switch back to the **Designer Persona** and create a new layer at the top of your layer stack in the **Layer Panel** called *frame*.

2 Draw a rectangle using the **Rectangle Tool** to the dimensions of the document *(6000x4000 px)*. Use the **Transform Panel** to get precise dimensions for your rectangle. Give this rectangle a black colour fill and use the alignment tools to centre the shape on your page.

3 Draw another rectangle as above but this time with the dimensions of *5120x2880 px*.

4 Select both rectangles and, on the **Toolbar**, select **Subtract** to create the final frame shape.

5 When you're happy with the frame, uncheck the *frame* layer entry in the **Layers Panel** to hide the frame.

Final adjustments to the concept

Finally add a **Black and White Adjustment Layer** to the *sketch* layer. There are two reasons for doing this; firstly to check if the perspective works and secondly to give a rough idea of the tones that will be required when we add in atmospheric perspective later on.

1   Select the *sketch* layer and select the **Adjustments** icon in the **Layers Panel**.

2   Choose *Black and White* from the pop-up menu.

> At this point, make sure both the *sketch* layer and the frame layer are locked.

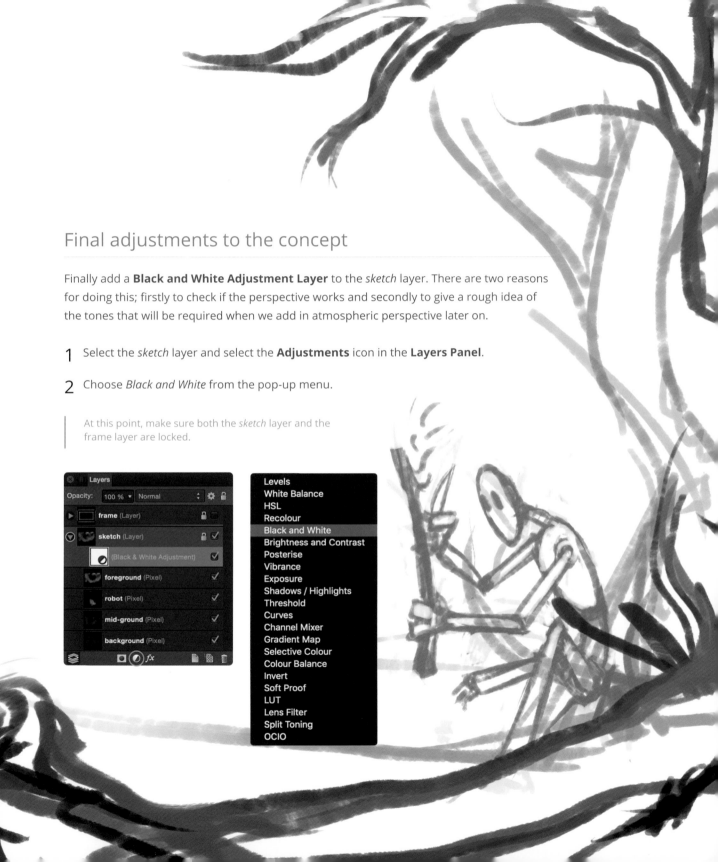

CREATE SHAPES AND LAYERS

Resource

whittler_03_shapes.afdesign

It is now time to define the layers and shapes in our illustration.

Setup

1 With the sketch layer selected, create two new layers called *illustration* and *canvas*.

2 On the **Layers Panel**, drag the canvas layer inside the the illustration layer to create a nested layer.

3 Switch to **Designer Persona** and then, on the *canvas* layer, use the **Rectangle Tool** to create a rectangle that is bigger than the page. Apply a grey to white elliptical gradient colour fill. Lock this layer and hide it so you it doesn't get in your way.

Vectorise your scene

We are now going to use the **Pen Tool** to vectorise our scene.

1 In the sketch layer, switch off each nested layer except for the foreground layer. Then create a new nested layer inside the illustration layer called *foreground* (to mirror the layers in the sketch layer).

2 With this new layer selected, with the **Pen Tool** (P) set to **Polygon Mode**. Start tracing over your foreground sketch. Add in details you like as you go, such as leaves and grass.

3 Apply a grey colour fill to your shape *(RGB 64,64,64)*.

4 Use the **Node Tool** (A) at any point to fix and smooth your curves.

5 Don't feel forced to keep to the structure of the sketch and add as many layers as you need. I needed three foreground illustration layers to replicate the depth of the illustration I envisioned from my original sketch.

6 Repeat the above steps for the other two planes, but for each new plane apply a lighter grey colour fill. Leave the robot for now; we will tackle him later.

> *Don't worry if you make a mistake! Because you are working in vector you can easily refine the shapes you make with the **Node Tool** at any time.*

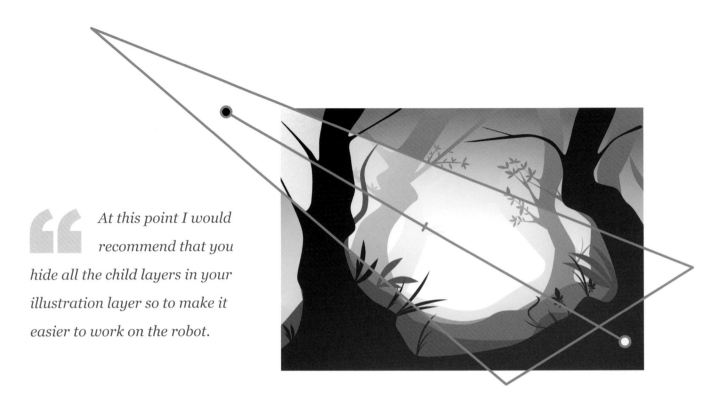

> *At this point I would recommend that you hide all the child layers in your illustration layer so to make it easier to work on the robot.*

Add the light source

Let's add a light source to our scene.

1 Create a new layer called *beam* just below the foreground layer(s) in the illustration layer.

2 Using the **Pen Tool**, trace a triangle shape from the top left corner of the page towards where the robot will sit.

3 Apply a pure white colour fill to your shape *(RGB 255, 255, 255)* and using the **Transparency Tool** (Y) fade the light strength towards the bottom right corner of the page.

4 Select each of the shapes in the illustration layer in turn and apply a linear gradient fill that reflects the light source you have just added.

Now we have set up our environment, let's get on with creating the robot.

Vectorising the robot

1. In the sketch layer, ensure only the robot layer is visible. Reduce the opacity of this layer to help you create your vector illustration on top.

2. In the illustration layer, switch off each nested layer and create a new nested layer called *robot*.

3. Select the **Pen Tool**, choose **Polygon Mode** and start tracing over your robot sketch.

4. As before, fill each shape with a grey fill, using darker grey values for closer body parts and lighter grey values the further away the body part is. For example, the right arm (holding the knife) should be lighter than the left one (holding the tree branch).

5. When you are finished, select all the objects you have made in this layer in the **Layers Panel** and group them.

Check your composition (using your frame layer if needed). Now is the time to tweak any of the colours of your shapes, add more details such as grass and plants, and to refine the light beam where it hits the tree's largest branches.

Now let's add some texture using both vector and raster paint.

Use the Add geometry operation to combine new shapes to your existing shapes.

VECTOR PAINTING

Resource

DAUB Vector Workbench.afbrushes
whittler_04_vectorpainting.afdesign

Let's now start adding some texture to our illustration using digital paint and vector brushes. We're going to be using the vector brush we made earlier (p. 200). If you have not completed that section, you can import the brushes provided in the resources.

Importing brushes

- From the **Brushes Panel**'s panel preferences, select **Import Brushes**. Select DAUB Vector Workbench.afbrushes and click **Open**.

The vector brush set will be imported into the **Brushes Panel** in **Designer Persona**.

Painting vector strokes

1   Select the shape which represents to closest trees and choose **Insert inside the selection** on the **Toolbar**. This shape will act as a clipping layer for our brush strokes.

2   Select the **Vector Brush Tool** (B) and the *DAUB Watercolour* from the *DAUB Vector Workbench* category in the **Brushes Panel**.

3   From the **Controller** pop-up menu on the context toolbar, select **Brush Defaults**. This will enable the pressure response on your graphics tablet.

4   Using the **Colour Picker Tool** (I), load the brush with a dark grey value taken from the gradient colour of the tree shape.

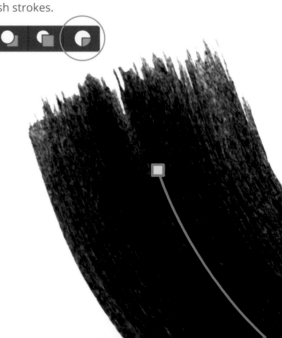

5   Paint random strokes on the page to give a pleasant textual look to the trees. Experiment with varying the width of your stroke using the **Width** slider on the context toolbar.

6   In the **Layers Panel**, select all of the painted curves and set their blend mode (via the pop-up menu) to *Multiply*.

7   Group all the brush strokes together to keep your **Layers Panel** neat and organised.

At this point we have only applied vector painting to the *foreground 1* layer. The main advantage of vector painting is the ability to scale and reshape strokes after being laid on the page. However, one of the arguments for raster painting (applying pixels to a page) is that it gives a more organic appearance. So in the next steps we will be incorporating raster painting into all of our 'scene' layers.

> *If you find the texture of the brush strokes too overpowering, drop the opacity of the group to make the effect subtler.*

RASTER PAINTING

Resource

DAUB Raster Workbench.afbrushes

whittler_05_rasterpainting.afdesign

We're going to be using the raster brushes we designed earlier (p. 192), if you have not completed this section you can import the brushes provided in the resources.

Importing brushes

- From the **Brushes Panel**, click panel preferences, select **Import Brushes**. Select DAUB Raster Workbench.afbrushes and click **Open**.

The raster brush set will be imported into the **Brushes Panel** in **Pixel Persona**.

Painting raster strokes

1   Switch to **Pixel Persona** and select the **Pixel Tool** (B).

2   In the **Layers Panel**, select the group containing the vector strokes we've just created in the foreground 1 layer, and choose **Insert behind the selection** on the **Toolbar**. Then add a new **Pixel Layer** to act as the shadows and midtones layer.

3   On the **Brushes Panel**, select the *Main Stroke* brush from the *DAUB Workbench* category and load the brush with a dark grey, varying this as you paint if desired. Vary the brush size, using the **Width** option on the context toolbar, as you paint your shadows and midtones to achieve a natural appearance to the tree's texture.

4   On the **Layers Panel**, select the group of vector brush strokes again, and add a new **Pixel Layer** to act as the highlights layer.

5   On the **Brushes Panel**, select the *Details Textured* brush from the *DAUB Workbench* category and load the brush with pure white. If you'd prefer a flatter look, select the *Details* brush instead.

6   Paint some highlights on areas of the tree where light would appear based on the light source. Then drop the opacity of the pixel layer, using the option on the **Layers Panel**, to make the effect more natural. A setting of around *18%* should do the job.

To get the most authentic painted appearance in your illustration, work at low zoom values, such as 25–30% for general painting and 60–70% for detail. Working at 100% zoom or more may encourage you to add more detail than is necessary and give the illustration an inauthentic painted look. The **Zoom Tool** and **Navigator Panel** give you full control over your preferred zoom level.

7   Repeat the previous process to all the layers in your scene to apply grey tone raster shadows and highlights to the remaining layers. To simulate diffused patches of light, try out the *Shade* brush from the *DAUB Workbench* brush set. Vary the opacity and set the blend mode of the layer to *Multiply* where needed.

8   When you think you are done, hide the beam and robot layers (if they are not already hidden) to check the global effect.

> *I prefer a crisper look to my painted pixels. The **Pixel Tool** provides this level of crispness by offering aliased strokes. The alternative option is the **Paint Brush Tool**, which offers anti-aliased strokes.*

Resource
whittler_06_robot.afdesign

BRINGING THE ROBOT TO LIFE

Making the robot layer visible once more, you'll see how odd it appears surrounded by a fully textured environment. We'll add shading detail to give the robot depth and will be working primarily within a clipping layer. Let's create this first.

Shading the robot

1 Select the grouped shapes within the robot layer and duplicate the group by selecting **Duplicate** from the **Edit Menu**.

2 Select all the shapes within the upper, duplicated group and then select **Add** from the **Toolbar** to combine all the shapes into a single curve.

3 Remove the fill from this new shape and set the layer to *Multiply*.

The layer we've just created will clip any strokes painted inside it and apply a **Multiply** blend to those strokes, giving us the ability to shade areas of the robot with great control.

> At this stage I chose to add more details to the robot's neck, drawing the shapes above the clipping layer. I added the shapes together to form one curve so I could clip raster paint strokes within it too.

4 Switch to **Pixel Persona** and add a new pixel layer nested inside the clipping layer. Begin defining the shadows on the robot using the *Main Stroke* brush with mid-to-dark grey and then the highlights using the *Details* brushes with light grey to white.

5 Use the *Shade* brush on another pixel layer to deepen the shadows on the right side of the robot and the rock it's seated on. Nest a raster layer inside the branch shape in the base layer and paint shadows and highlights as before. Repeat for the detail shape on the neck, if you drew this before step 3.

The robot looks too dark considering it's sitting directly in the beam of light, so we'll create a highlights layer to simulate this.

> When shading your robot, remember to use darker shades of grey for the areas closer to the foreground and lighter shades for those further back.

6 Duplicate the original robot group base layer and move it to the top of the stack within the *robot* layer. The **Layers Panel** should be structured like the screenshot below.

7 **Rasterise** the highlights layer by selecting the option from the **Layer Menu** and set its blend mode to *Add* and its **Opacity** to *30%*.

8 On the **Layers Panel**, ensure the highlights layer is active and then select the **Mask Layer** icon. Paint on this mask layer using the *Shade* brush loaded with black to remove unwanted highlight areas. Vary the brush size to create subtle shadows such as the one cast under the left (front) arm.

Resource

whittler_07_details.afdesign

ADDING DETAIL TO THE SCENE

Now let's use the painting techniques we have learned to add some final details.

Painting on haze

1 Switch back to **Designer Persona** and add two new layers called *haze*. Position these above the *robot* layer.

2 Select the **Vector Brush Tool** once more, load it with a stroke colour of *RGB 81,60,72* and set the brush type on the **Brushes Panel** to *DAUB Watercolour*. Increase the size of the brush to *1024 pt* by typing in the **Width** input box or by using the] key.

3 On the lower haze layer, paint strokes across the bottom half of the illustration and then set all the strokes to *50%* **Opacity**. Repeat this for the upper haze layer but concentrate strokes on the right side of the picture.

> At this point I will also add more details to my scene, like more grass. Depending on the details you want to add and the effect you want to create, you may want to use vector tools or brushes.

Character details

To enhance this illustration's story, we need to add movement and give the robot a soul.

1 In **Pixel Persona**, add a new pixel layer directly underneath the highlights layer within the robot layer. I have called this layer *speckles*.

2 Using the **Pixel Tool** and the *Details* brush, paint wood chippings flying through the air. Ensure the chippings are a similar grey tone to the held branch.

3 Paint across the edge of the branch to give it a roughened appearance and add an area which is in the process of being sliced.

4 Locate the top eye layer within the robot base group's head layer and copy it to the clipboard (**Edit > Copy**).

5 Select the curves layer within the shadows group and, from the **Edit Menu**, select **Paste Inside**. With this new eye layer still selected, from the **Edit Menu**, select **Paste Inside** once again. This will result in one ellipse being nested inside the other.

6 Select the parent eye layer and set its fill to dark grey and then set the nested eye layer's fill to pure white. With the nested ellipse still selected, use the **Move Tool** (V) to reposition it and resize it.

7   Add a new pixel layer underneath the nested ellipse (but still inside the parent eye layer) and paint highlights at the bottom of the ellipse to simulate the socket being lit from the robot's glowing eye.

8   Repeat the above procedures to define the second eye.

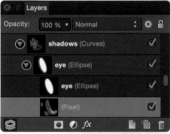

ADDING TONE AND ATMOSPHERE

We've finished painting for the moment so let's make all our layers visible, sit back and see what our illustration looks like.

As we've worked in a greyscale environment, we can now quickly tweak the tonal values of our illustration and add colour using adjustment layers.

Add Curves Adjustments

1 On the **Layers Panel**, select the top level illustration layer and then click on the **Adjustments** icon. From the pop-up menu, select **Curves**.

2 Drag the curve in the dialog to fix the overall tone and refine grey transitions. Lift up the shadows a bit to achieve an analog film aesthetic.

> The curves layer is automatically applied to the illustration layer, meaning it will affect the entire composition.

3 Then warm the highlights and cool the shadows. To do this, select a channel from the pop-up menu. Increase the level of **Red** and **Green** in the highlights, and increase the level of **Blue** in the shadows.

4 Continue to add **Curves Adjustments** to other layers to adjust their tone and add colour. I applied a **Curves Adjustment** to the foreground 1, foreground 3 and mid-ground layers.

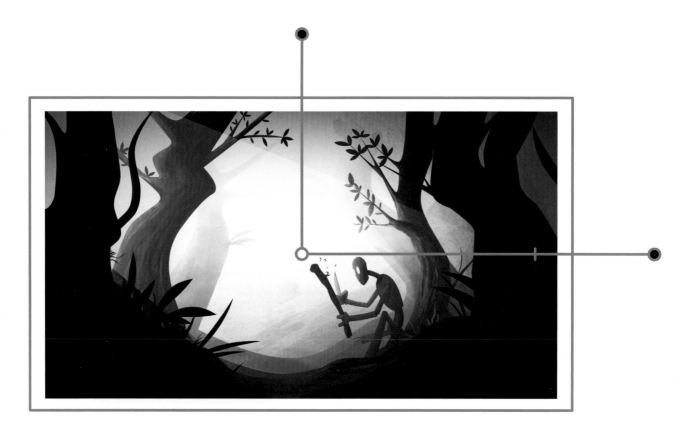

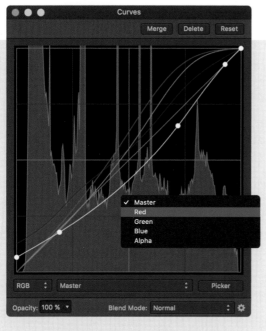

Soften the look

1 Following all our **Curves Adjustments**, the light beam looks particularly harsh. To soften it, set the beam layer to a *Linear Light* blend mode and an **Opacity** of *60%*.

2 Create a new layer at the top of the illustration layer and call it *atmosphere*. In this layer add a violet rectangle. Then use the **Transparency Tool** to apply an elliptical transparency from *0%* transparency at the corners to *100%* transparency at the centre to create a vignette effect.

Resource
whittler_09_finaltouches.afdesign

FINAL TOUCHES

Earlier in this project we added movement to the robot to bring it to life. We can do the same with the forest environment. We'll add spots of light where floating dust particles are illuminated and create a depth of field to add realism.

Illuminating Dust

1 Switch back to **Designer Persona** and add a new layer (I called mine *spots*) and position it behind the closest foreground layer.

2 Using the **Ellipse Tool** (M), draw a tiny circle about *20 px* in diameter on the page. Apply a light grey, almost white, colour to its fill.

3 Copy the circle as many times as desired and place the copies randomly around the page where they would catch the light from the beam. Reduce the size of some of the circles as you go to enhance the natural appearance of the illuminated dust.

4 When you have finished, set the layer blend mode to *Glow*.

Repeat the above process to add dust spots between other layers. I added some more before the *robot* layer.

Glows on the robots broken leg

1 Add a new pixel layer directly above the *beam* layer. Call this layer *glows*.

2 In **Pixel Persona**, using the **Pixel Tool** and the *Details* brush, paint some 'glows' on the end of the robot's broken leg using a light grey, almost white, colour fill.

Depth of Field

We have already established a depth of field using the tones of each layer, with closer layers being darker. However, we can improve this perception by non-destructively taking some of the planes and details out of focus.

1 Select the closest foreground layer and then switch to the **Effects Panel**. Select the **Gaussian Blur** effect and increase its **Radius** to approximately *4 px*. This should retain some details while taking the foreground a little out of focus.

2 Repeat this step for the foreground, background and beam layers, plus any spots layers, using a radius between *2–4 px*.

Final touches

After completing the project, walk away from the composition. Returning with refreshed eyes, you can evaluate your artwork more objectively.

When I returned to this piece, I decided to add a **Selective Colour Adjustment** to my illumination to subtly boost the red and blue tones.

Wine Cellar

Isometric illustration
by *Kevin House*

Learn from Kevin how to create isometric illustrations with this project creating a topsy-turvy wine cellar rich in colour, shading and texture.

BEFORE YOU GET STARTED

Resources

 You can get all the resources that are referenced in this project from:
https://affin.co/winecellar

Knowledge of Affinity Designer

To get the most from undertaking this project, you will need to:

- Know how to use the **Pen Tool** in Affinity Designer. Master the **Pen Tool** by completing Pen Tool: Curves & Shapes on p. 97.

- Be familiar with the interface of Affinity Designer. You can learn more about the interface in the Interface Tour chapter, starting on p. 13.

- Have good core skills. See the skills table below to see which additional aspects of Affinity Designer you need to be confident with to complete this project:

Objects	p. 80
Geometry Tools	p. 95
Colours & Gradients	P. 106
Effects & Adjustments	p. 112
Design Aids	p. 118

CREATING
THE CONCEPT

The idea for Wine Cellar started as a rough client sketch for a winery. I then revised the sketch to conform to an isometric grid and fine-tuned the composition to really play up the theme of multiple perspectives.

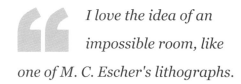

I love the idea of an impossible room, like one of M. C. Escher's lithographs.

The great thing about an isometric image is that optically it's rather easy for the eye to shift from top, side and bottom, making the different viewpoints a bit easier to grasp.

Orthographic projection doesn't allow for the usual type of perspective depth, so our image will need a bit of help in the form of light, shadow and colour to suggest depth and move the eye around.

We'll cover all this and more in this project.

DOCUMENT SETUP

Let's set up our document to place our scanned sketch.

1 Select **File > New**.

2 Choose a document **Type** of *Print (Press-Ready)* to set up a CMYK document. Set **Document Units** to *Pixels* and **Page Width** and **Page Height** to *5120 px* each.

3 From the **View Menu**, select **Grid and Axis Manager** and check the **Show grid** option. Select the **Advanced** tab, set the **Grid type** to *Triangular*, the **Spacing** to *128 px* and the **Divisions** to *5*.

> I know what you're thinking: why use Triangular and not Isometric? The Isometric grid only has oblique angle guides and I want vertical guides as well. Triangular has the same guides as Isometric but with the additional vertical guides I want.

I have set the spacing to double that of the default because of the relatively large dimensions of the file. The increase in divisions allows for more accurate snapping, to keep everything lined up and in its proper place.

4 On the **Toolbar**, select the drop-down arrow on the **Snapping** icon to set the snapping preferences shown to the right.

> You can toggle the grid on and off using the Show Grid option on the View Menu. Remember to keep in mind that not everything has to adhere or snap to the grid. However, the grid will allow you to line your shapes up accurately and help keep the isometric perspective.

5 From the **File Menu**, select **Place**. Select winecellar_lockin_sketch.jpeg (or your own scanned sketch) and click **Open**.

6 Click anywhere in the document to drop the image. Drag the corners of the image to scale it up slightly, then position the image so the sketch's outside border pencil lines go slightly beyond the document's page edge.

Uncheck **View Mode > Clip to Canvas** from the **View Menu** to reveal the canvas. This helps size your image.

7 On the **Layers Panel**, with the image still selected, set the **Opacity** to *75%*, the blend mode to *Multiply* and lock it using the **Lock/Unlock** icon.

> We will keep this layer at the top of the layer stack throughout so that we can always see the sketch while building all of the shapes. You can toggle the visibility of the layer at any time using its checkmark.

8 On the **Layers Panel**, select the **Add Layer** icon to add a new layer and then, on the **Toolbar**, select **Move to Back**. This new layer will accommodate all the shapes needed to vectorize the sketch.

DRAWING

I complete a great amount my drawing using the Pen Tool. However, as this project focuses on constructing an isometric drawing, the operation of the Pen Tool will not be covered in detail. If you're new to using the Pen Tool and Bézier curves, you may wish to periodically refer to Pen Tool: Curves & Shapes on p. 97.

I also use some of the Shape Tools found in the Tools Panel. I then make use of Boolean operations in Affinity Designer to create more complicated shapes from overlapping simpler shapes where necessary.

> As you may have noticed, there are some repeating elements in this piece, such as the arches, barrels, crates and steps. For these, you only need to create once instance and then duplicate it.

Using the sketch as a guide and the Grid and Snapping settings we set up, let's work through one example to get you familiar with isometric drawing: we'll focus on the barrel at the top right of the sketch.

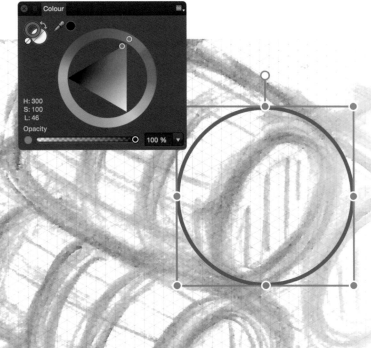

Barrel

1   On the **Layers Panel**, select Layer1 and then select the **Ellipse Tool** (M) from the **Tools Panel**.

2   Drag over the barrel end while holding the shift key (⇧) to constrain the drawn shape to a circle and use the **Colour Panel** to remove the shape's Fill and define a bright colour for the Stroke. I used magenta.

> From the context toolbar, I increased the stroke on my shape to *2 pt* for clarity, but you may wish to leave your strokes set to *1 pt*.

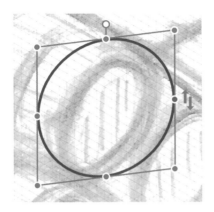

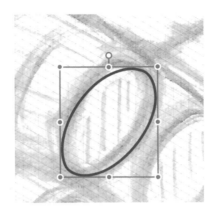

3 Skew the circle so it adheres to the proper isometric angle by hovering just outside the bounding box near a side handle and dragging when you see a double-arrow cursor.

4 Continue to skew, resize and reposition the circle until it lines up neatly with the sketch and grid.

5 Duplicate the skewed circle by selecting **Duplicate** from the **Edit Menu** and offset the duplicate slightly up and to the left of the original circle.

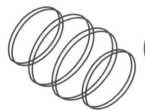

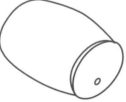

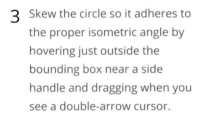

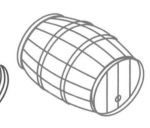

6 Duplicate this set of circles and reposition, then perform a **Divide** operation (p. 96) on each set.

7 Use the **Pen Tool** (P) to define the remainder of the barrel.

To help positioning, you can temporarily disable snapping by moving objects with the option ⌥ key (Mac) or alt key (Win) pressed.

When coloured, shaded and textured (we'll look at this later), this single barrel can be duplicated and repositioned (and sometimes flipped) to create all the other barrels which lie down. The upright barrels will need constructing as described before, but again only one is needed and then it can be duplicated.

Ceiling

Another area of design I'll cover now in detail is the ceiling in the lower left chamber room.

1 Draw an ellipse with a curvature which follows the archway and then draw a thin rectangle with a width that expands beyond the ellipse and a height of *100 px* or so. Rotate it by *30°* and place it about halfway down the ellipse to line up with the plank closest to the wall in the sketch.

2 **Duplicate** the rectangle using the command from the **Edit Menu** and position the duplicate higher up on the ellipse. Without deselecting the duplicate, reuse the Duplicate command again to create another rectangle which is also repositioned by the same amount again. This is known as **power duplicating** and can be continued to cover the top half of the ellipse with rectangles.

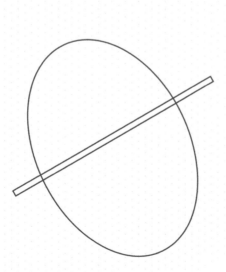

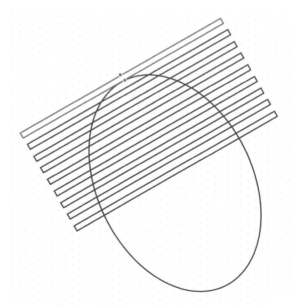

Using the techniques covered so far, continue to draw the remaining objects from supplied geometric shapes on the **Tools Panel**.

- The doorway can be formed from a skewed ellipse and skewed rectangle, subjected to an Add operation (see p. 95). Then the resulting doorway shape can be subtracted from a rectangle representing the wall to leave the final shape.

- The arch of the archway can be built using overlapping skewed ellipses in a similar way to the barrel hoops. Two skewed, overlapping rectangles can be subtracted from each other to create the wall. A Divide operation can then be undertaken on the arch and wall to create constituent parts of the archway. Delete the unnecessary shapes and then perform an Add operation on the remaining shapes.

- Crates can be formed from skewed rectangles and Divide operations.

- The hanging light is constructed from an ellipse, a triangle, a rectangle and a Pen drawn shape.

- Steps (not shown) are built from skewed rectangles.

3 Select the ellipse and all the rectangles and use a **Divide** operation (p. 96) to create new shapes which represent the ceiling's boards and the lower wall. The shapes outside the ellipse can be deleted.

It was only necessary to create every other rectangle because the divide operation creates the in-between rectangle shapes for us.

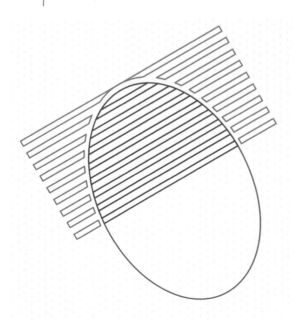

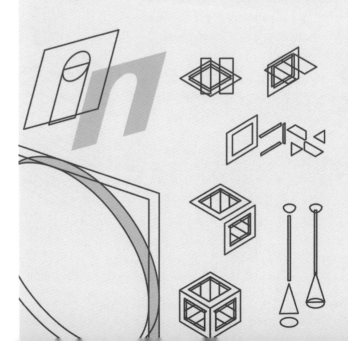

Resource

winecellar_lockin_03_structure.afdesign

STRUCTURE

We'll assume all went well with creating your repeating objects. Let's now take a step back from drawing for a moment and concentrate on getting our layers organized.

Right now you have a lot of objects on the same layer (Layer1) below the scan layer. If we were to continue to draw on one layer, we would very quickly run into some difficulty as the design becomes more complex. When working on specific subject areas (e.g., a barrel) it's beneficial to be able to select and edit just that area of the design, without unrelated overlapping or underlying objects being incorrectly selected instead.

Fortunately, the Layers Panel can help us organize related objects into identifiable named layers so you're able to focus on just that design area for selection and editing.

With better management of your design using layers, your design process becomes less frustrating and infinitely more enjoyable.

The most important aspect for me is the ability to lock a layer or the ability to lock all the layers except the one I am working on. It's a great workflow to adopt, especially on complex pieces such as this.

1   On the **Layers Panel**, select Layer1 and then add a new layer (it should be added between Layer1 and the sketch layer).

2   Click on the layer's name and then type a more useful name, such as *hanging light right*.

3   Select the hanging light objects on the page, and then **Cut** them using the command on the **Edit Menu**.

4   On the **Layers Panel**, select the hanging light right layer and **Paste** the objects using the command on the **Edit Menu**.

> Alternatively, you can drag selected objects from one layer to another directly in the Layers Panel. A good way to know which objects have been assigned a layer is to hide each new layer as you complete it.

Have a look at your drawing and decide which objects or shapes warrant their own layer, for example, I decided to split my chamber objects over two different layers – *chamber interior wall* and *chamber ceiling*.

Layers can be moved up or down in the Layers Panel, duplicated, deleted and so on to give you full control over your illustration. Alternatively, you may wish to use Edit All Layers (bottom left icon on the Layers Panel). When this option is off, only the current, active layer will be editable. This is very powerful and useful when you're having difficulty selecting objects in a crowded piece. This is another reason for containing subjects on their own layer.

Keep in mind that objects higher up on the Layers Panel will display in front of objects on layers below. This image is particularly tricky to separate out objects and organize the layer structure because of its multiple-perspective nature, so don't scrimp on the number of layers you use (there are no limits!) and feel free to make and change decisions as you go.

Resource
winecellar_lockin_04_puzzle.afdesign

ASSEMBLING THE PUZZLE

Return to the Pen and Shape Tools to ink in the remaining, unique objects of the sketch on their own layers.

Most of the sketch's elements will need to be created as closed shapes to allow us to colour them in afterwards. Many of the edges of elements within the image connect up, as with a jigsaw puzzle. Ensuring your shapes conform to the grid as closely as possible, and with Snapping switched on, should allow the edges of your shapes to line up perfectly and leave no gaps.

Occasionally you may need to hold down the option ⌥ key (Mac) or the alt key (Win) to temporarily deactivate snapping to allow you to draw with a creative eye and ignore the restrictions of the grid.

> To check if objects line up perfectly you can switch to **Outline view mode** using the icon on the **Toolbar**. This will display all page objects as paths (with no strokes) and allow you to see the exact placement of a shape's edges.

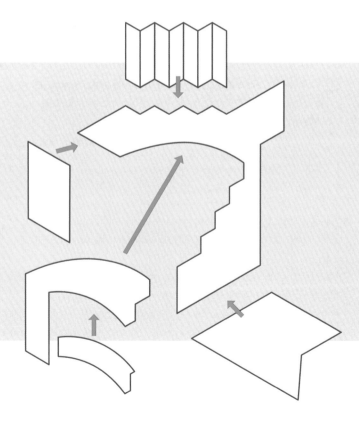

Resource

winecellar_lockin_05_colour.afdesign

COLOUR

Whether you use the Colour Panel, Swatches Panel or the Colour Picker to choose your colour scheme, I recommend saving your base colours in a custom palette in the Swatches Panel.

1 From panel preferences on the **Swatches Panel**, select **Add Document Palette** and then select **Rename Palette** from the same menu to rename the new palette to *Winecellar*.

2 Create a new layer above the sketch layer called *colour swatches* and hide all the layers below, and then create a set of small squares on the page using the **Rectangle Tool** (M).

3 Use the **Colour** or **Swatches Panel** or **Colour Picker Tool** (I) to apply colours to the squares on the page and tweak them until you're happy with the base colour scheme.

4 Select all the colour squares, ctrl-click (Mac) or right-click (Win) the selection and choose **Add to Swatches > From Fill As Global**.

Alternatively, choose Add Application Palette to create a palette which all Affinity Designer documents can access.

This will add the colours to your palette as Global colours.

Global colours can be changed at any point in the future and all objects using that global colour will automatically update to match the changes made.

> *I keep image files of pleasing colour schemes I come across on a daily basis and dig them out for future projects. For this illustration, I chose a limited colour scheme I've been wanting to use for a while.*

Now we can go about applying colour to our shapes and objects from the swatches we just created. In the beginning stages, I like to apply flat base colours to objects that help create a pleasing composition with some nice eye movement around the piece.

Continue by adding gradients to build the depth of the illustration. Use the **Fill Tool** (G) to drag a gradient path across each object in turn, then set the colour of the circular end points using the Swatches Panel or Colour Panel.

As I introduce more hanging lights later, I may want to adjust these gradients with the new lighting in mind.

Hold down the shift key (⇧) and click to select multiple objects (click them again to remove from the selection, if they were incorrectly selected) and then apply a global colour.

SHADING AND EFFECTS

I'll take you on an in-depth look at how we can bring the barrels to life using shading and effects.

I'll hide everything except the barrel right top layer so as to concentrate on just one element of the illustration.

1 Select the shape which represents the body of the barrel and, using the **Fill Tool**, add a gradient fill to add some basic top-down light direction.

2 On the **Effects Panel**, select **Inner Shadow**, and apply the settings. The colour used is *CMYK 66,71,60,53*.

3 Repeat the previous steps for the head of the barrel and add a gradient fill to the spout hole. Draw a light coloured curve below the hole and apply a **Pressure** profile to it on the **Stroke Panel**.

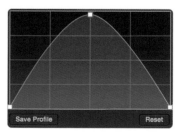

Shading and Effects for me is where the fun happens!

4 Add a gradient to the hoops to suggest a metal finish by adding highlight areas at the centre, where light will hit, and shade at both ends of the hoop as it disappears from view around the barrel.

5 Duplicate all hoops except the head hoop, recolour the lower layers to be dark grey and offset them under the original hoops to give the appearance of thickness. Use **Back One** on the **Toolbar** to order the duplicated hoops.

6 Select the ellipse representing the top of the head loop and apply a metallic gradient to its Stroke. To do this, with the **Fill Tool** selected, choose **Stroke** from the context toolbar's **Context** pop-up menu. Then recolour the remaining curves brown to give the barrel's staves a natural appearance.

7 To simulate the hoops casting a shadow on the barrel, draw curves with a dark stroke and set them to *Multiply* blend mode and *50%* **Opacity** on the **Layers Panel**.

On the **Effects Panel**, apply a **Gaussian Blur** of *2–3 px* to each curve.

8 Duplicating the curves defining the staves, recolouring, offsetting and blurring them is a great way of adding soft highlights. Furthermore, you can add stronger highlights in a similar way by using the **Transparency Tool** (Y) to fade out the highlights, rather than blurring them. This is a great way of adding depth to the staves of the barrel.

Adjusting the width of the Stroke is a good way to tweak the thickness of a shadow or highlight.

The barrel is looking pretty awesome, but if I reveal the sketch layer, it appears to be floating in the air. We can 'ground' it by adding shadows beneath.

9   To give the wood an organic appearance, select the body of the barrel and, on the **Colour Panel**, select the toggle icon below the word **Opacity** to switch to the **Noise** setting, and set the shape's Fill to have **Noise** set to *40%*. Repeat this for the barrel's head and spout hole.

10   Draw a rounded shape below the barrel, give it a dark colour, a **Gaussian Blur**, and set it to *Multiply* blend mode and an **Opacity** of *43%*. Repeat the process to add another shape closer to the barrel's base. This shape can have a sharper edge than the first.

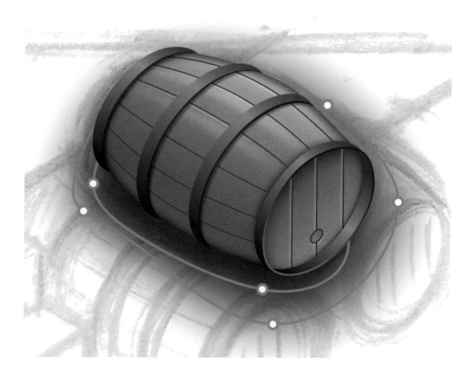

Over the years, I've learned not to be afraid of the dark. Shadows, particularly ground shadows or shadows in corners and crevices, are really dark. Use a very dark colour, or black, and always set the blend mode to Multiply for realistic results.

Incorporated effects

I usually prefer to create my visual effects by hand, using the techniques already discussed, rather than using gimmicky 3D and Emboss effects. However, as Affinity Designer's implementation of these effects is subtle and powerful, I do occasionally use them to speed up my workflow. I'd encourage a good exploration of these Effects to see how they can help you.

1 For the grapes picture, after applying a linear gradient, add an **Inner Shadow** to a grape to establish a dark, rounded surface. Then add a **3D Effect** to add a quick highlight and overall shading.

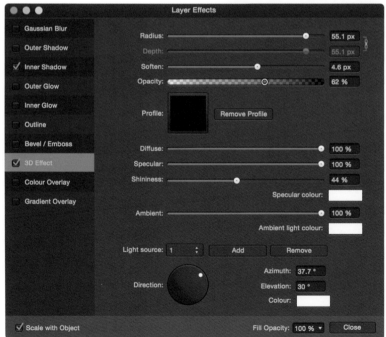

2 The **Bevel/Emboss** effect can be put to great use on the grape bunch's stem.

3 Again, for the ceiling boards, the **Bevel/Emboss** effect applies shading and highlights efficiently.

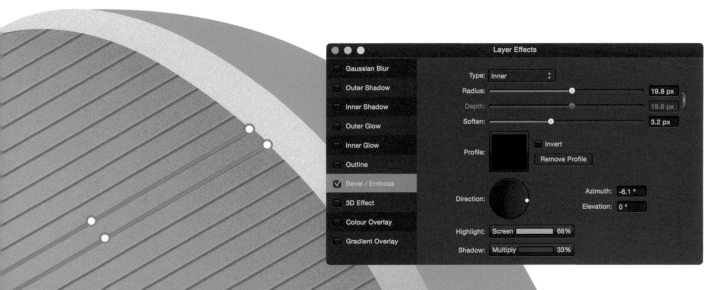

TRANSPARENCY

Extra shadows, highlights and other lighting effects can be applied at the top of layers to heighten the dimensional realism.

1   Select the layer containing the hanging light and draw a simple trapezoid shape, using the **Pen Tool** or **Trapezoid Tool**, extending from the bottom of the light. Set the Fill of the shape to *white* and add Noise (*40%*). Move the light beam to the bottom of the layer.

2   On the **Tools Panel**, select the **Transparency Tool** and drag from the top to the bottom of the trapezoid shape.

   This will fade the shape's Fill from *100%* opacity at the top to *0%* at the bottom, giving the appearance that the light softens as it spreads into the room.

   Once you're happy with the look of repeating features such as the barrel and light, you can go ahead and duplicate the original and then reposition (rotate and flip, if necessary) the duplicates to create all the remaining instances. Change the light beam's Fill colour to complement objects behind it and, if needed, adjust colour gradients on walls to fit with the new light direction.

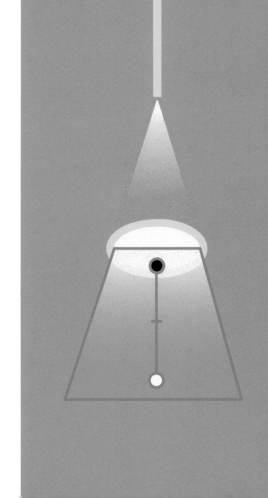

The same technique can also be used to create areas of fading shadow, such as those under archways.

For truly realistic effects, duplicate the existing solid shadow, and give the overlaid new object a white fill and a linear transparency gradient (*0%* to *100%*) using the **Transparency Tool**.

Resource

winecellar_lockin_08_texture.afdesign
winecellar_lockin_texture.png
DAUB Dry Media.afbrushes

TEXTURE

Adding interest using texture can push your image that little bit extra. We've already covered using visual noise in a previous section, so let's look at two other techniques.

Adding an image

1 Place winecellar_lockin_texture.png on your page using the same method as you used to originally import the sketch.

   Then use the **Cut** command on the **Edit Menu** to move it to the Clipboard.

2 Select one of the wall shapes you wish to texture and, from the **Edit Menu**, select **Paste Inside**. Drag the pasted image to the wall shape so the texture shows, then skew the image so it overlays the shape in a desirable manner.

3 On the **Layers Panel**, change the texture layer's blend mode to *Multiply* and, if you feel the effect is too strong, reduce the layer's opacity or use the Transparency Tool for focused softening.

   Feel free to use a different blend mode you like – each will give a unique result.

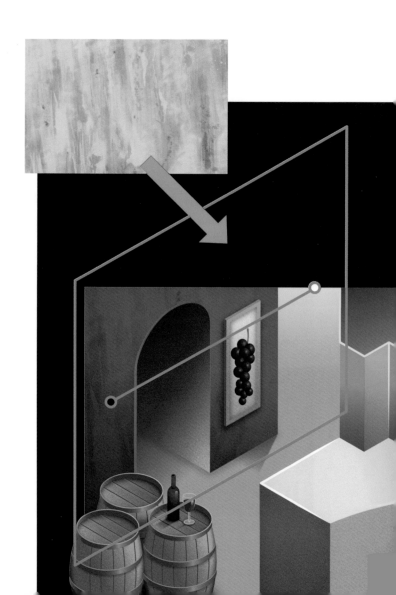

> *Adding noise is the easiest and quickest method for adding a consistent, regular type of texture and is the most common method I use. I really like it. Pixel painting is a more advanced technique and can result in a more professional finish.*

You can also colour pick from anywhere on the page by dragging with the option ⌥ key (Mac) or alt key (Win) pressed.

Pixel Painting

1 Switch to **Pixel Persona** by selecting its icon on the **Toolbar**.

2 From the **Brushes Panel**'s preferences menu, select **Import Brushes**. Select DAUB Dry Media.afbrushes and click **Open**.

3 On the **Layers Panel**, select a layer to which you want to add texture and, on the **Toolbar**, select the **Insert inside the selection** icon.

4 Select the **Paint Brush Tool** (B) from the **Tools Panel**, a brush from the **Brushes Panel**, a colour from the **Colour** or **Swatches Panels**, and drag on your page to apply texture. Painting will be confined to the previously selected object. A *100 px 'Scatter Chalk'* brush works well here, set with *Global Colour 6*, a lowered **Flow** setting (about *32%*) and a layer blend mode of *Multiply*.

The DAUB Dry Media brushes were created by Paolo Limoncelli. For more information on creating and applying raster brushes, see The Whittler: Creating Raster Brushes and The Whittler: Raster Painting on p. 192 and p. 222, respectively.

FINAL TOUCHES

One more object I added to my illustration and then skewed to fit the isometric grid, was a text object.

- Select the grapes art frame layer and select the **Artistic Text Tool** (T). Click on the page and set the font and size via the context toolbar. Type the word *wine* and then skew the text object to align with the grid.

Lastly, I often want to tweak or adjust certain properties of the image globally after all of the drawing, painting and texturing is finished. Perhaps to warm up the design a bit or adjust its overall brightness or contrast. This can be done by placing an adjustment layer at the top of your layer stack. For this illustration, I subtly applied both **Brightness/Contrast** and **Vibrance** adjustments.

Hopefully this project has given you enough information or sparked some interest to go forward and experiment adapting these methods in your own work with Affinity Designer.

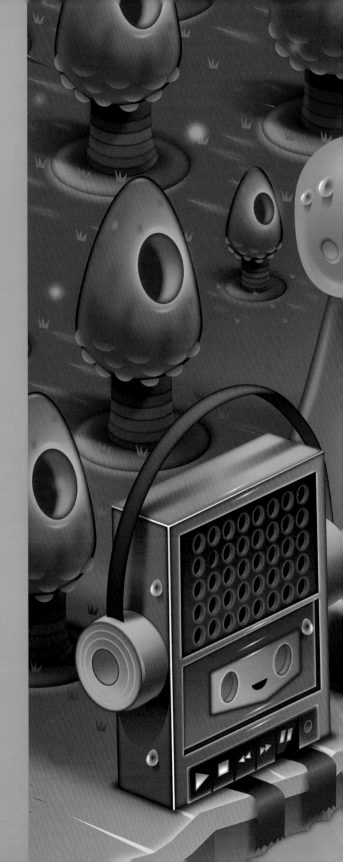

The Fisherman

3D character illustration
by *pokedstudio*

pokedstudio takes you through his process of creating a
3D style character in this project, and the result pops out
of your screen!

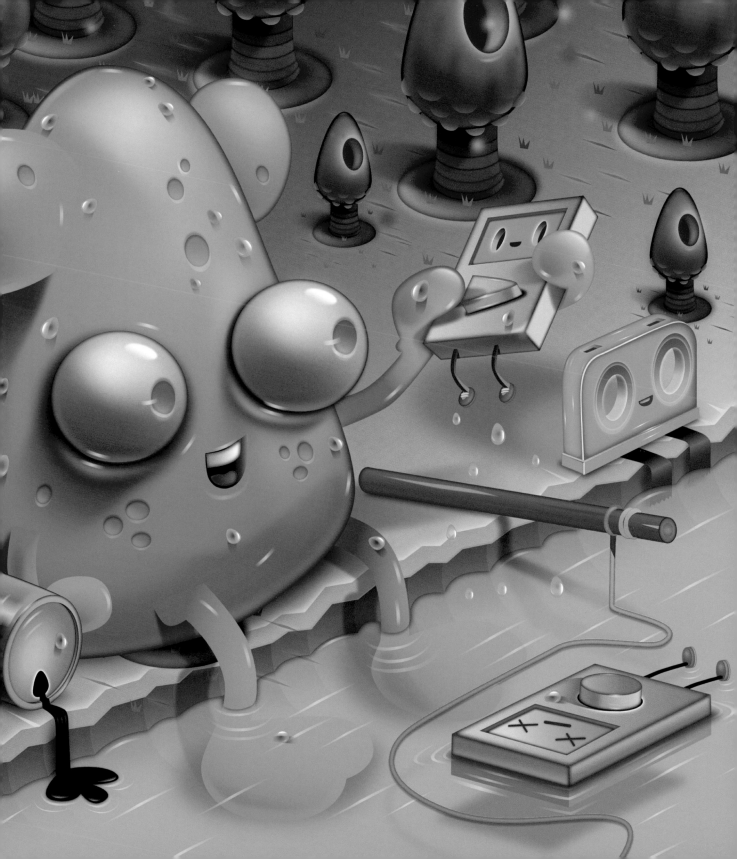

BEFORE YOU
GET STARTED

Resources

 You can get all the resources that are referenced in this project from:
https://affin.co/fisherman

Knowledge of Affinity Designer

To get the most from undertaking this project, you will need to:

- Know how to use the **Pen Tool** in Affinity Designer. Master the **Pen Tool** by completing Pen Tool: Curves & Shapes on p. 97.

- Be familiar with the interface of Affinity Designer. You can learn more about the interface in the Interface Tour chapter, starting on p. 13.

- Have good core skills. See the skills table below to see which additional aspects of Affinity Designer you need to be confident with to complete this project:

Objects	p. 80
Geometry Tools	p. 95
Clipping	p. 90
Colours & Gradients	p. 106
Effects & Adjustments	p. 112

CREATING
THE CONCEPT

I start off any project by creating concept sketches with pencil and paper. This lets me come up with ideas before committing to anything, and also lets me get sign off from the client.

Think about lighting

Decide where lighting will originate from—below, behind, above, or from left or right. With this in mind, drawn arrows on your sketch will help you introduce shadows and highlights to your main sketch which look natural and consistent.

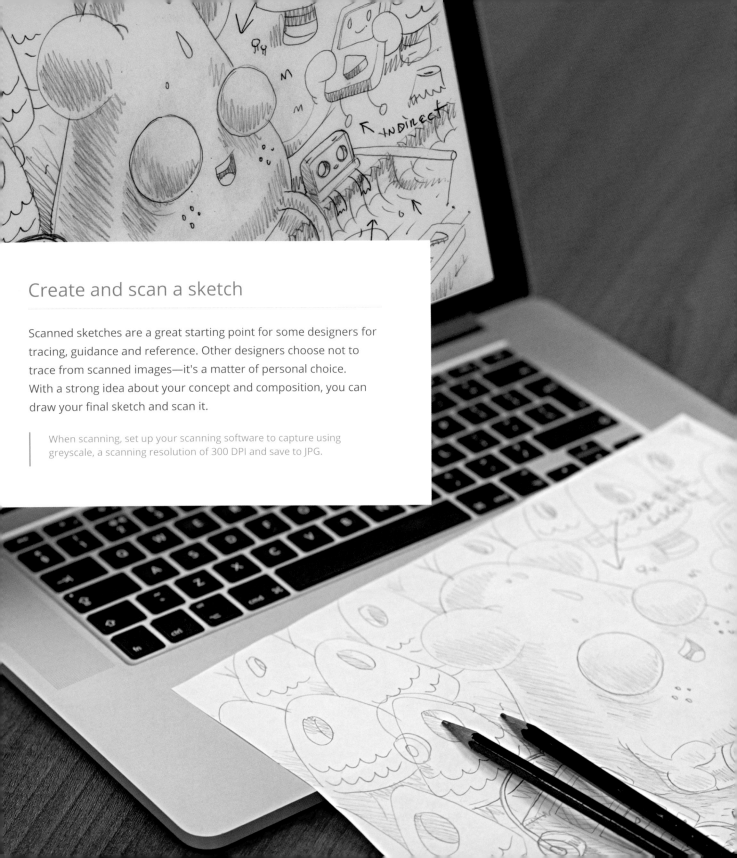

Create and scan a sketch

Scanned sketches are a great starting point for some designers for tracing, guidance and reference. Other designers choose not to trace from scanned images—it's a matter of personal choice. With a strong idea about your concept and composition, you can draw your final sketch and scan it.

> When scanning, set up your scanning software to capture using greyscale, a scanning resolution of 300 DPI and save to JPG.

Resource

fisherman_01_sketch.afdesign
scan_390.jpeg

DOCUMENT SETUP

Set up the document to place the scanned sketch.

1   Select **File > New**.

2   Set **Document Units** to *pixels*.

3   Use the **Colour Profile** called *sRGB IEC61966-2.1*, then
    a **Page Width** and **Page Height** of *5120x3475* pixels.

4   Click **OK** to create a blank page.

Importing the sketch

1   From the **Tools Panel**, select the **Place Image Tool**.

2   Navigate to, select and open the scanned image
    scan_390.jpeg.

3   Enable **Snapping** from the toolbar.

4   Drag the cursor from the top-left corner until the
    image snaps to the bottom page edge.

5   Drag the image's top-right corner handle up and to
    the right until the image snaps to the right page edge.
    Notice that the image is placed as a new image layer
    in the **Layers Panel** using the image's name.

6   Click the **Lock** icon.

If designing artwork for professional printing,
photo printing, web, or mobile device, choose
a suitable Type and Page Preset combination.
These set up the document correctly for your
intended delivery method.

DRAWING THE FISHERMAN

Resource

fisherman_02_drawingcurves.afdesign

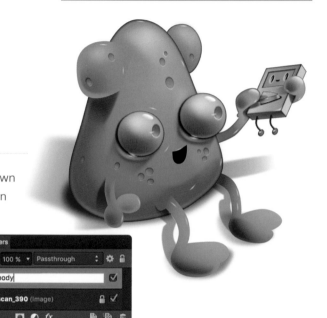

Adding layers

To keep your design organized, you'll need to create your own layers to store your objects as you progress, especially when starting a new component of your design.

1 From the **Layers Panel**, click **Add Layer**.

2 Click the layer name and give it a new name such as *body*.

Drawing curves over outlines

Now use the **Pen Tool** to draw over the main character's features on the scanned image.

1 From the **Tools Panel**, select the **Pen Tool** (P).

2 Click and drag around the character's features in your sketch, making closed shapes from the drawn curves. You can use the **Ellipse Tool** (M) on the **Tools Panel** to make the eyes.

3 Reorder the shapes in the **Layers Panel** by dragging up/down so they are placed in front or behind the main body.

4 Using the **Colour Panel**, block in each shape with a solid fill for now. Colour the body and ears (*HSL 120,100,35*), eyes and arms (*HSL 124,100,20*) and legs (*HSL 120,87,22*). The mouth can be solid black.

> *We will use our sketch as a guide so we can draw over it. However, I often find that further down the illustration process I will need to break away from following the sketch exactly. This might be to move some part of the design, scale the design up or down or to improve the composition in general.*

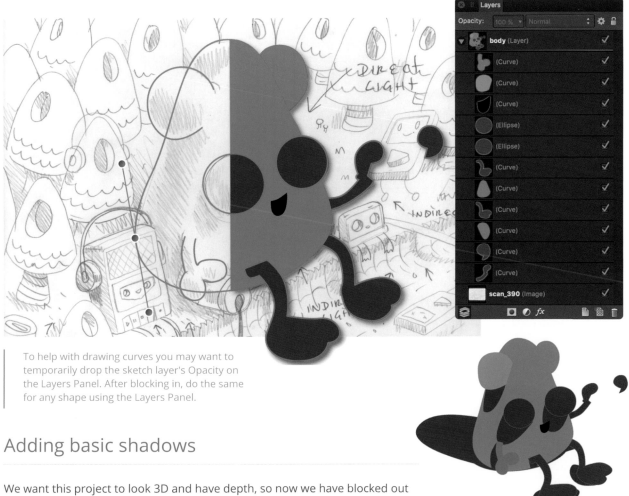

To help with drawing curves you may want to
temporarily drop the sketch layer's Opacity on
the Layers Panel. After blocking in, do the same
for any shape using the Layers Panel.

Adding basic shadows

We want this project to look 3D and have depth, so now we have blocked out
the basic shape of our character we need to think about lighting again.

Using the light sources noted on the sketch, think about where shadows would
fall on your character and block them in using the following steps as a guide.

1   Draw 'shadow' shapes cast from existing shapes.

2   Arrange the shape's order by dragging in the **Layers Panel**.

3   Give the shapes a darker green fill (*HSL 125,100,20*) to represent shadow.

Use deep shadows just under
where parts join. Keep these
quite small so they're just
under edges. For the direction
of shadows, follow the
direction of the direct light as
indicated in your sketch.

271

Resource

fisherman_04_realisticshadows.afdesign

Making shadows realistic (direct light)

Our shadows are basic but they need to appear natural, i.e. they should fall away from the 'shadowing' shapes. We can create this look by using **Opacity control**.

1 Select a basic shadow with the **Fill Tool** (G), available on the **Tools Panel**. We'll apply a shadow to the right eye.

2 Drag across the shadow away from the direct light source, in this case downwards and to the left to create a **linear gradient**.

3 The selected end stop can be made transparent by dropping the **Colour Panel's Opacity** slider to *0%*. The shadow now falls away nicely.

To speed things up, copy the first shape with the desired radial gradient (**Edit > Copy**), select all other shapes, then select **Edit > Paste Style**. Simply adjust each object path with the Fill Tool to finish.

Don't forget to experiment with blurring and gradient control when working with shadows. Each gradient path may need its length and direction adjusted for best results.

4 To make the shadow appear diffuse and softer, use the **Effects Panel** to apply a **Gaussian Blur**. Also, change the shape's **Opacity** and blend mode in the **Layers Panel** to *60%* and *Multiply*, respectively.

5 Repeat for other shadows created from direct light.

Adding highlighted areas to shapes

To remove flatness, let's apply a gradient fill to any shape that is affected by a light source, either directly or indirectly. The scanned sketch should have a light direction arrow to help you envisage how the design is to be lit.

Radial gradients are perfect for highlighting rounded shapes in a natural way. We'll use the main body as a great example, so here goes...

1   Select the main body.

2   From the **Tools Panel**, select the **Fill Tool**.

3   On the context toolbar, change the gradient **Type** to *Radial*, and click **Reverse gradient**. A **radial gradient** path appears with its end stop colours reversed.

> Most of the shapes are rounded so a Radial gradient is perfect; for flatter shapes, use a Linear gradient.

4   Drag the cursor across the body from the top right away from your light source towards the base of the body.

5   Select the end stop at the opposite end of the path, then from the **Colour Panel**, choose a suitable lighter colour. Go with *HSL 81,82,54*.

6   Repeat for other shapes.

> The basic principle is that you're applying a path along which the colour lightens towards your light source.

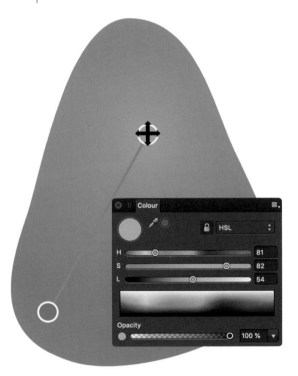

Adding overlaid highlights and shadows

You can also draw multiple highlights and shadows as their own independent shapes that can be placed over your main shapes. These are drawn at the areas where the light will fall most strongly, so shape them with this in mind.

For highlights:

1   Draw shapes and fill with a solid "highlight" colour (*HSL 65,84,70*).

2   With the **Fill Tool** create a radial fill, then tail it off to *0%* opacity. To add softness, apply a **Gaussian Blur** of *37 px*; set the blend mode to *Normal*.

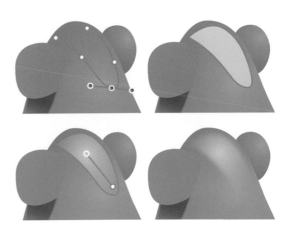

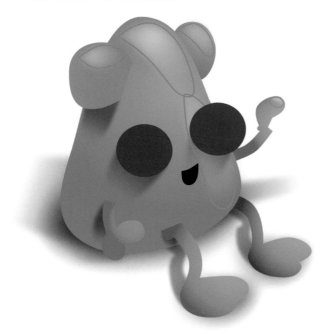

For shading, use the same principle, but draw shapes with a radial fill of *HSL 120,100,27* falling away to *0%* opacity towards the direct light source.

> Some highlights, called specular reflections, can be drawn as simple ellipses with a linear gradient of 100% white falling away to 0% opacity.

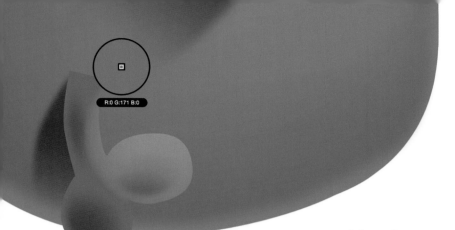

Resource

fisherman_07_mergingarms.afdesign

Merging arms into body

The introduction of shadows has made the join between the right arm and the body appear unnatural. Let's fix this before further highlighting.

1   On the **Colour Panel**, click the **Colour Picker** and hold down the mouse button.

2   Drag the cursor to the body closest to where the arm is joined. Release the mouse.

3   Select the **Fill Tool**, then click the right arm.

4   Click the stop nearest to the arm-body join to select it.

5   Select the **Colour Picker**'s colour swatch on the **Colour Panel**. This applies the picked up colour to the fill, merging the arm into the body.

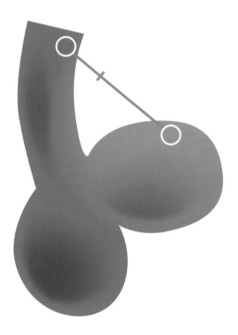

Adding edge highlights

Highlights can be added sparingly and naturally at object edges as fine detail. For example:

- From direct light: top of ears and head.

- From indirect light: under right ear.

For direct light, we'll need a **three-stop linear gradient** to simulate how the highlight falls away at either end of the shape. ▶

For indirect light, i.e. reflected from the river, you can use linear fills from light blue (*HSL 184,100,50*) to *0%* **Opacity**. We'll do this now for under the right ear, then later for under the eyes. ▼

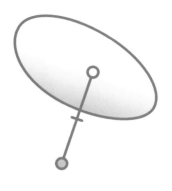

From the **Tools Panel**, select the **Pen Tool**. Draw a sausage-like shape at the prominent edge of your shape. In this case, a sphere represents the ears or head.

With the **Fill Tool**, drag along the shape to create a simple linear gradient. Double-click the middle of the path to create a new stop.

On the **Colour Panel**, assign the new stop a colour of *HSL 72,58,62*. Select each end stop and assign *0%* **Opacity** from the same panel to both.

Finish off with a subtle blur (**Gaussian Blur** at *0.3 px*).

Darkening edges

For more depth, edges can be made to appear more rounded by using darkening. We'll work on the fisherman's body.

1 On the **Effects Panel**, select **Inner Glow**.

2 Select a **Colour** and **Radius** of *HSL 71,85,21* and *59.2 px*, respectively.

3 Click the **cog icon** and change **Blend Mode** to *Multiply*.

4 Repeat for left arm and ear.

Around the edges of many shapes you can use inner glow effects with a darker colour than the shape's fill. By also setting a Multiply blend mode, I get a nice rounded darker edge. An inner glow effect may suggest a bright edge, but for my needs a darker edge is perfect.

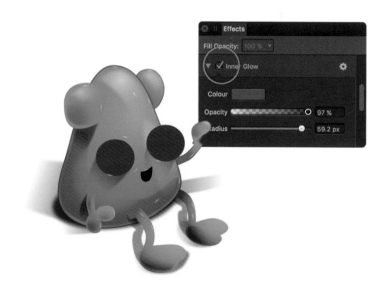

Making the eyes

We've overlooked the eyes for now but let's fix these.

Using the same principles as before, add an ellipse over the blocked in eye and apply a radial gradient to it (*HSL 318,100,41 > 301,100,80*), with a dark-blue Inner Glow effect (*HSL 223,49,23*). The shadows, highlights and specular reflections all use linear or radial gradients, some falling away to *0%* as shown in the exploded view. The iris possesses a linear fill with a red **Inner Glow** effect.

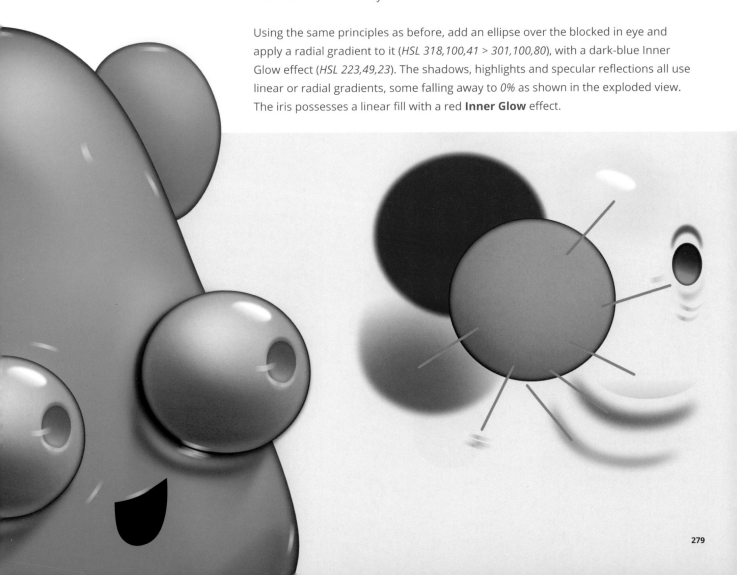

Making spots

The spots on the body are made up from an interesting combination of techniques learnt so far plus a technique called **divide**. This splits up overlapping shapes into separate smaller shapes, some of which can be used to simulate depth.

1 With the **Ellipse Tool** (**Tools Panel**), draw an ellipse and give it a solid fill *(HSL 91,100,50)*.

2 Duplicate the shape, making the shape underneath a darker green *(HSL 125,88,32)*, then stretch it top and bottom simultaneously by dragging the top middle handle upwards while the cmd ⌘ key (Mac) or ctrl key (Win) is pressed. Drag its right-hand side handle inwards slightly with the key still pressed.

3 Select both ellipses, then from the **Toolbar**, select **Divide**. Three main shapes are produced.

4 Move the remaining light-green ellipse to the back using **Move to Back** on **Toolbar**.

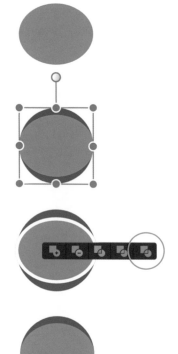

There are two other techniques you could use to produce similar spots:

By shape clipping: Offset a duplicated ellipse from its original, and apply a radial fill to the top ellipse. On the Layers Panel, drag the top ellipse's layer under the lower ellipse's layer to clip. Experiment with glow and shadow effects.

By effects only: With a single ellipse, apply two layer effects, An **Outer Shadow** and **Inner Shadow**, both with an angle of *270°*. Ensure **Offset** is applied.

Top crescent	Ellipse	Bottom crescent

Enable the **Node Tool**, click the downwards crescent, then drag the lower middle node downwards and change colour (*HSL 101,62,17*).

On the **Layers Panel**, apply a **Multiply** Blend Mode, click **Layer Effects**, and apply **Gaussian Blur** with a **Fill Opacity** of *64%*.

Apply a **linear gradient** (*HSL 91,100,50 > 120,100,27*) and an **Inner Glow** effect (*HSL 118,22,23*) with **Radius** of *20 px*.

For a highlight effect, give the bottom crescent a yellow **three-stop linear gradient** (*HSL 74,100,53*) falling way to *0%* **Opacity** at each end of the path.

For other spots, copy and paste to other areas of the body and rotate and reshape using handles according to the spot's position. Realign their linear fill paths to light sources if needed.

MAKING THE POD GUY

The fisherman has got lucky and caught a pod! We'll now concentrate on drawing the held pod, looking at how light falls onto its flat, rather than round, surfaces.

1   On the **Layers Panel**, select the *body* layer and click **New Layer**. Drag this layer under the body layer and name it *pod*.

2   Let's place the fisherman's left arm and fingers into this layer. Right-click the arm and select **Find in Layers Panel**. Also select the 'fingers' layer using the cmd key ⌘ (Mac) or ctrl key (Win), then cut and paste both shapes to the pod layer.

> Now you're finished with the body layer, lock it to prevent accidental repositioning.

Making the pod case

1   With your scanned sketch visible, use the **Pen Tool** to draw the three faces of the pod.

2   Using the **Fill Tool**, apply a subtle linear gradient across each face, going slightly darker towards the direct light source. Each gradient's end stop colours continue on from each other (the side face *HSL 0,11,81 > 0,11,83*, the top face *0,11,83 > 0,4,52*, and the bottom face *0,4,52 > 0,5,30*).

3   From the **Effects Panel**, apply an **Inner Glow** to give each face a more rounded appearance.

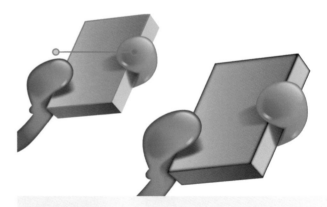

Instead of drawing symmetrical shapes with the **Pen Tool**, you could consider using the **Rectangle Tool**. Drawn rectangular faces can be rotated and sheared, which will preserve the correct geometry.

Pod screen

1 Draw the screen with the **Pen Tool**, making the screen's shape match with the pod front.

2 Add a **linear gradient** (*HSL 136,100,50 > 165,100,33*) and a strong blue **Inner Glow** effect (*HSL 220,100,36*).

3 For the recessed look, draw an L-shape (*HSL 203,100,50*) that touches the top and left edge of the screen with an **Inner Glow** effect (*HSL 258,99,61*).

4 The mouth is a drawn closed shape with a solid fill.

Eyes

Each eye on the screen is simply one ellipse clipped inside another ellipse to give the impression of depth.

1 Create an ellipse with a solid fill of *HSL 12,67,21*, rotate it *-25°* from the shape's top rotation handle, then duplicate and offset the top ellipse to the left.

2 Apply a **linear fill** (*HSL 232,82,29 > 178,100,50*) to the top ellipse.

3 To clip the bottom shape to the top shape, drag the lower ellipse's layer inside the upper ellipse's layer.

4 To finish, apply a white **Outer Glow** effect.

5 Repeat for the other eye.

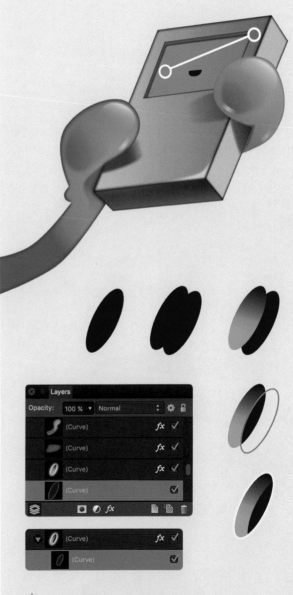

This dragging operation is the same as *Insert inside the selection* but here we are replicating the original ellipse.

Play button

The play button possesses basic/complex linear gradients, warm rounded edges and several highlight areas. This give the button a sense of depth.

For a complex linear gradient, we'll introduce new stops on the fill path to bring other colours into the fill.

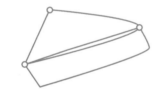

1 Draw the top 'iron' shape and the overlapped side shape with the **Pen Tool**, giving a linear gradient (*HSL 48,100,50 > 27,100,50*) to the top shape.

2 For the 'side' shape, apply a gradient of *HSL 357,100,39 > 32,100,57* then add a new node by clicking halfway along the fill path, and change its colour to *HSL 28,100,50*. Add another node close to the right end stop, giving the node a colour of *HSL 348,100,50*—this adds a deep red to the gradient. Reposition the perpendicular midpoint markers either side of this deep red node to be closer to the node. This limits the spread of the red colour to a smaller area.

3 Apply an **Inner Glow** effect to both objects of colour *HSL 327,79,41* and **Blend mode** of *Normal.*

4 Add three edge highlights as before (p. 277) using a three-stop linear gradient on each. The middle stop's colour can be *HSL 56,100,50.*

5 Add the main shadow using an **Inner Glow** and **Outer Glow** effect.

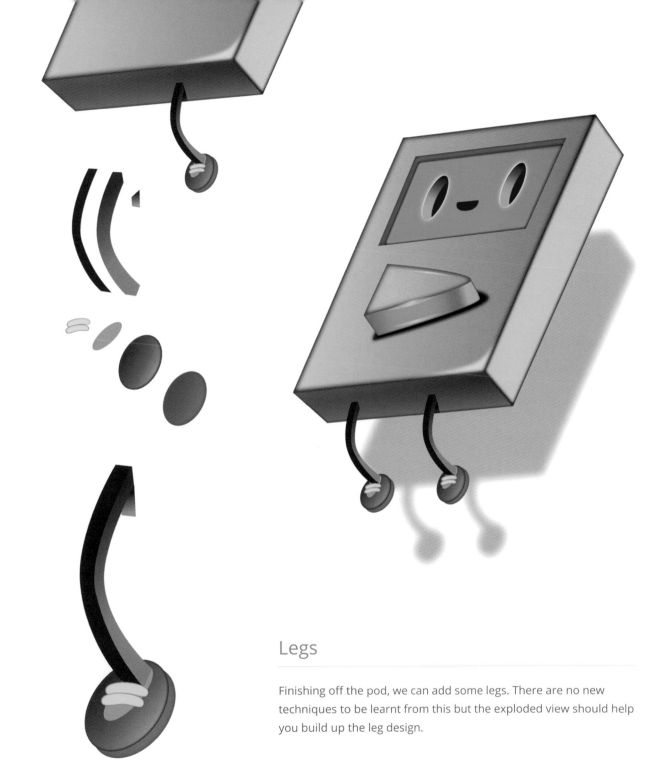

Legs

Finishing off the pod, we can add some legs. There are no new techniques to be learnt from this but the exploded view should help you build up the leg design.

CREATING THE BACKGROUND

No design is complete without a background that complements the main character. We'll be creating the land, water's edge, some trees, and, of course, the river itself, before finishing off the main character.

Background

Let's start by creating a new layer for containing the background elements of our design.

1 Select the pod layer.

2 From the **Layers Panel**, click **Add Layer**.

3 Name the layer as *background* and drag it below the pod layer.

Land

The land is made by overlapping multiple duplicated shapes, with each shape protruding more the lower it is. In doing so, we can create the basic impression of the water's edge.

1 Using the **Pen Tool**, draw a shape that covers the page background but which also reserves a triangular area in the bottom right of your design for the river. The serrated water's edge section of the shape can be drawn by repeating your clicks in alternating directions. Apply a **linear gradient** of *HSL 28,67,27 > 52,65,67* to the shape.

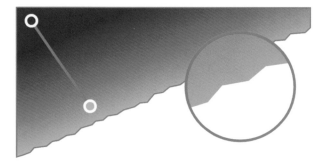

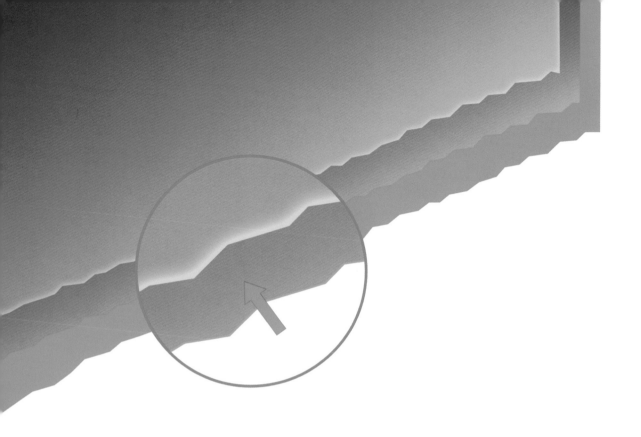

2 Make two copies of the shape and offset each one by dragging.

3 With the Fill Tool, reposition the gradient on the middle shape to make the edge a darker brown.

4 To the top and middle shapes, apply a white **Inner Glow** and subtle **Gaussian Blur** effect, respectively. The bottom shape can take a turquoise colour (*HSL 167,100,47*) to suggest indirect lighting from the soon to be designed river. Position it so only a faint edge is shown (as circled above).

> The large shapes that make up the bulk of the background can happily extend over the page edge. Alternatively, you could choose to enable **Snapping** on the **Toolbar** and snap the shapes precisely to the page edge.

5 The small channels running towards the water's edge, can be drawn as acute isosceles triangular shapes with a solid fill (*HSL 49,61,82*).

6 To finish off the land, add a triangle (*HSL 48,32,68*) in the blank area of the background design.

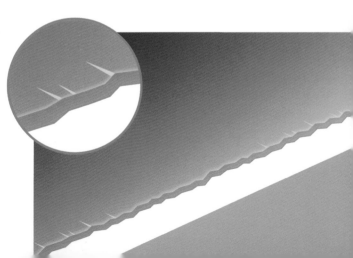

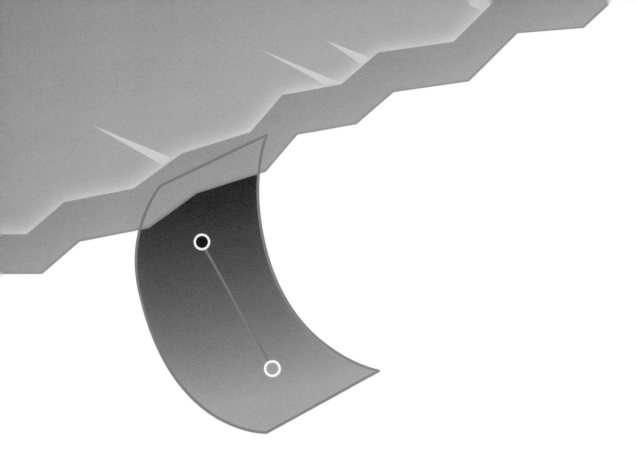

Forming the water's edge

We'll now make more of the water's edge by creating a curved shape, then duplicating and repositioning the duplicates along the edge so they slightly overlap.

1 On the **Layers Panel**, select the turquoise background shape.

2 On the **Toolbar**, enable **Insert behind the selection**.

3 Draw a curved shape with a linear gradient (*HSL 48,32,68 > 12,22,30*) that underlaps the land.

4 Copy and paste the shape, then reposition duplicated shapes along the river edge. It's important to overlap shapes then reposition each one by one to make them less uniformly positioned.

River

Adding a river that meets the waters' edge naturally requires some delicate work using the **Pen Tool**. As a rule, the water should be made to fit the contours of the water's edge naturally.

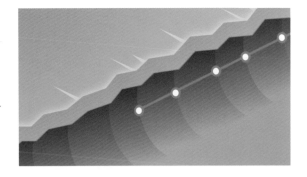

1   Create a new layer at the top of the layer stack, named *river*.

2   Draw the river shape with the **Pen Tool**, ensuring that you click at each ridge along an imaginary straight line that follows the water's edge. Press the shift key (⇧) while drawing to ensure a straight line all along the water's edge.

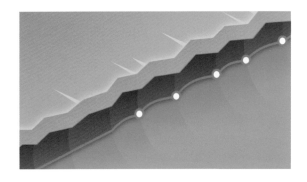

3   Give the shape a solid fill of *HSL 180,74,56* and *59%* opacity, plus an **Inner Glow** effect (*HSL 226,65,33*).

4   To bend each segment at the water's edge, with the cmd ⌘ key (Mac) or ctrl key (Win) pressed, drag upwards from the centre of each segment to fit the curve to the contour of the water's edge. Curved segments are formed from straight-line segments.

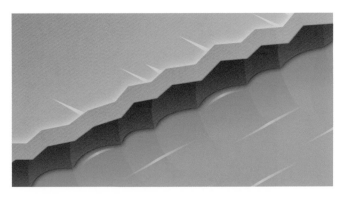

Water creases and swirls are created from narrow shapes with a white three-stop **linear gradient** falling way to *0%* **Opacity** at each end of the path as described on p. 272.

Now you've completed the layer, lock it in the **Layers Panel**.

Trees

Let's make a forest! By creating a single tree, we can duplicate it, then make many differently sized trees.

1 Select the *background* layer.

2 From the **Layers Panel**, click **Add Layer**, then name the layer *trees*.

3 Draw a circle using the **Ellipse Tool** (**Tools Panel**), remembering to constrain the shape to a circle by keeping the shift key (⇧) pressed.

4 To make the circle fully editable, click **Convert to Curves** on the context toolbar. Using the **Node Tool** (**Tools Panel**) with the shift key (⇧) pressed, drag the top node upwards. The shift key (⇧) constrains the node's movement to vertical.

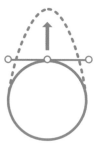

5 Apply a radial gradient (*HSL 224,4,38 > 182,100,43*) across the shape, then an **Inner Glow** effect (*HSL 309,80,24*) with a **Blend Mode** set to *Multiply*. Make the lighter region face the direct light, then make the darker region stop short of the bottom of the tree to suggest a little indirect light.

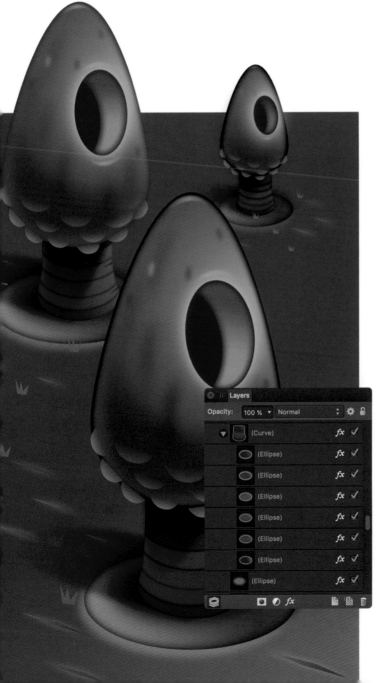

For the tree trunk, we'll introduce a **clipping layer** that means we can easily reposition the trunk sections later which would be impossible to do if using a destructive and more complex divide operation:

1 Draw the trunk shape with the **Pen Tool**.

2 Select **Insert inside the selection** from the **Toolbar**.

3 Draw an ellipse over the base of the trunk and apply a **linear gradient** (*HSL 25,100,16 > 16,17,50*) then both an **Inner** and **Outer Glow** (*HSL 204,100,62* and a **Blend Mode** set to *Multiply* for both).

4 Copy and paste duplicates of this ellipse up the trunk, subtly recolouring each ellipse's **linear gradient** by changing end stop values—experiment a little here. You'll see the trunk sections being clipped to the trunk shape.

5 Finish off the 'clipping' trunk with the same **Inner Glow** effect as the trunk sections.

The eye can also benefit from clipping where the 'pupil' can be clipped inside the eye socket. This was done similarly to the pod eyes.

1 Draw an ellipse for the socket, then duplicate it.

2 Offset the top ellipse so it's above and to the right of the bottom ellipse. Give the bottom ellipse a colour of *HSL 25,100,16* and **Outer Glow** of *HSL 29,91,19*.

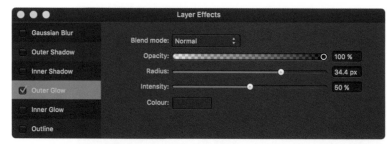

For the top ellipse, apply a **linear gradient** (*HSL 23,100,50 > 0,100,36*), an **Outer Glow** (in *white*) and **Inner Glow** (*HSL 29,91,19*).

3 On the **Layers Panel**, drag the bottom ellipse under the top ellipse so it is nested (clipped) inside the top ellipse.

The bumps on the tree body are open curves that have a linear gradient of *HSL 182,100,43 > 224,4,38*. To ensure they blend into the body, use the **Colour Picker Tool** (I) on the **Tools Panel** to sample the body colour for matching with the fill end stop.

Add some patterns and textures to the tree using some subtle fills and also introduce some shapes at the tree base. Add a deep shadow under the tree, and then a longer shadow that fades out over length. Keep the shadow directions consistent with the light direction.

FLOATING POD

The floating pod seems to have drunk too much river water. In terms of design, there's nothing new here as we're using the same principles as those described on p. 282. One exception is the pod's shadow below the waterline which we'll look at now.

1   On the **Layers Panel**, create a layer named *floating pod* above the *river* layer.

2   Draw the pod similarly to the pod drawn previously.

3   Create another layer below the river layer and name it *floating pod shadow*.

4   Extend the sides of the pod into the water using new shapes filled with colour (*HSL 356,19,20*) so the sides appear continuous. Notice that the semi-transparent river shape allows these shapes to show through naturally. Add an offset shadow under the pod to suggest it is floating.

> Always tweak and adjust as you go. I found I needed to move my whole design up a bit so the main character was more central as it made a better composition.

Let's add a few final details.

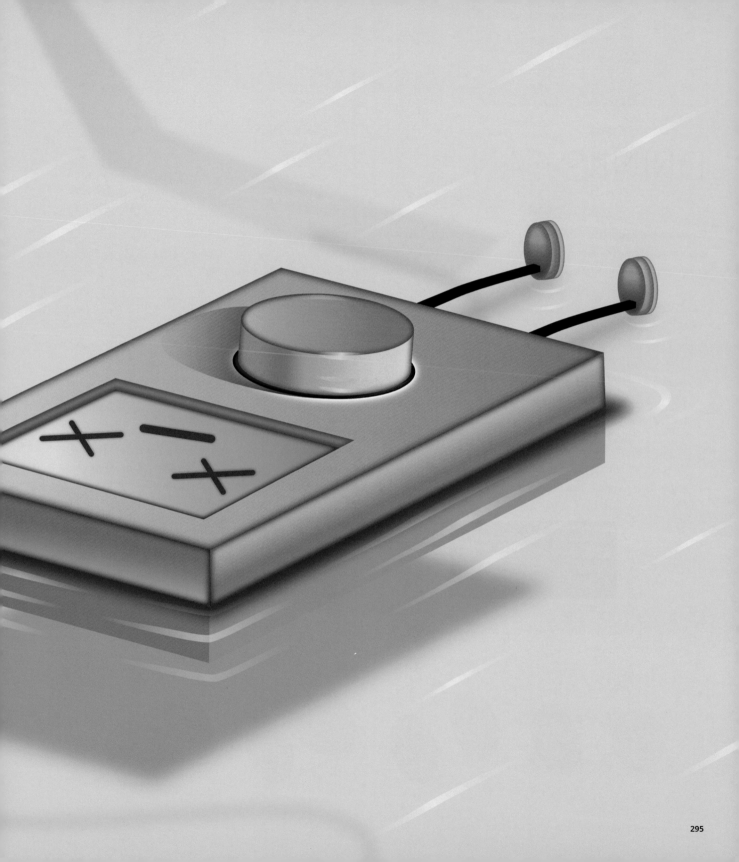

DRINKS CAN

We'll finish off with a soft drinks can, slowly emptying into the fisherman's swim. We'll focus on the can's cylindrical shape and how light can be made to fall across the can's body using a multi-colour linear gradient. Other shadow and highlight techniques you've learnt before can then be applied.

- On the **Layers Panel**, create a layer named *drinks can* above the floating pod layer.

For the can shape:

1 Draw an ellipse with **linear fill** (*HSL 315,0,64 > 182,100,50*) and **Inner Glow** effect (*HSL 171,0,35*) for the can front.

2 Rotate *anti-clockwise* from the top rotation handle, then shear from the top-centre edge handle towards the right. Check that your **Transform Panel** looks like this.

3 Duplicate this shape and move it to where the back of the can would be.

4 On the context toolbar, click **Convert to Curves** to allow the shape to be modified.

5 Select the **Node Tool** (**Tools Panel**) and click at the top and bottom of the shape to add new nodes. This ensures the back of the can will remain symmetrical with the front.

6 Drag the two nodes closest to the front of the can so they touch the front can shape top and bottom. You may have to adjust the control handles on these two nodes, reforming the curves to ensure the can sides are linear and parallel.

7 Move the shape back using **Back One** on the **Toolbar**.

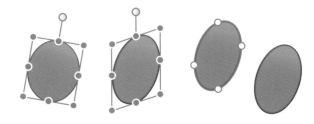

For the multi-colour linear gradient:

1 Select the can body.

2 On the **Tools Panel**, select the **Fill Tool** then drag across the can body from bottom to top.

3 For the **linear fill**, colour the end stops (*HSL 28,52,42 > 80,100,45*) with your direct light source in mind.

4 Now we can introduce further colours along the fill path to simulate lighting. Simply click on the path for each new stop and recolour.

5 Fine tune the positioning of stops by dragging or reposition the midpoint markers between stops to shrink or grow the extent of the stop colour.

For the can front, add some detail:

- An overlaid sheared ellipse shape over the can front with an **elliptical gradient** (*HSL 175,83,73 > 315,0,55*) and **Inner Glow** effect (*HSL 215,26,47*). This gives the can front a realistic raised rim.

- A dark bevelled edge created using the Divide operation (see p. 280).

- A drinking hole 'tear' shape (*HSL 0,0,11*) creating from an elongated ellipse with a white **Outer Glow** effect.

- Curving highlights (p. 277) at the can front's edge.

- Some blurred shadows under the can.

For the drink spill:

- Draw some drink spilling into the river using the **Pen Tool**. Make sure the angles match the shape of the can rim, ground, water's edge and river surface. Add details like highlights and shadows.

FISHING ROD AND ROPE

Resource

fisherman_16_fishingrod.afdesign

A fisherman isn't a fisherman without a rod! This relatively straightforward design uses identical principles to those used in creating the drinks can. However, one new operation to learn is the **Expand Stroke** option, used to convert the pen-drawn fishing rope to curves. This mainly allows us to apply a linear gradient making the rope naturally lit.

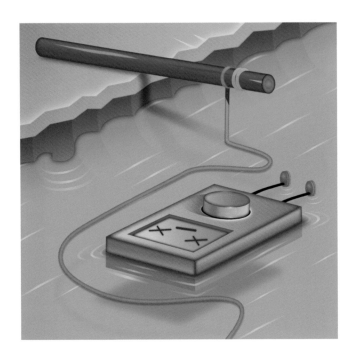

- On the **Layers Panel**, create a layer named *fishing rod* between the drinks can layer and the floating pod layer.

For the basic rod design:

1 Draw the elliptical rod end, duplicate it, then offset the duplicate so it rests on the land (this is the rod butt). As for the can previously (p. 296), extend the nodes on the duplicate back to touch the rod end top and bottom.

2 Apply a linear gradient (*HSL 39,100,50 > 13,77,35*) along the rod length.

3 Make the wood appear more natural using lighter and darker streaks running along its length. Rings are drawn shapes with linear gradients. Use a subtle blur on each streak.

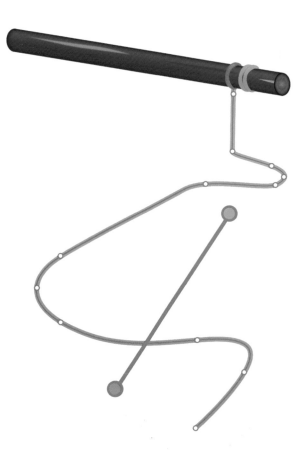

For the fishing line:

1 On the **Colour** and **Stroke Panels**, choose an orange stroke colour (stroke *HSL 27,100,50*; no fill) and a stroke width of *5 pt*, respectively.

2 With the **Pen Tool**, draw the fishing line from the rod tip so it drops vertically from the rod, then plays out across the water surface.

3 On the **Layer menu**, convert the line to curves using the **Expand Stroke** option.

4 Finish off by applying a **linear gradient** (*HSL 27,100,50 > 42,87,59*).

For shadows, apply as before but introduce a subtle fishing rope shadow within the *floating pod shadow* layer instead of the *fishing rod* layer.

Adding extra characters

The cassette tape guy and cassette player (a 70's thing!) are designed using the same principles as those used for the pod characters (p. 282).

> You could make both designs in separate .afdesign files to concentrate solely on these designs. Once you're happy with them you could place them as **Embedded documents** using **File > Place**.

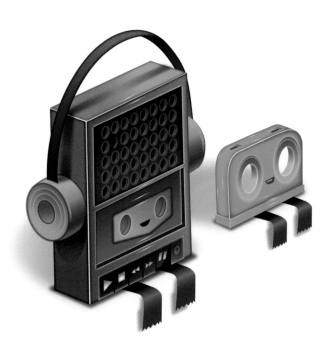

Drips

Drips offer a bit of added realism to the fishing trip. These can be introduced underneath the freshly caught pod guy and as more general splashes over the fisherman.

All drips in the design share two main features—they possess a transparent centre, just like their natural counterparts, and they're also derived from a pre-supplied Tear shape which makes them very easy to create. We'll draw these now.

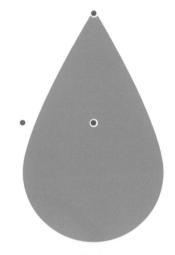

1 On the **Layers Panel**, create a layer named *drips* above the *cassette player* layer.

2 On the **Tools Panel**, select the **Tear Tool.**

3 Drag across the page to create a tear shape. Give it a solid fill (*HSL 192,100,47*) for now.

4 Drag the red handle at the left edge of the shape's selection box to fill out the upper area slightly.

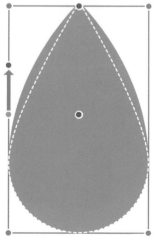

The drips look good but you might want to give them a little more punch, making them jump out of the page. A trick to do this is to simply duplicate the *drips* layer, making a new layer called *drips boost*. The results are both more pronounced and quick to accomplish.

The **Corner Tool** is really useful here, as the pointed tip of the tear needs to be more rounded, to make the shape drop like.

1   On the **Tools Panel**, select the **Corner Tool** (C), then drag the top edge node downwards to round the pointed tip.

2   The drip just needs a three-stop **radial gradient** (*HSL 192,100,47*) that falls away to *0%* **Opacity** at each end of the path.

Once you've completed the drop shape, rotate and scale to suit, then apply directly and indirectly-lit highlights; follow this with a blurred shadow cast by the drop. Note the colour of the underlying shape showing through.

FINISHING OFF –
A LITTLE SPARKLE
AND MOOD

Resource

fisherman_19_finishingoff.afdesign

Final flourishes can now be added to the design. These include coloured sparkles around the trees and a dark vignette to bring more attention to the centre of the design.

Adding sparkles

1 Create multiple layers (named *sparkle1*, *sparkle 2*, etc.) at the top of the layer stack.

2 Draw random circles sparingly in each layer using the **Ellipse Tool** (**Tools Panel**) with the shift key (⇧) pressed. Storing circles in different layers gives more flexibility if some circles need to be hidden in the final piece.

3 Experiment with some contrasting solid colour fills for the circles, then apply a **Gaussian Blur** effect to each layer for a diffuse look.

Adding a vignette

1 Create a layer named *vignette* at the top of the layer stack.

2 Draw a rectangle within the layer slightly larger than the page.

3 Select the **Fill Tool** and the fill **Type** to be **Radial** from the context toolbar.

4 Drag from the centre of the page to its top-left corner. This sets the fill path.

5 Using the **Colour Panel**, give a green colour (*HSL 130,78,15*) to the selected top-left end stop and *0%* Opacity to the opposite end stop.

6 Apply a *Multiply* blend mode via the **Layers Panel**.

Finally, take a little time to review your work. Make last minute changes, including shadow and highlight positioning, to ensure good composition.

If you're happy then you've completed your project! Congratulations and tight lines!!

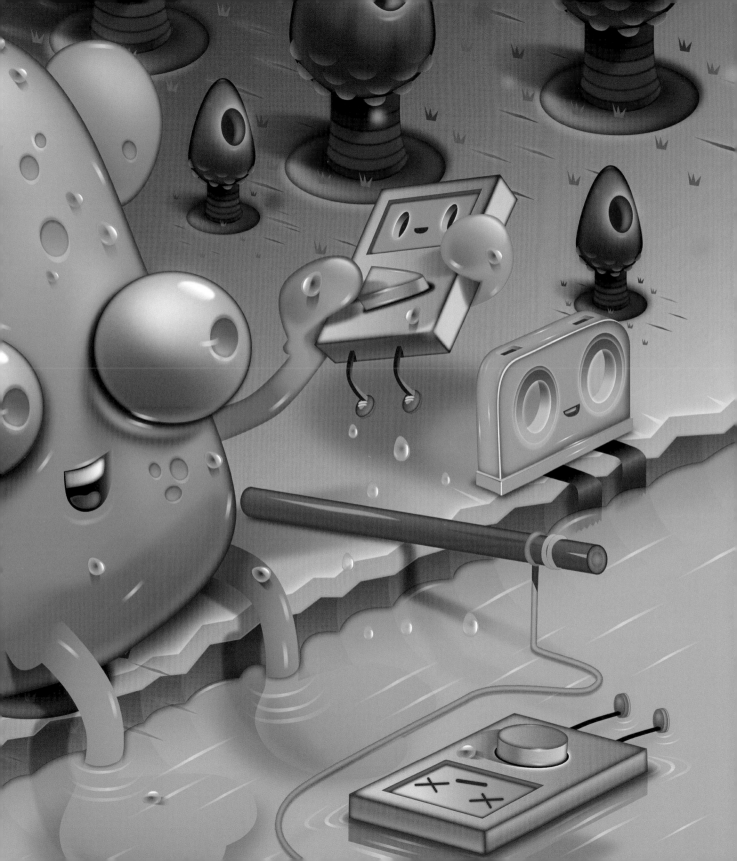

CHAPTER 4

Design Projects

In this chapter learn from Affinity's own Creative Director about how to approach designing collateral and logos for brands and how to design for print.

Plus, join Tom Koszyk, lead designer at Hologram, for lessons in UI and UX design and how to design icons in Affinity Designer.

1

Lace Frame
Galleries 1

Brand collateral and logo design by *Neil Ladkin*

This project looks at client-designer relationships and realising designs to the customer's satisfaction. Neil also shows you how to develop a chosen logo design.

BEFORE YOU GET STARTED

Resources

 You can get all the resources that are referenced in this project from:

https://affin.co/lace1

Knowledge of Affinity Designer

To get the most from undertaking this project, you will need to:

- Be familiar with the interface of Affinity Designer. You can learn more about the interface in the Interface Tour, starting on p. 13.

- Have good core skills. See the skills table below to see which additional aspects of Affinity Designer you need to be confident with to complete this project:

Artboards	p. 74
Objects	p. 80
Geometry Tools	p. 95
Colour & Gradients	p. 106

YOU AND YOUR CLIENT

Working with a client can be tricky, particularly if it's a new client. My best advice is to ensure clear communication throughout the process. Start by extracting as much information as possible at the briefing stage and kick-off meeting.

Listen to your client! They know their business and their customers. Try and find your client's unique story and exploit this in your design.

> " *You need to open their eyes to new ways of thinking and help them achieve brand clarity.*

If you have a client who has a fixed idea of what they want from their brand, but you feel this is not right for them, then it's your job to explain your reasons why. Remember, just because your idea is ground breaking, don't expect your client to immediately be willing to spend their hard earned cash to see it through. They might need convincing.

One trick in winning them over is to present your own take on ideas as well as developing the client's ideas exactly as asked of you. With this, give clear reasons to why you feel your version will benefit their product, service or brand. Nine times out of 10, if your idea is genuinely stronger, the client will agree with your vision.

Seven key questions to ask your client

1 What does your business do, produce or sell?

2 Who are your current and potential customers?

3 What problems do you solve and how do you benefit customers?

4 What is the primary message you want to convey to customers?

5 Do you have any market research about potential customers you can share?

6 Who are your five main competitors?

7 Why do, or should, customers choose you over these competitors?

THE BRIEF

By the end of the kick-off meeting, it's vital that you and your client have an agreed brief. This should outline exactly what is expected from the project and should reduce miscommunication and lost time.

Seven key questions to ask your client

1 What is the purpose/objective/context of the project?

2 What are the deliverables for the project?

3 What do you expect me to deliver?

4 Do you have your own specific design dos and don'ts?

5 What brands, logos and websites do you like and dislike?

6 Who is my main point of contact and who is the decision maker on the project?

7 What are the timescales and budget for the project?

Once you have your brief and an insight into your client's business, you can begin the design process.

If your client already has an existing brand, you might want to ask why their current brand/identity is not working and if they have any current collateral which will need updating with the new identity.

STARTING THE PROCESS

Let's give ourselves a focus for the remainder of this section by taking on a job for a fictional client...

Name: Lace Frame Galleries

Client Details: Contemporary art sales gallery with a separate coffee shop and retail space selling novelty and creative products. Newly established and based in an old warehouse located in the Lace Market in Nottingham, UK.

Your Brief: Design a contemporary logo that hints at the history of the location but also identifies with the contemporary display space. The logo should also be flexible in its ability to focus on different aspects of the brand, i.e. the gallery or the café.

When working on a brand project, look outside your day-to-day world and immerse yourself in a new way of thinking. Put yourself in the shoes of your client's new potential customer. As a designer it's important to absorb information like a sponge, so take in the environment around you—inspiration can come from the strangest of places.

Take photos, think about colours and create mood boards. Don't rush this stage of the process and don't get fixed on one idea too early. Try and keep your mind free and open.

> *It's often a good idea to sketch in a different environment to where you usually work.*

Once you have some ideas, or a direction, start sketching them. This enables you to remain free without the constraints of sitting at your computer.

Work on basic form, keep it simple and let ideas develop as you sketch. Don't be too prescribed and never throw anything away. Don't worry about being precise, as long as you know what that scribble is supposed to be, it's enough for you to work up into a firm idea later.

Start with basic form. Think about the brand name and your mood boards but try not to think too literally. Make notes about colour and form as you sketch – even random words can sometimes develop into great visual ideas.

Once you're happy with your sketched ideas, scan or take photos of them and place them into Affinity Designer to create your rough designs.

As you put together your rough designs, think about the intended use, consider what will fit with your new brand and think about the impression and message you'll create for the intended customer. Use your mood boards, sketches and ideas to inspire your choices.

This is also the perfect time to consider the strength of the typeface, which will need to work at all various sizes, from small labels on takeout coffee cups to the large building signage.

Once you have several strong candidates, say three rough ideas, it's time to approach your client.

YOUR CLIENT PROPOSAL

Ensure you communicate your idea fully at this proofing stage. Don't just send over a pdf with no explanation—take time to articulate the ideas behind the designs and this will save you a lot of pain. I find the best results come from taking time to prepare a full presentation, not only illustrating for the present day, but also predicting how a brand could develop in the future.

I felt the first 'six circle' design was the strongest. The arrangement of circles coming together around a central point have two meanings which illustrate the history of the client's location and their business name:

After the client looked at the first design, I felt the font choice needed to be looked at again before seeking approval.

As a solution, I took font inspiration from vintage sign writers. I especially liked the clean, block, monospaced type that was commonly painted directly onto old industrial buildings and warehouses—the kind of building that now houses the gallery. This was the perfect way to combine the historic nature of the area with the contemporary look the client was seeking.

I convinced the client that, with further development, this reworked design would be the most appropriate to deliver what they were looking to achieve.

- The circles echo the symmetrical patterns and linking structure found in lace, as well as the circular rollers on the mechanical lace machine that was invented in Nottingham.

- The linking structure of circles creates a frame.

When selecting a font, it's important you consider its final use cases. It needs to be readable at small sizes but also have a refined look at large sizes. Generally, for main logo type, it's standard practice to adjust character spacing and curves manually, unless you've created a specific font set for the brand.

FONT: MONTSERRAT - BOLD

FONT: MONTSERRAT - REGULAR

LACE FRAME
GALLERIES

Next, I'm going to show you how the final design was created, try out a few different finishing techniques and then export it for future use.

Resource

laceframe_logo_01_layout.afdesign

CREATING THE BASIC LAYOUT

Once you've had the initial, proof design signed off by the client, it's time to begin building the final design. I'd recommend starting with a new slate and reconstructing the logo from scratch in Affinity Designer. This will result in a cleaner final design and will allow you to break away from the proof, when needed, to give a stronger final design.

1   Select **File > New**, and set up the document as below then switch **Snapping** on from the **Toolbar**.

2   On the **Tools Panel**, select the **Rectangle Tool** (M) and drag on the page with the shift key (⇧) pressed down to draw a *60 mm* square.

> The Transform Panel can be used to apply precise values for the size of objects.

3   Apply a mid-grey *(CMYK 0,0,0,50)* to the square's fill and centralize it on the page using the **Alignment** pop-up panel on the **Toolbar**.

4 Using the **Ellipse Tool** (M), draw a circle, with the shift key (⇧) pressed down, measuring *29 mm* and move it to the top, centre of the square. On the **Stroke Panel**, give it a **Width** of *10 pt*.

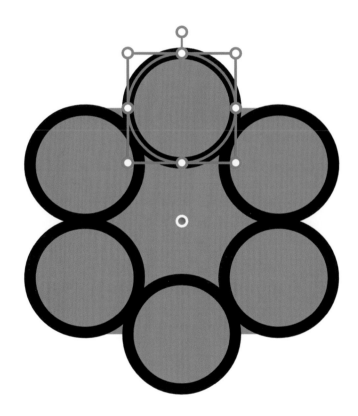

5 With the circle selected, on the context toolbar, click **Show Rotation Centre** and move the circle's rotation centre to the middle of the square.

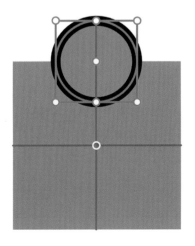

6 **Duplicate** the circle using the command on the **Edit Menu** and then rotate the circle to *−60°* while holding the shift key (⇧). Then, without deselecting, duplicate the circle four more times using cmd ⌘ + J (Mac) or ctrl + J (Win). Affinity Designer will duplicate the circle and include the applied rotation. This is known as **power duplicating**.

USING BOOLEAN OPERATIONS

Resource

laceframe_logo_02_boolean.afdesign

The Shape tools in Affinity Designer have allowed us to quickly build up our logo's basic structure, but it's now time to break away from this to move the logo toward my envisioned final design. Geometry operations, otherwise known as Boolean operations, allow me to create the shapes inside the circles with ease and accuracy.

For an overview of geometry operations in Affinity Designer, see p. 95.

1 On the **Layers Panel**, select all six circles and then, on the **Toolbar**, select the **Add** icon. Then, from the **Layer Menu**, select **Expand Stroke**. You'll see that in our **Layers Panel** we now have a separate lower fill layer and the stroke is now one, single complete vector shape.

2 Select the square and use the **Forward One** icon on the **Toolbar** to place it on top of the 'fill' shape. Now, with the square selected, hold down the shift key (⇧) and select the bottom 'fill' layer. Then, on the **Toolbar**, select the **Subtract** icon. You should be left with two clean shapes.

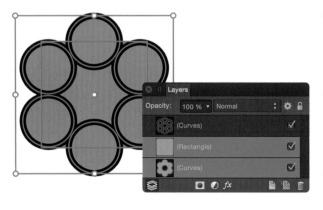

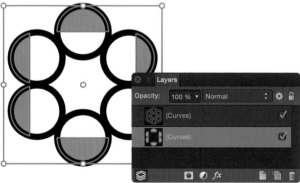

3 With the new 'fill' layer still selected, apply an *18 pt* white stroke and, in the **Transform Panel**, set the **Y** value to *35 mm*.

4 From the **Layer Menu**, select **Expand Stroke** and then select the two resulting shapes and perform another **Subtract** operation. Then select the final two layers and perform another **Add** operation. You should now have one simple shape that forms the main logo.

Resource

laceframe_logo_03_type.afdesign

LOGO TYPE

When I came to add the text to the final design, I abandoned the font I'd used in the original proofs. I kept to the same theory I presented to the client, of a contemporary style which hinted at the block type used on old industrial buildings (p. 316), but chose to adopt the Montserrat family instead (with a few modifications). I also used guides to help me lay the full logo out accurately.

Downloading and installing fonts

1 Go to fonts.google.com (or search online for *Google fonts*) and download the **Montserrat** family (Regular and Bold).

2 Open the downloaded zip file and open and read the **OFL.txt** file.

3 *For Mac:* Double-click the downloaded font files and select **Install Font**.
or:
For Windows: Right-click the downloaded font files and select **Install**.

Adding logo type

1 Select the main layer and reposition it based on the values shown on the **Transform Panel**.

2 Ensure you have rulers displayed (**View > Show Rulers**) and then drag a horizontal guide from the top ruler to the bottom of the main logo, which should be at *93 mm*, and another to *103 mm*.

Use View > Guides Manager to be millimetre accurate.

3 Using the **Artistic Text Tool** (T) on the **Tools Panel**, click on the page and type *LACE FRAME*. Highlight the text and, on the context toolbar, select *Montserrat* from the **Font** pop-up menu and set it to *Bold*. Make the text *48 pt* and *Centre Align*.

4 Switch to the **Move Tool** (V) and position the top of the text to snap along the lower ruler guide and central to the page.

Carefully examining the text, you can see there are some spacing issues that require fixing if we want to achieve a clean monospaced look. To fix this we can select the characters from each word and manually adjust the spacing.

5 With **Move Tool** enabled, select the text then click **Convert to Curves** on the context toolbar. Select **Ungroup** from the same toolbar.

6 Select the letters from *LACE* and distribute them evenly using the **Alignment** pop-up panel (**Space Horizontally** option). Now manually space each letter to create an evenly spaced look, using your eye as judgement. Repeat this procedure to neaten up the *FRAME* letters.

Use the shift key (⇧) as you move each letter to restrict their vertical movement and keep them aligned. You could also use your left or right arrow keys to nudge letters in small increments.

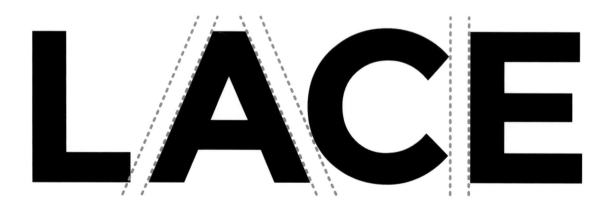

7 Drag a horizontal guide to *122.5 mm* and click on the page with the **Artistic Text Tool**. On the context toolbar, select **Character** and then, in the **Character Panel**, set the text to *Montserrat, 27 pt, Regular*, with *210%* tracking. Type *GALLERIES* and centralize the text on the page and snapped to the *122.5 mm* guide.

I'm not going to convert the text to curves this time as I need the ability to edit the text for various logo versions, and using the Artistic Text Tool will enable scalability.

8 Regroup *LACE FRAME* and realign it as necessary. Then make the logo black, then group everything together. We now have a scalable, finished logo.

CREATING LOGO VARIATIONS

Resource

laceframe_logo_04_variations.afdesign

Using the logo that we've created, we're now going to create a few different versions using different tools and techniques available in Affinity Designer. We're going to create the various logo options on separate artboards within the same document. These artboards will be created at our original page size.

The first variation we will create will be for a logo specifically for the café.

1 Select the logo group and centralize vertically and horizontally on the page using the options from the **Alignment** pop-up panel.

> Now we've repositioned our logo, our guides now longer line up correctly. We can therefore hide these guides, using cmd ⌘ + ; (Mac) or ctrl + ; (Win), or remove them entirely by dragging them off the page

2 On the **Tools Panel**, select the **Artboard Tool**. On the context toolbar, ensure the **Size** is set to **Document** and then click **Insert Artboard**. On the **Layers Panel**, click on the artboard's name and type a new name, e.g. *Master logo*.

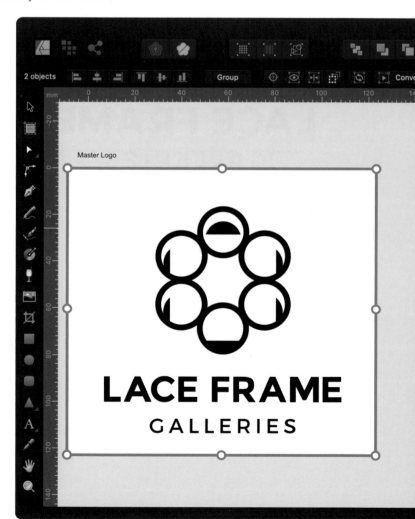

3 With the artboard selected, **duplicate** it using the option from the **Edit Menu** and then select both artboards. From the **Toolbar**, click the **Alignment** icon to display a pop-up panel. Select **Space Horizontally** then uncheck **Auto Distribute** to set a custom distance between the artboards. Rename the new artboard to *Cafe logo.*

4 Press the V key to switch to the **Move Tool**. Hold down cmd ⌘ key (Mac) or ctrl key (Win) then click on the word **GALLERIES** on the **Cafe logo** artboard.

5 Press the T key to switch to the **Artistic Text Tool**, drag to select the **GALLERIES** text and type **BEANS & BAKES**. The new text will automatically honour the spacing originally applied to the text so we keep consistency across the brand logos.

DISTRESSED LOOK

Resource

laceframe_logo_05_distressed.afdesign

Next, I'm going to show you how to give our logo a distressed look, while still keeping it in a scalable vector format.

1   Duplicate the Master logo artboard, distribute the three artboards evenly using the **Alignment** pop-up panel as before. Rename the new artboard to be *Option 1* and then from the **View Menu**, select **Zoom to Selection** (Mac) or **Zoom > Zoom to Selection** (Win).

2   On the **Layers Panel**, expand the group in the **Option 1** artboard and duplicate the six-ring section of the logo. Then, to the duplicate, apply the settings shown on the **Stroke Panel** (below-right), then colour the stroke white and remove the fill colour.

The custom pressure profiles in the pressure chart are created by clicking along the top of the chart to introduce nodes, then dragging nodes downwards selectively to shape the profile. The lower the node the less the simulated pressure contributed to the stroke.

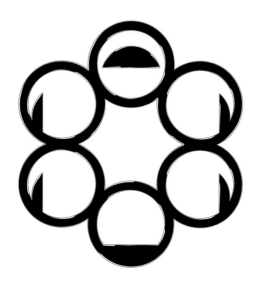

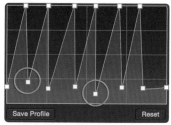

Click **Save Profile** on the **Pressure** pop-up panel so we can then use this again if needed.

3 Change this duplicate object's blend mode to **Erase** and then drag it inside the parent six-ring logo object in the **Layers Panel**. Move it off-centre to enhance the ragged look.

4 Press the esc key to deselect any layers and then select the **Pencil Tool** (N) from the **Tools Panel**. Now, on the context toolbar, change the **Controller** to *None*, and set the **Stroke Panel** up as shown below left.

5 Set the stroke colour to anything other than black or white and draw lots of small lines and squiggles over the top of the logo.

6 Select all of the new lines and squiggles and group them, then set the blend mode of the group to **Erase**. Move this group inside the six-ring layer.

7 Duplicate this group a few times and vary the scale and rotation until you achieve the amount of distress you want.

By creating the effect in this way you can still edit any individual elements at any point in the future.

Try experimenting with different colours to finish the look.

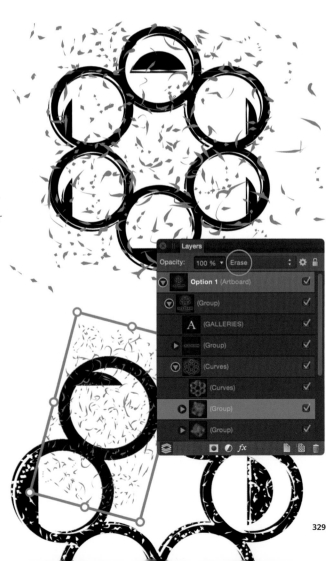

ANAGLYPHIC LOOK

Resource

laceframe_logo_06_anaglyphic.afdesign

For this alternative take on the logo, we'll use offset red and cyan versions of our logo shape to recreate the look you get when viewing an anaglyph 3D image without red-cyan glasses.

1 Duplicate the Master logo artboard, reposition it neatly in the document, rename it appropriately and then zoom into it.

2 Duplicate the six-rings layer twice and then change the fill colour of the two lower layers. Set one to cyan (*CMYK 100,0,48,0*) and the other to red (*CMYK 0,100,80,0*).

3 Hold the shift key (⇧) and move one left and one right then select all three ring layers and horizontally distribute evenly.

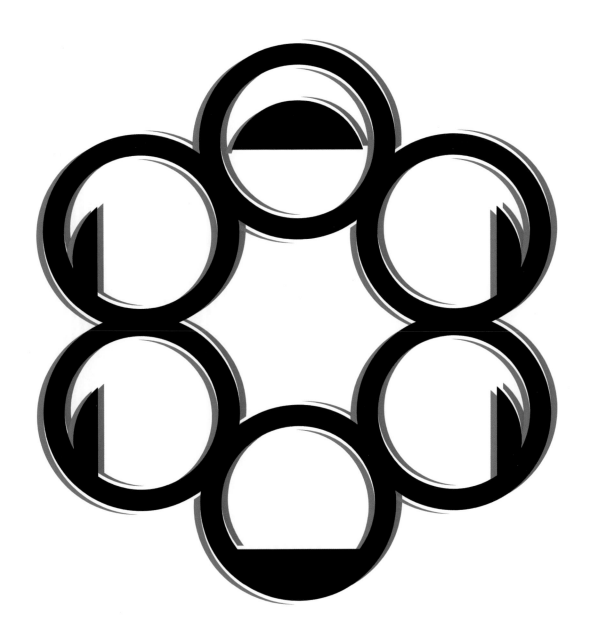

4 Now duplicate the top, black ring layer two more times.
Select one of the duplicates and one of the coloured
lower layers and perform a Subtract operation. Repeat
this with the other duplicate and coloured layer. Then,
directly on the artboard, move one coloured layer up and
one down an equal distance to offset them.

5 Duplicate the black ring layer again then, using the **Rectangle Tool**, draw a box on the page and then use the **Transform Panel** to resize it to *1 mm x 75 mm* (WxH). With this box selected, duplicate it and then use the **Transform Panel** to move the duplicate *2 mm* to the right. You can do this by typing the expression *+=2* in the **X** input box.

Typing *+=2* into the **x** input box will add two units to the selected object's current horizontal position. In this case, the selected rectangle will move 2 mm to the right. For more, useful expressions, see the Advanced Text, Expressions & Gestures insert.

6 Press cmd ⌘ + J (Mac) or ctrl + J (Win) repeatedly to power duplicate (i.e. duplicating multiple times without deselecting), creating a square of lines that cover the size of our logo (approximately 40 are needed).

7 Group the lines, choose a black **Fill** (*CMYK 0,0,0,100*) and no **Stroke**, and centralize the group over the black rings using snapping.

8 Rotate the group *-45°* while holding the shift key (⇧) and then place it **inside** the duplicate of the black rings (avoiding making it a Mask layer). This clips the group to the ring shape. Change the colour of the base ring layer to white and remove the Fill from the parent ring layer which now contains the 'lines box' group.

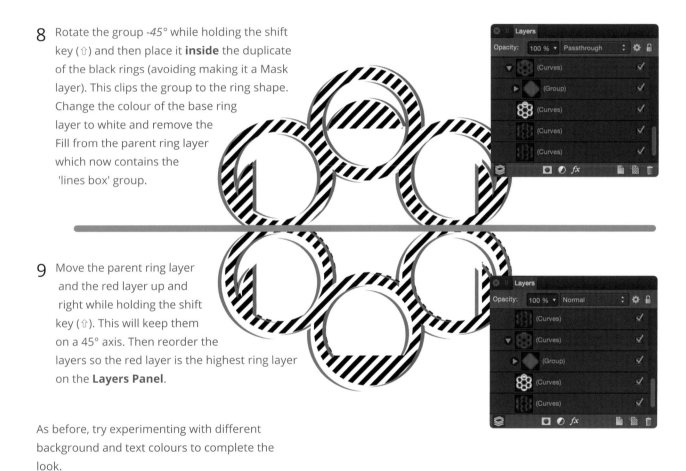

9 Move the parent ring layer and the red layer up and right while holding the shift key (⇧). This will keep them on a 45° axis. Then reorder the layers so the red layer is the highest ring layer on the **Layers Panel**.

As before, try experimenting with different background and text colours to complete the look.

EXPORTING AS SVG

With our final logo designs complete, and possible variations on the theme, we can present them to the client, discuss the choices made along the way, and seek their final approval.

Once approved, we need to get the design into a format which allows it to be used on a lot of platforms. The best option is to export the design as a Scalable Vector Graphic (SVG). SVGs are XML-based text files which are displayed as vector images when viewed in a variety of applications including web browsers. If the SVG contains no rasterized content, its file size is extremely small. This makes SVGs perfect for graphics and logos which will appear on the web. Also, SVGs with no rasterized content are equally important in a printing environment because they can be scaled up or down with no loss in quality.

Before we export our approved designs to SVG, it's good practice to convert each logo to a 'single shape' so it cannot be easily modified by external parties. This helps protect your design and your client's brand. However, you may wish to also keep the designs in a project you can return to later to amend and update, should the need arise. This can be done by saving your current project as two separate files.

Snapshots

If you'd rather work on a single project file only, you may wish to consider using Snapshots. From the **View Menu**, select **Studio > Snapshots** to display the **Snapshots Panel**. Click the **Add snapshot** icon to save a copy of the project in its current state—you can name this anything you like. Regardless of any changes you now make to your document, you can always return to this point in the process by selecting the snapshot and clicking **Restore snapshot**.

1 From the **File Menu**, select **Save As** and save the document as lace-frame-logo-master.afdesign. Repeat this procedure to save the document as lace-frame-logo-converted.afdesign.

The Master file can be returned to at any point to quickly modify the logo design while the Converted file will eventually contain the fixed 'single shape' logos.

We'll use the scenario that the client has approved the Master and Café logos.

2 In the **Layers Panel**, select the group on the **Cafe Logo** artboard and then on the **Layer Menu**, select **Ungroup All**. This will split the logo into all its separate components but will leave the logo looking identical. With all the objects still selected, select the **Add** operation on the **Toolbar**. The logo still looks identical, but it's now a single object (listed in the Layers Panel as 'Curves') made up of numerous curves.

The Café logo is ready for exporting to SVG.

If you export to a raster format, such as PNG or JPG, step 2 is not necessary.

3 From the **File Menu**, select **Export**.

4 From the pop-up dialog, select **SVG**, set the **Preset** to **SVG (for export)** and the **Area** to **Cafe logo**, and then click **Export**.

5 Save the file as 'lace-frame-logo-cafe', navigate to a folder of your choice and click **Save**.

We'll use this exported Café logo in the next project when we explore designing for print.

Feel free to follow the procedures for the **Master logo** artboard.

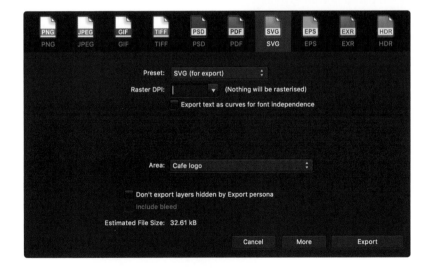

If you wish to export the distressed version of the logo, you'll need to use Expand Stroke for all the objects set to Erase blend mode, then add them together before subtracting from the base logo. To maintain the colour variation between logo and text, Add the text together only. To export the anaglyphic version, because of the colour variations, I'd recommend only performing an Add operation on the text.

INSIGHT: GLOBAL COLOURS

Resource

laceframe_logo_08_aqua.afdesign
laceframe_logo_08_gold.afdesign
laceframe_logo_08_rose.afdesign

You may wish to experiment with the colours in the designs and introduce global colours. This will allow the logo's colour to change dynamically in the event of future brand development and redesign.

Let's explore global colours using a previously referenced Affinity Designer file, as we can build our global colours based on colours we have already used in our anaglyphic logo.

1 Open the resource called laceframe_logo_06_anaglyphic.afdesign.

2 Duplicate the anaglyphic logo artboard, reposition it neatly in the document, rename it appropriately and then zoom into it.

3 From panel preferences on the **Swatches Panel**, select **Add Document Palette** and then, from panel preferences again, select **Rename Palette** to give the document palette a unique name, e.g. *Lace Frame Galleries*.

4 On the **Layers Panel**, select the GALLERIES artistic text layer and then, on the **Swatches Panel**, ensure the Fill selector is active and then select the **Add current colour to palette as a global colour** icon.

Affinity Designer uses the colour values currently applied to the active selector to create our first global colour. This is given the automatic name of 'Global Colour 1'.

> This newly created global colour is **not** automatically applied to the selected object.

5 Right-click on the global colour swatch and select **Rename Global Colour**, then rename the colour to better identify its purpose, e.g. *text*. With the artistic text still selected, select the **Text** global colour swatch to apply that global colour to the text's Fill. Apply this global colour to the grouped letters which make the word LACE FRAME.

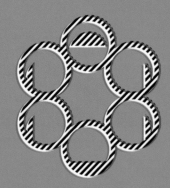

LACE FRAME
GALLERIES

To display the names of colours within the Swatches Panel, select Appearance > Show as List from panel preferences.

6   Repeat steps 4 and 5 for the remaining five colours within the design and, although your logo design should look identical, your document palette should be populated as above.

With these global colours defined and applied to the various layers in our logo, we can tweak the colours in the design without needing to touch the Layers Panel again.

7   Right-click on the global colour which is applied to the background and select **Edit Fill**. In the pop-up panel, select a colour mode from the pop-up menu, and then define a new colour. I used *CMYK 70,0,35,0.*

Continue to edit the global colours until you have high contrast designs which you're happy with.

> *Using global colours is a fantastic way of protecting yourself against unexpected design change when it comes to colours. If your client decides they want to change the colours in a logo, you can simply head straight for the Swatches Panel. Imagine how much extra time you'd also save if these global colours were applied throughout the entire brand collateral — you could make the change in seconds rather than hours!*

2

Lace Frame Galleries 2

Designing for print
by *Neil Ladkin*

This second project for Lace Frame Galleries covers the professional printing of a poster and table card. Both incorporate the logo design created in the previous project.

LACE FRAME
BEANS & BAKES

TAKE
ME
OUT

**Fairtrade full
roast freshly
ground to order**

LACE FRAME
BEANS & BAKES

LACE FRAME
BEANS & BAKES

BEFORE YOU GET STARTED

Resources

 You can get all the resources that are referenced in this project from:
https://affin.co/lace2

Knowledge of Affinity Designer

To get the most out of undertaking this project, you will need to:

- Be familiar with the interface of Affinity Designer. You can learn more about the interface in the Interface Tour chapter, starting on p. 13.

- Have good core skills. See the skills table below to see which additional aspects of Affinity Designer you need to be confident with to complete this project:

Objects	p. 80
Geometry Tools	p. 95
Colours & Gradients	p. 106

CONTINUING
THE CAMPAIGN

Alongside designing a logo, the brief I discussed with the Lace Frame Galleries company included developing a campaign to advertise their café's takeaway option. The expected deliverables were a poster and table card.

" *For brand consistency, the poster and table card should have complementary designs which also match the aesthetics established with the logo.*

LACE FRAME
GALLERIES

Resource

laceframe_print_01_document.afdesign

PRESS-READY DOCUMENTS

Affinity Designer can help us manage the two printed deliverables through the use of artboards. This means all our designs are contained within a single document which is easier to manage, rather than multiple documents, and helps us maintain a design consistency across the deliverables.

1 Select **File > New** and then set up the document for professional press-ready printing as shown. This time we'll create our first artboard from the outset, so ensure you check **Create artboard** before clicking **OK**.

2 On the **Layers Panel**, click on the artboard's name and rename it *Lace Frame Poster*. Now go to **File > Document Setup**, click on the **Margins** tab and check **Include Margins**. Type *20 mm* in all four margin input boxes. This demonstrates that you can change document settings anytime after document creation.

The Transform Panel can be used for precise size settings. Bleed extends the printable area beyond the artboard edge to allow artwork to be trimmed. This will allow for slight movements that the print finishers may get when trimming the poster to size.

Now we have our first artboard setup, we can create a second artboard for the table card within the same document.

3 On the **Tools Panel**, click the **Artboard Tool**.

4 On the context toolbar, click **Insert Artboard**. Name this new artboard *Lace Frame Table Card*.

5 With the table card artboard still selected, go to **File > Document Setup** and set the margins to *5 mm*.

These margins are the safe area around the edge where we don't place any important images or text. This is often requested by printers in order to ensure nothing gets lost in the finishing stage.

I'd recommend chatting to your print shop to get their specific safe area requirements.

6 On the **Transform Panel**, set the size to **W** *105 mm* x **H** *210 mm*. This is the final size of our table card.

7 Go to **View > Guides Manager** and add three horizontal guides at *100 mm*, *105 mm* and *110 mm*. To add a new guide, click the **Add new horizontal guide** icon. Then, to edit its position, click on the text and type a new value.

Now we have an artboard dedicated to the poster and another which defines the front and back sections of the folded card.

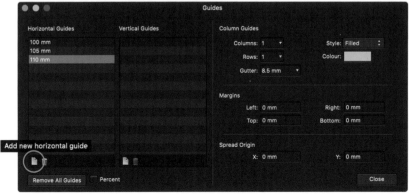

POSTER DESIGN

Resource

laceframe_print_02_poster.afdesign

lace-frame-pattern.svg

lace-frame-logo-cafe.svg

lace-frame-photo-cafe.png

Let's start work on our poster...

1 Select the **Lace Frame Poster** artboard and click the
Rectangle Tool (M) from the **Tools Panel**. Drag on
the page to draw the rectangle and then, using the
Transform Panel, set its size and position.

Next we'll recolour the rectangle, but for consistency and
easy maintenance we'll use global colours.

2 Using panel preferences on
the **Swatches Panel**, add a
global colour using *CMYK
40,0,25,0*. Then apply this
global colour to the
rectangle's fill.

3 On the **Tools Panel**, select the **Place Image Tool** and
open lace-frame-pattern.svg. Drag the image across
the artboard.

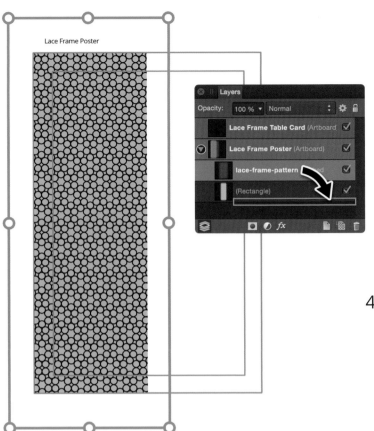

Lace Frame Poster

4   On the **Layers Panel**, drag the **lace-frame-pattern** layer entry inside the rectangle so that it clips the pattern to the edges of the rectangle. Then, with the pattern still selected, on the context toolbar, click **Edit Document**. This will open our pattern in a new window and allow us to edit it.

> When making changes in this new window, the embedded document will update but won't harm the original file. You can make changes to placed images if they support vector information. These include afdesign and afphoto files as well as SVG, EPS, PDF and PSD.

5   In the Embedded document window, select the layer and change the fill to *CMYK 38,43,0,0*. When you switch back to the main file, you'll see that the pattern colour has changed.

> If you work in Separated Mode (Mac only), you'll be able to edit the embedded document and see the changes taking place in the parent document in real time.

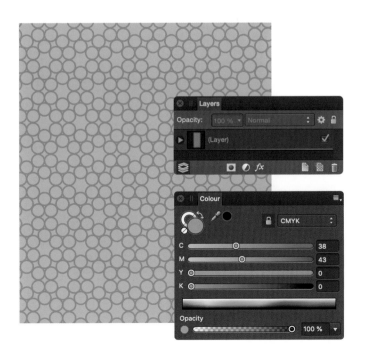

6 Press the esc key and then, using the **Rectangle Tool**, draw a box and apply a new global colour to its Fill, set to *CMYK 38,43,0,0*. Give it a stroke of *3 pt*, coloured using the first global colour. Size it to *80x80 mm* and position at *20 mm and 20 mm* (**X,Y**). Then place the lace-frame-logo-cafe.svg logo graphic using the same size and position as the box.

7 Draw another rectangle (*180x426 mm*) and position at *120 mm and -3 mm*. Then select **Move to Back** on the **Toolbar**. Place the lace-frame-photo-cafe.png image on the artboard to cover the purple section and the bleed area.

8 On the **Layers Panel**, drag the image entry inside the purple rectangle entry to clip it to the shape. Set the blend mode of the image to **Average**.

It's now given us a nice purple hue, but we've lost a bit too much contrast. We can rectify this with an adjustment layer.

9 Select the rectangle containing the image and, on the **Layers Panel**, click the **Adjustments** icon and select **Brightness and Contrast.** Adjust the sliders in the dialog to liven up the image. With the rectangle still selected, select the Fill selector on the **Colour Panel** and click the icon under **Opacity** to switch to the **Noise** slider. Set this to *60%*.

We've achieved a nice stylized image that is toned and muted, ready to take some text.

10 On the **Tools Panel**, select the **Artistic Text Tool** (T), then click on the right edge of the **Lace Frame Poster** artboard.

11 On the context toolbar, set the **Font** to *Montserrat* (*Regular*) with a size of *64 pt* and enable the **Right Align** option. As a fill, choose the green global colour from the **Swatches Panel**. Add the words **TAKE ME OUT** to the poster, adding line breaks after each word. Drag the bottom left corner of the text's bounding box downwards to the left so the scaled text touches the pattern's right edge. Reposition and scale the text so it also touches the right artboard edge.

12 On the **Paragraph Panel**, switched on via **View > Studio**, pull in the **Paragraph Leading** to *170 pt*.

Use the **Frame Text Tool** (T) to draw a text frame below the artistic text and type 'Fairtrade full roast freshly ground to order'. Adjust the font, size, alignment and colour to suit.

13 In the **Layers Panel**, make sure the text objects sit under the green rectangle on the left but above the image on the right.

I chose Montserrat Bold, 48 pt, with white fill.

Downloading and installing fonts

1 Go to fonts.google.com (or search online for *Google fonts*) and download the **Montserrat** family (Regular and Bold).

2 Open the downloaded zip file and open and read the **OFL.txt** file.

3 *For Mac:* Double-click the downloaded font files and select **Install Font**.
or:
For Windows: Right-click the downloaded font files and select **Install**.

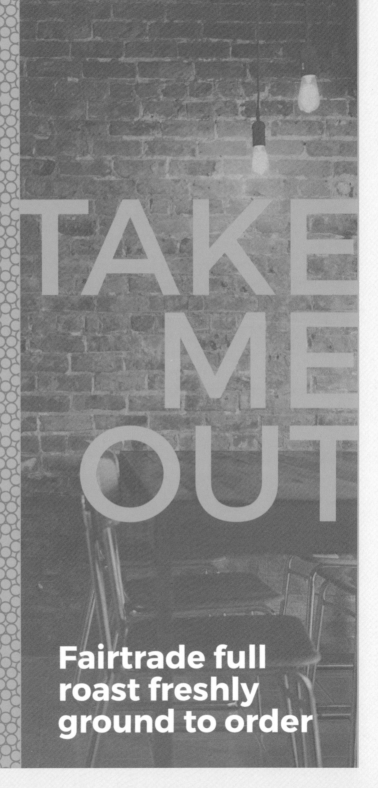

LACE FRAME
BEANS & BAKES

TAKE ME OUT

Fairtrade full roast freshly ground to order

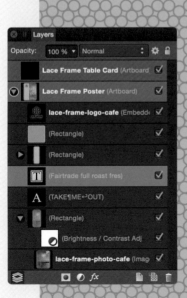

Layers

Opacity: 100 % ▾ Normal ▾ ⚙ 🔒

■ **Lace Frame Table Card** (Artboard) ☑
▼ **Lace Frame Poster** (Artboard) ☑
  lace-frame-logo-cafe (Embedd ☑
  (Rectangle) ☑
▶ (Rectangle) ☑
  T (Fairtrade full roast fres) ☑
  A (TAKE¶ME↵OUT) ☑
▼ (Rectangle) ☑
  ◐ (Brightness / Contrast Adj ☑
  lace-frame-photo-cafe (Imag ☑

◧ 🔘 fx   📄 ▦ 🗑

TAKEOUT CUP GRAPHIC

We're going to create a realistic looking, scalable takeout coffee cup that we can use for all our various sizes of marketing material, including the poster and table card.

1   Select the **Lace Frame Poster** artboard and then, with the **Artboard Tool** selected, on the context toolbar, click **Insert Artboard** and rename the new artboard *Takeaway Cup*.

2   From the **View** menu, select **Show Grid** and then add a central, vertical guide via **View > Guides Manager** (click **Add new vertical guide** to place automatically). Using the **Trapezoid Tool**, draw a trapezoid measuring *150x230 mm*.

The **Trapezoid Tool** is located on the **Tools Panel** and is grouped with a variety of other shape tools.

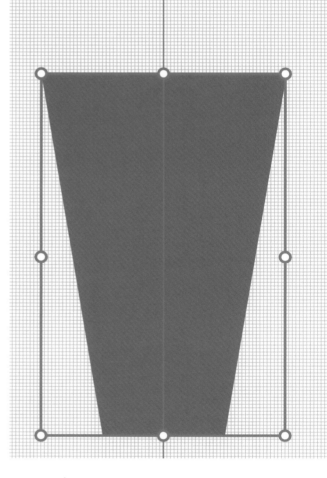

Snapping settings can be activated and updated from the Toolbar.

Resource

laceframe_print_03_graphic.afdesign

3 Switch to the **Move Tool** (V) and rotate the shape **180°** and snap it to the vertical centre of the artboard. On the **Swatches Panel**, remove the shape's **Stroke** and recolour the **Fill** to mid-grey.

4 Switch to the **Node Tool** (A) and, with the cmd ⌘ key (Mac) or ctrl key (Win) held down to keep the shape symmetrical, drag the shape's lower left red handle outwards (the context toolbar's **Right point** option changes to around *84%*). Then, on the context toolbar, select **Convert to Curves** and add a central node at the bottom of the cup. Select the node and move it downwards and then convert it to a **Smooth** node from the context toolbar. Hold the shift key (⇧) and drag each node handle to form a neat curve.

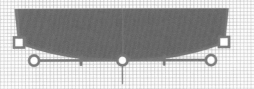

You'll know when both handles are equal as they will snap in place and display a small crossbar.

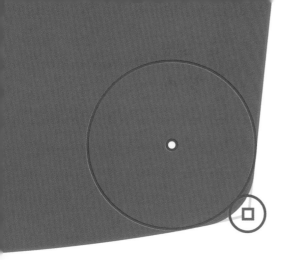

5   Select the **Corner Tool** (C) from the **Tools Panel** and, holding down the shift key (⇧), click to select the two nodes which define the bottom corners of the cup. Drag one of the nodes inwards (the other will copy).

6   Use the **Fill Tool** (G) to create a realistic lighting effect by setting the **Type** to **Elliptical** on the context toolbar. Drag from the top of the cup horizontally to the left to set the elliptical gradient, then position and colour the handles and stops as shown. I introduced an extra stop by clicking on the top path for more lighting control.

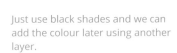

Just use black shades and we can add the colour later using another layer.

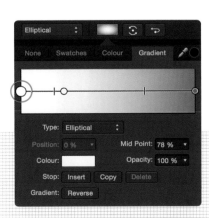

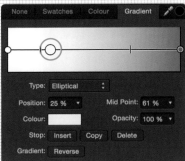

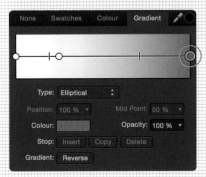

7 Select a dark end stop of the gradient, which is creating the shadow. Then in the **Colour Panel**, set the **Noise** to *20%*. This will help our cup look photo realistic.

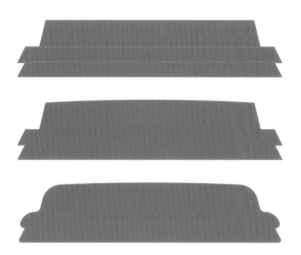

8 Using the **Trapezoid Tool** again, draw the bottom of the lid using a mid-grey solid fill and set the context toolbar's **Left point** and **Right point** options at *3%* and *97%*. Switch to the **Move Tool** and then drag the shape upwards while holding the cmd ⌘ key (Mac) or ctrl key (Win) to create a copy which overlaps a fraction. Also press the shift key (⇧) to constrain positioning vertically for precision. Repeat to make a third copy higher up and make it taller and narrower.

Use the **Add** operation on the **Toolbar** to convert them to a single shape and then curve the top in a similar way to how we curved the bottom of the cup (step 4). Then round off those sharp edges with the **Corner Tool** again as in step 5.

We want the lid to be symmetrical, so make sure you adjust the opposing nodes on either side of the lid in pairs by using the shift key (⇧) to select them.

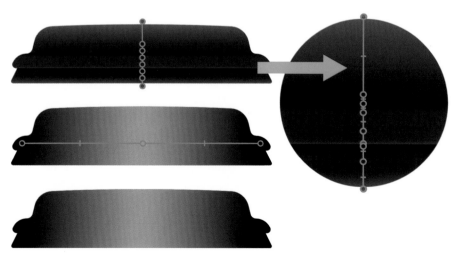

9 Using the **Fill Tool**, add a vertical linear gradient to the lid and then add and adjust the stops to create the contours of the lid. I used nine stops set to various shades of black with varying midpoints to define the look. Then duplicate the lid layer and give it a simple horizontal black-grey-black gradient. Set this layer to a **Overlay** blend mode to create a highlight.

10 Duplicate the main body of the cup, set the
    shape's **Fill** to the green global colour and
    then apply a *Multiply* blend mode. Using the
    Crescent Tool (grouped with the Trapezoid
    Tool) draw and rotate a black crescent across
    the top of the body of the cup. On the **Layers
    Panel**, set the crescent's **Opacity** to *15%*, the
    blend mode to *Multiply* and then drag it
    inside the main body of the cup (the
    greyscale layer).

Instead of duplicating the main cup layer you can apply a
Colour Overlay effect. Simply select the main cup layer and
switch to the Effects Panel. Activate Colour Overlay and set
the colour to the green global colour.

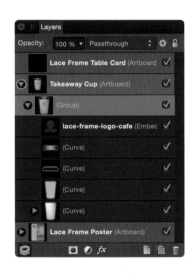

11 Place the lace-frame-logo-cafe.svg logo graphic on the cup at a size of approximately *90x90 mm*, centre it and, from the **Layers Panel**, set its **Opacity** to *70%*. Group all the layers on the artboard together.

We now have a realistic coffee cup graphic we can use in our other deliverables! (Feel free to hide the grid now.)

Now it's a grouped object, be sure to hold down the shift key (⇧) when scaling to keep the aspect ratio.

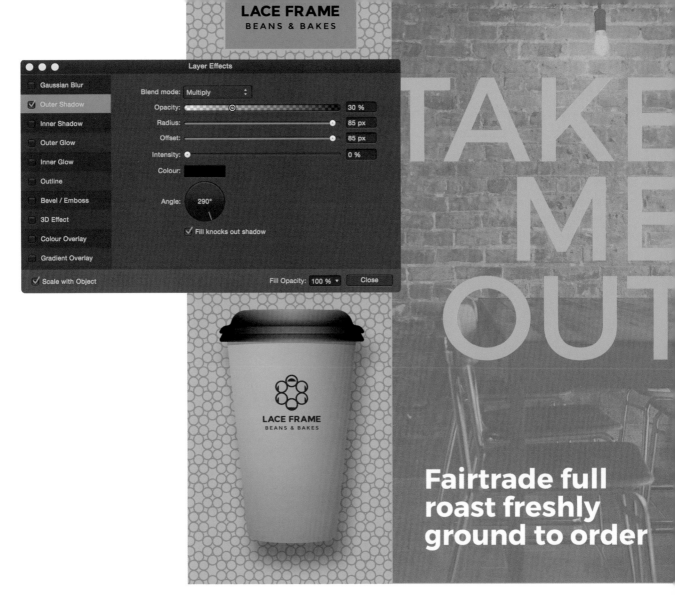

12 Select the takeaway cup group and copy it over to the **Lace Frame Poster** and position it bottom-left. Then, with the group still selected, select the **Layer Effects** icon on the **Layers Panel** and apply an **Outer Shadow** to the group.

Be sure to select the **Scale with Object** option in the bottom-left corner so the shadow will remain consistent, regardless of the group's dimensions.

Resource

laceframe_print_04_card.afdesign

TABLE CARD DESIGN

We can now use the elements from our poster to create the table card. Not only does this keep the deliverables consistent, it also speeds up the design process.

We'll start with the background elements and work from the fold on the lower half of the **Lace Frame Table Card** artboard.

1 Copy the rectangle containing the photo from the poster and paste it onto the table card artboard. Reposition it so its top-right corner handle is positioned directly over the fold at the right.

Remove its stroke and then, holding the shift key (⇧), scale the rectangle from its lower left-hand corner handle to fill the lower-right half of the card, remembering to leave enough bleed area outside the artboard. On the context toolbar, select **Lock Children**. Now you can widen the rectangle without distorting or moving the photo itself. You can also select the photo inside the rectangle by double-clicking with the option ⌥ key (Mac) or alt key (Win) pressed and reposition it.

At this new size, the noise applied to the rectangle is too harsh and the photo looks a little too washed out. We can correct this.

I chose to leave off the top-left logo as I wanted to make use of the space to really highlight the product.

2 Select the rectangle and reduce the **Noise** to *42%* then double-click the **Brightness/Contrast adjustment** layer and reduce the brightness to *-28%*.

3 Copy the poster's pattern element and paste it onto the table card artboard. On the context toolbar, switch off **Lock Children** and then scale it in the same way as we did previously. Then copy the rest of the poster elements over to the card, scaling as necessary. The frame text (unlike artistic text) will not scale by nature so adjust the Fairtrade text to be *14 pt* after scaling.

4 Group all the objects on the **Lace Frame Table Card** artboard and then duplicate the group. On the context toolbar, click the **Show Rotation Centre** icon and drag the rotation centre (shown as a target icon centred on the group) to the top-centre of the group. Then rotate the group *180°* using the group's rotation handle.

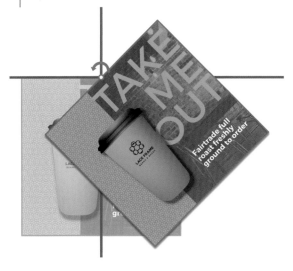

Hold the shift key (⇧) as you rotate as this will help you snap to *180°*.

Your deliverables are now ready to be presented to the client and, if approved, sent to the print shop.

EXPORTING TO PDF

High-resolution PDFs are the ideal way to share your artwork with professional printers. However, PDFs also provide an efficient way of creating proofs for your client to approve.

Let's create an electronic proof for the Lace Frame Poster and then the Lace Frame Table Card.

1 From the **File** menu, select **Export**.

2 From the pop-up dialog, select **PDF**, set the **Preset** to **PDF (for web)** and the **Area** to **Lace Frame Poster**, and then click **Export.**

3 Save the file as 'lace-frame-poster', navigate to a folder of your choice and click **Save**. Then repeat the procedure but select the **Lace Frame Table Card** area and save it as 'lace-frame-table-card'.

This will provide us with two PDFs with small file sizes which are ideal for sending to the client electronically for them to approve. Once they have, you can export the designs as hi-res versions for the printers.

4 Follow steps 1-3 but this time, set the **Preset** to **PDF/X-1a:2003**, check **Include bleed** and select **More**. From the dialog, check **Include printers marks** and click **Close**.

You can save this updated PDF profile as a custom preset by clicking Manage Presets and selecting Create preset.

TAKE ME OUT

LACE FRAME
BEANS & BAKES

LACE FRAME
BEANS & BAKES

**Fairtrade full
roast freshly
ground to order**

3

Tix App 1

UX and UI design for an app
by *Tom Koszyk*

This project, and the subsequent project, looks at developing a 'To Do' mobile app for iOS devices—we'll cover the UX/UI design of the app here, while the next project focuses on developing a complementary icon for the app.

In this project, three design files are expected to be created—one each for UX design, UI design, and Constraints (a key Designer layout feature).

BEFORE YOU
GET STARTED

Resources

 You can get all the resources that are referenced in this project from:
https://affin.co/tix1

Knowledge of Affinity Designer

To get the most from undertaking this project, you will need to:

- Be familiar with the interface of Affinity Designer. You can learn more about the interface in the Interface Tour, starting on p. 13.

- Have good core skills. See the skills table below to see which additional aspects of Affinity Designer you need to be confident with to complete this project:

Artboards	p. 74
Colours & Gradients	p. 106
Clipping	p. 90
Symbols	p. 122
Guides	p. 121

CREATING
THE CONCEPT

I'd been commissioned by a client to design a 'To Do' app, called **Tix App**. After discussions, I had a pretty strong concept: the client wanted it to be very simple and straightforward, but with functionality that would allow power users to squeeze out more from it.

The most basic use cases envisaged were:

- Adding a new task

- Completing the task

- Creating work tasks separate from personal tasks

- Browsing between different Task Boards

- Creating custom Task Boards

- Adding a due date if task is time related and get a clear message if the task is overdue

- Reminders about closing due dates

- Searching multiple tasks

PLANNING

For app design, I'd recommend establishing a design process which should consist of at least these few steps:

- Research

- Preparing a Design Doc

- UX Design*

  ○ Information architecture / Flow maps design

  ○ Designing Mock-ups

  ○ Test

- UI Design

> * from this point, you should also test your design as frequently as possible.

Research

Know exactly what you're designing.
Sit down with your client and talk about the concept. Let's say you're designing a To Do app for a start-up company. Is there enough information to begin work? If not, look at To Do apps currently available on the market. There are many available and almost every app takes a different approach. You can design a very simple app like **Clear** or something more complicated such as **Things for Mac** (with projects, areas of responsibility, recurring tasks), or even a true combine like **Asana**. Maybe your client wants something based on completely different methodology like kanban-based **Trello**.

Get to know your target audience and age demographics.
Why should they use the app you're designing? What do they really need? How would they interact with the app?

Try to write down a few basic use cases.
The use cases will be completely different for the app designed mainly for personal use and for the app designed for big teams in corporations. If you have them written down, you have a check list; when you have mock-ups designed you can go through them with your list of main use cases in hand and check if you can perform all of them and if it's easy enough.

Preparing a Design Brief

Collate all of these findings into a Design Brief. It will make a freelancer's life easier, and would be a life saver if you work in a bigger team.

UX Design

For me this is the whole process of translating things you learnt during your research into real solutions and finally designs. UX design is all about designing interactions, app flows, where to display information and how and where to place elements so the user can easily see it and interact with it (if a button). It's not about creating shiny gradients and choosing beautiful typography. You'll work on this later as part of UI Design (p. 370).

I prefer a bottom-to-top approach, i.e. starting at the lowest level of detail and progressing up to the highest finer detail. I usually start by sketching an "app tree" or wireframe with different app screens drawn as rectangles (with titles) and connected together in a logical manner.

TASKS CARDS

TASKS LIST

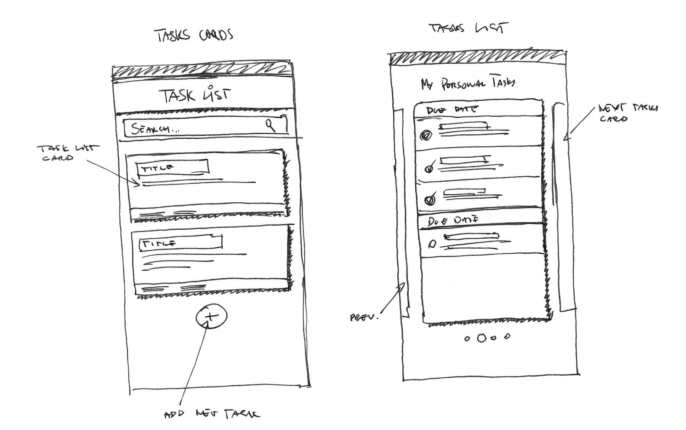

TASK LIST

SEARCH...

TASK LIST
CARD

TITLE

TITLE

ADD NEW TASK

MY PERSONAL TASKS

DUE DATE

DUE DATE

NEXT TASKS
CARD

PREV.

Meanwhile, I'm also working on information architecture. I plan what information should be shown on every screen without thinking how and where exactly.

Next, I start to focus on another level, i.e. the screens and views themselves. Let's say I've drawn a screen rectangle representing a Task List previously, so I'll now add specific features to this screen, like an Add Task button or a list of tasks. I'm also planning which button triggers which interaction, and which action leads where and how.

I'm a big fan of animations in UX design (UX choreography) so I think about how the user should be taken to another screen. For example, if tapping an Add Task button, should the animation transition to the next screen via the bottom of the current screen, or maybe from the right-hand side of the screen?

Test

At this point, you should test your designs whenever possible. Show your basic mock-ups to other people, ask them questions ("How would you add another task?" etc.). You can do that on a very simple prototype or even on a printed mock-up. When you collect feedback, go through it, think about it and correct your designs, then test again.

> Remember that testing a design with one user is better than not testing.

UI Design

Finally, the most fun part. UI design is where you take your plain 'boring' mock-ups and play with visuals, choose colours, and define typography. This doesn't suggest complete design freedom as you still need to think about your client branding, target audience and medium. For example, you wouldn't use green and violet colours if your client's brand colours are red and blue.

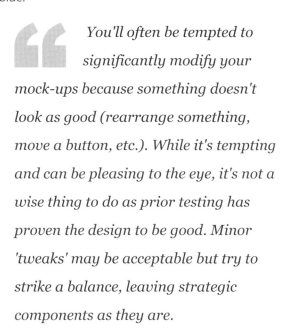

You'll often be tempted to significantly modify your mock-ups because something doesn't look as good (rearrange something, move a button, etc.). While it's tempting and can be pleasing to the eye, it's not a wise thing to do as prior testing has proven the design to be good. Minor 'tweaks' may be acceptable but try to strike a balance, leaving strategic components as they are.

THE PROJECT APPROACH

In response to my client, I'll be designing a To Do App for Apple's iOS platform, called **Tix App**. We'll look at how to apply theory and act on the client's requirements to create a real project, and how to use Affinity Designer for both UX and UI Design. The principles and techniques in the project can also be applied to Android app development equally. At relevant points through the project, I'll point out Android-specific issues that you may need to consider.

Technical Aspects

The screen size

There are many iOS devices available on the market and almost all of them have different screen sizes and resolutions. For this project, we'll be mocking up an app design for iPhone 6, 7 or 8 devices (all 375x667 pt).

Pixel Density

Because of the many different screen sizes and resolutions of iOS devices they have different **pixel densities**. Pixel density refers to the number of pixels squeezed into a screen inch.

Non-Retina (x1) devices have a resolution half that of a Retina (x2) device if screen sizes were the same. That means that for every inch of the screen there are twice as many pixels displayed on the Retina (x2) device. As a result, a button (or any other graphic) on an iPhone with a Retina (x2) display has to have four times the number of pixels as the one from a non-Retina display. And that may create confusion as to what the button size should be? 88 px or 44 px height? To avoid such problems, the mobile app developer always works in **points** rather than pixels.

Points (pt) are device-independent metrics. 1 pt equals 1 px on non-Retina (x1) displays, 2 px on Retina (x2) displays, and 3 px on Retina HD/Super Retina HD (x3) displays. This means that you can define a button as being 44 pt tall and any device will multiply the button size by its pixel density factor: 1x, 2x or 3x for Apple devices.

DPI

Along with measurement units being set to points, a **DPI** of 144 dpi is recommended for Retina (2x) app design; 216 dpi for Retina HD or Super Retina HD. This ensures graphics appear crisp and of good quality at higher pixel densities. Fortunately, when you set up your document, the device presets available will set measurement units to points and DPI to 144 or 216, which gives you a solid foundation for excellent app design.

DOCUMENT SETUP

For app design, it makes sense to start from a device-specific artboard so you're designing using the same dimensions as the app owner's mobile device. You can introduce differently sized artboards for other devices later.

1 Select **File > New**. From the document setup, ensure you select *Devices* and *iPhone 6 (Retina)* from **Type** and **Page Preset** pop-up menus, respectively. Ensure the **Create artboard** check box is selected.

2 On the **Layers Panel**, click on the artboard's name and rename it *myapp-main-screen*.

> When designing for iPhone 7, use the iPhone 6 (Retina) preset.

> If you're developing for Android devices, enter custom Page Width and Page Height dimensions to match targeted devices.

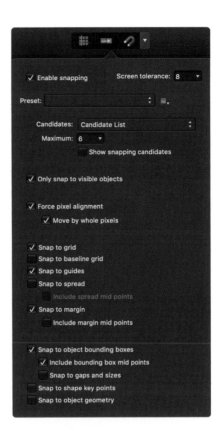

Design aids

To make life easier, turn on **snapping**. This will ensure pixel accuracy and that objects align perfectly.

1   On the **Toolbar**, select **Snapping**.

2   Click the button's drop-down arrow and select the *UI design* preset. A series of snapping options are enabled—for my design I'll adjust these settings so I can use up to six objects (as a Candidate List) that can be snapped to at any time. I unchecked some other options I felt I didn't need.

The **Force Pixel Alignment** option is important as you can snap to (and position) by whole pixels.

Colour panel setup

Let's set up the Colour Panel so you can easily and repeatedly enter RGB Hex values.

1   On the **Colour Panel**, click panel preferences icon.

2   Select **Sliders** from the pop-up menu.

3   Click the **RGB** pop-up menu, then select *RGB Hex*. The # input box can be used for hex colours, although I also use the **Fill** swatch (Colour tab; RGB Hex sliders) on several context toolbars too.

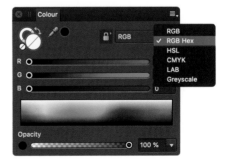

Resource

tix1_02_uxelementsmainscreen.afdesign

UX DESIGN: CREATING ELEMENTS (MAIN SCREEN)

The initial UX design involves laying out 'building blocks' in the design. Bars, cards, and supporting text form a good framework for later, more visually appealing, UI design.

In this section, use the **Transform Panel** (**X, Y, W,** and **H** input boxes) to accurately size rectangles with point accuracy.

Creating a Status Bar

Always leave enough space for device-specific components. You definitely need a Status Bar at the top of the screen area as it's always visible on iOS devices.

1 With the **Rectangle Tool** (M), draw a 375x20 pt rectangle and snap it to the top of the screen.

2 Name this shape *status bar* and apply a temporary black fill.

Navigation and Search Bars

1 Draw a 375x44 pt rectangle and place it just below the Status Bar (**Y** *20 pt*), then change its name to *nav bar*.

2 Duplicate it (**Edit > Duplicate**) and place below (**Y** *64 pt*), then change the duplicate to be named *search bar*. Now draw a 359x30 pt white rectangle and place it on the search bar, naming it *search input*. Use **Alignment** options on the **Toolbar** to align it horizontally and vertically—place it exactly at the centre of the search bar.

3 On the **Layers Panel**, drag the search input rectangle inside the search bar rectangle to nest it.

4 For search input, on the context toolbar, change **Corner** to *Rounded*, select the **Absolute sizes** check box, then enter a Corner value of *4 pt* to mimic standard iOS input.

5 Change nav bar and search bar fills to be *#CACACA* and *#E4E4E4E*, respectively.

> *UX is about functionality and not about being pretty. Keep your mock-ups in greyscale and use basic fonts to concentrate on UX issues and avoid visual UI distractions.*

Creating nav bar text

1 On the **Tools Panel**, select the **Artistic Text Tool** (T).

2 Hover over the nav bar, then click and type *TASK LISTS*.

3 Format the text using the **Character Panel**, which can be switched on via **View > Studio**.

4 Position the text at the centre of the nav bar until horizontal red and vertical green lines appear to indicate snapping.

5 On the **Layers Panel**, clip the TASK LISTS text entry inside the nav bar entry by dragging.

> The Character panel gives some flexibility but you can also use the Text context toolbar as it's more at hand.

Creating Task Cards

On the main screen you'll create several categorised **Task Cards** that will jump to different categories of Task Boards, plus a button to add a new one. You'll create My Personal Tasks, Work Tasks and My Secret Project task cards.

1 Draw a *359x90 pt* rectangle, name it *task-board-card*, and change its fill to *#E4E4E4*. Apply rounded corners with an Absolute size of *4 pt*.

2 Draw another rectangle (*359x20 pt* with fill *#CACACA*) over the task-board-card rectangle, and change its name to *bottom-bg*.

3 On the **Layers Panel**, drag to indent the new rectangle under the task-board-card entry until you see a blue highlight and release.

4 Move the bottom-bg rectangle so it snaps to the bottom of the task-board-card rectangle—make it snap horizontally too.

5 Snap the task-board-card shape centrally and set a Y value of *117 pt* (**Transform Panel**).

Creating task card text

The card needs some text showing the card name, a brief description, and the number of tasks (plus those overdue).

1 Select the task-board-card shape.

2 Using the **Artistic Text Tool**, add the following text:

- *My Personal Tasks (fill #000000, 16 pt Arial).*

- *A sample list of my personal tasks. (fill #000000, 12 pt Arial).*

- *4 Tasks, 2 Tasks Overdue (fill #FFFFFF, 12 pt Arial).*

3 On the **Layers Panel**, drag the three text layers into the task-board-card layer and arrange them neatly on the page as shown.

UX: SYMBOLS

Symbols give you incredible power in Affinity Designer. They can be used instead of identical repeating elements in your design so that, in the event of design change, a single edit on any one instance of that symbolised design will simultaneously and automatically update all other 'repeated' symbolised elements. Magic!

In this project, symbols can initially be used to make simultaneous text changes across multiple task cards.

Creating a symbol

1 On the **Layers Panel**, select the task-board-card layer.

2 Switch on the **Symbols Panel** (via **View > Studio**), then click **Create Symbol** on the panel.

3 Drag the created symbol from the panel onto your artboard twice, placing each symbol instance below the lowest symbol at 10 pt increments.

> Snapping (enabled previously) will let you align symbols horizontally, while measurement guides will show the distance between symbols as you move them. Zoom into the gap between cards for a better readout if needed.

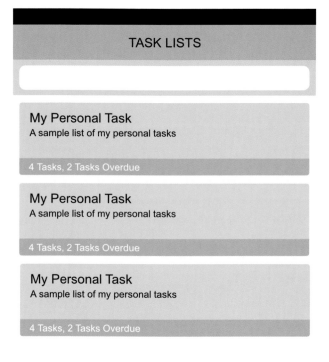

Simultaneous global editing using symbols

While reviewing the cards, I decided that the description text on the cards is too dark.

- On the **Layers Panel**, locate the *'A sample list...'* text layer in any task-board-card (Symbol) layer, and change its colour to *#959595*. Designer will automatically change the colour of all the text descriptions across all other symbols simultaneously. Slick!

If you need to make an edit in isolation to any 'symbolized' object, simply switch **Sync** off on the **Symbols Panel**, make the edit, then switch it back on again. We'll look at synchronisation later on p. 391.

Resource

tix1_04_uxelementsmainscreen2.afdesign

UX: CREATING ELEMENTS 2 (MAIN SCREEN)

It's time to finish up the first screen mock-up. Continuing with the main screen development, let's add an Add Task Board button, a Search button and label up each card for each task category.

Adding an Add Task Board Button

1 Switch on the **Assets Panel** (via **View > Studio**), then navigate to the **Icons** category.

2 Select the myapp-main-screen artboard.

3 Drag the Add icon to the right-hand side of the nav bar. Snapping should centre it vertically.

4 Give the icon a white fill, then rename it to *ico-btn* and move it into nav bar shape you've created before.

Text edits

The Task Board cards are set up as symbols, but at the moment they show the same text information. Once the look of the cards is agreed upon, the text can be changed to be specific to the card. Let's change Task Board names as well as descriptions.

These edits can be done by temporarily disabling synchronisation.

1 On the **Symbols Panel**, click **Sync** to disable synchronisation.

2 Select and edit the text on the second and third cards as shown opposite.

3 Switch synchronisation back on by enabling the **Sync** button.

Although the text changes seem like usual text editing, the symbol properties of other card elements in each card are retained, which means global editing can be performed at any point in the future. Try resizing the bottom-bg rectangle of any card to demonstrate this!

Adding Search text

Let's add Search text to the search input box so users know what the box is for.

1 With the **Artistic Text Tool**, type *Search...*, and use a font size of *12 pt* and a fill of *#959595*.

2 On the **Layers Panel**, drag and nest the text entry inside the search input entry (within the search bar).

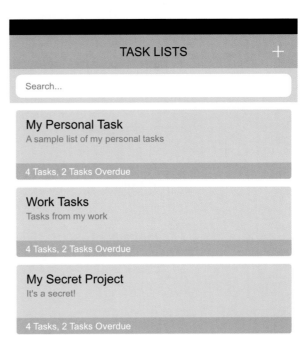

UX:
CREATING ELEMENTS 3
(TASK LIST SCREEN)

Now it's time to move on, starting with creating a new artboard for the Task List Screen design. This will contain all the tasks for My Personal Tasks, Work Tasks, or My Secret Project. My Personal Tasks will be used as an example.

Creating an additional artboard

1   Select the **Artboard Tool**, and from the context toolbar, click **Insert Artboard**. The existing document's settings are used.

2   On the Layers Panel, change its name to *myapp-task-list-screen*.

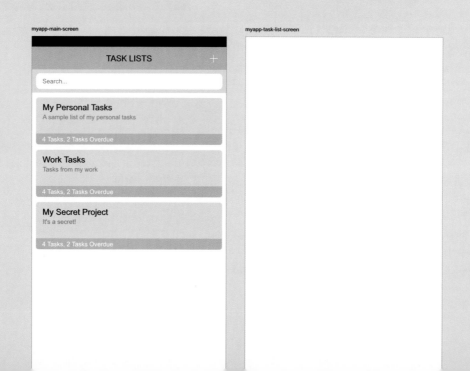

Adding content

Build up content on the artboard using the following guidelines.

- Copy status bar and nav bar shapes from the previous screen, as they will make a good base.

- Change the nav bar title to *My Personal Tasks*, centre the text on the bar, then delete the + icon as a new Add Task button will be added later.

In this view we'd like to have a bright single card foreground and dark background. You'll have many information displays here and the text should be more readable on the brighter foreground (to be added later).

- Change the artboard background to be the same as the nav bar background. On the **Layers Panel**, select the entire myapp-task-list-screen artboard and change its colour to *#CACACA*.

myapp-task-list-screen

My Personal Tasks

Creating a Task List Card and Side Cards

On the Task List screen, a single card is all that's needed to contain the task list.

1 Create a *315x515 pt* rectangle (fill *#EAEAEA*) and centre it on the page. On the **Transform Panel**, set **Y** to *85 pt*.

2 From the context toolbar, make its corners rounded—check **Absolute sizes** and set a **Radius** of *8 pt*.

Additional Side Cards help indicate that navigation is possible between Task List Cards by the user swiping/left or right.

The user will get to this view after selecting a task board on the previous screen, but won't have to move back to select another—instead the user will be able to swipe right/left to change the current task board. Adding a sneak peak of the other boards at the side lets the user know that there's something more there to explore.

3 Create another rectangle of size *15x485 pt* and snap it to the edge of the artboard (**Y** 100 pt).

4 To selectively round corners, select the **Corner Tool** (C). Select the top and bottom inner corners with the shift key (⇧), then drag inwards to a context toolbar Radius of *6 pt*.

5 Select the rectangle with the **Move Tool** (V), duplicate it using **Edit > Duplicate**, then **Flip Horizontal** on the **Toolbar**. Move the duplicate with the shift key (⇧) pressed until it snaps to the opposite side of the screen.

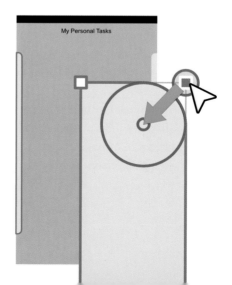

Adding Task Cards

I will add some tasks onto the board—to do this, use the same methods as you used to create Task Cards on the main screen. Symbols are used for the list bullets in case I want to change them in the future—maybe I won't but it's a great insurance policy!

That's it for the UX design. The mock-up is created and will now be subject to review and testing.

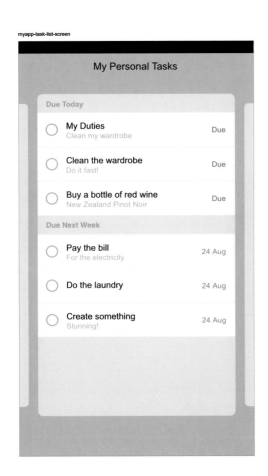

UI DESIGN: BACKGROUNDS AND BARS (MAIN SCREEN)

Going forward, we've assumed that the review process and testing were successful. You can now concentrate on UI design, using the mock-up as a base. Now the fun begins!

You can find out more about the UI design process on p. 370. As a quick recap, UI Design is all about making the app look amazing and easy to use, but without compromising the underlying design structure.

Creating a copy

You can leave the UX design file now as it has served its purpose.

- In your folder, create a copy of your mock-up UX design file, rename it (e.g., to tix-app-ui.afdesign), and open it in Affinity Designer.

Downloading and installing fonts

Firstly, I've decided that the font I'd like to style most of my text with will be Montserrat, a font family downloadable from Google Fonts.

1 Go to fonts.google.com (or search online for Google fonts) and download the **Montserrat** family (Regular and Bold).

2 Open the downloaded zip file and open and read the **OFL.txt** file.

3 For Mac: Double-click the downloaded font files and select **Install Font**.

or:

For Windows: Right-click the downloaded font files and select **Install**.

Background

Let's get onto some page design—starting with changing the screen background.

1   On the myapp-main-screen artboard, select the status bar rectangle.

2   On the **Toolbar**, select **Insert behind the selection**.

3   Draw a rectangle from the bottom-left to top-right corner of the artboard, covering it completely. Name it *bg-gradient*.

4   Using the **Fill Tool** (G), create a linear fill by dragging upwards across the shape. With the **Colour Panel**, set a gradient of *#FFFFFF* to *#000000* top to bottom, assigning both stops an **Opacity** of *5%*.

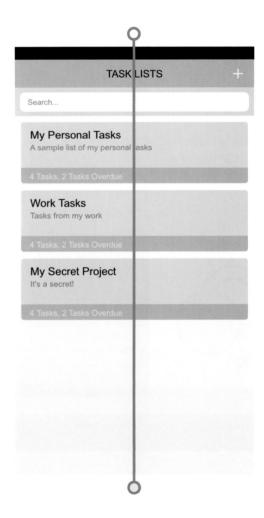

Nav Bars and Search Bars

I'd like the nav bar to look more interesting by utilising a new font and making use of the newly created background.

1   Select the nav bar shape and remove its fill by clicking the None swatch on the **Colour Panel**.

2   Give the Task Lists title and Add Task Card button a fill of *#979FB1*.

3   On the context toolbar, assign the Montserrat font to the title and apply toolbar settings below.

For the Search bar, its container can be removed, leaving just the Search input box. The latter could also do with being narrower and deeper. We'll also adopt a shadow effect to make the input box stand out and recolour the text.

1   On the **Layers Panel**, move the search input rounded rectangle out of its parent layer and delete the search bar rectangle—this was used for UX reasons only.

2   On the page, select the search input box and check **Lock Children** on the context toolbar. This preserves the text's aspect ratio prior to resizing its parent. Resize the search input rectangle to *335x36 pt*, then uncheck **Lock Children** again.

3 The search input has become invisible so it needs a shadow effect. From the **Effects Panel**, check **Outer Shadow** and apply settings.

4 Reposition the Search text in the Search input box and assign a new fill (*#BEC7DC*).

Now the design has some appeal! While all of the components from the mock-ups were left in place a few visual details were changed, e.g. the size of the search input. As long as you don't mess with the overall flow or don't make buttons, input boxes or text too small (or too big) to use them comfortably, you have room to experiment. It's not like UI design is only about changing colours!

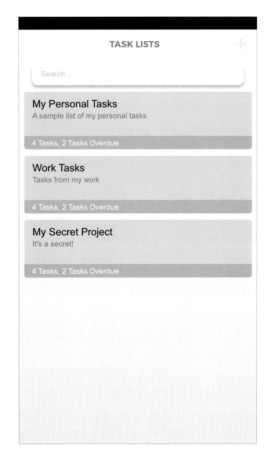

<table>
<tr><td>Resource</td></tr>
<tr><td>tix1_07_uitaskcards.afdesign</td></tr>
</table>

UI: TASK CARDS (MAIN SCREEN)

At the moment, the Task Cards look bunched up and a little dull. Let's make them pretty by using vibrant colours and the Symbols feature.

Spacing and Expressions

The cards need to be moved away from the search feature a little more so it's easier for a user to distinguish them and to ensure that fingers don't inadvertently tap the Task Card instead of the Search input. Spacing is a vital thing in UX/UI design.

1 With snapping enabled, select the search input box. This adds it as a candidate to allow the cards to snap to it.

2 Select all Task Cards with the shift key (⇧) pressed, then drag the selection up so it snaps to the bottom of the Search input box.

3 On the **Transform Panel**, set the **Y** value to be an **expression** rather than an absolute position. In this case, make it shift the selection down by *20 pt.*

Symbols revisited

We've not seen symbols in action too much but this is the point where they can really demonstrate their power. You can use the symbols functionality to modify all cards simultaneously—switching off synchronisation when you need to make isolated changes (and back on again!).

Changing card dimensions

As the search bar was previously narrowed I now want to do the same to every card. If I had many cards this would be a time-consuming and boring job. Here's how symbols make this easy.

1 Select the Search box to make it a snapping candidate.

2 On the **Layers Panel**, select the task-board-card rounded rectangle on any card, and check **Lock Children** on the context toolbar. This ensures that the text is not stretched or squashed when subject to resizing.

3 With the cmd ⌘ key (Mac) or ctrl key (Win) pressed, drag an edge handle inwards until the card is resized to the Search boxes width (i.e., *335 pt* wide).

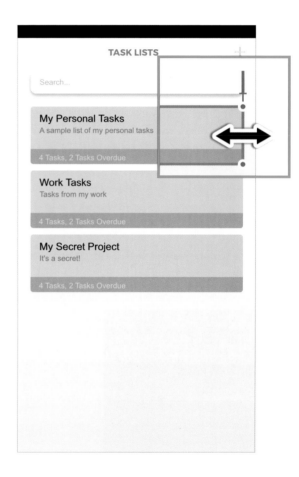

This leaves the text slightly out of alignment, so using the in-built symbols again, select all of a card's text objects and nudge to the right with the right-arrow key to suit.

Applying effects

Like the search bar, each card needs some shadowing to 'lift it' off the page. You can access layer effects directly from the bottom of the Layers Panel but try the dedicated Effects Panel instead. In any case, all the cards should have the effect applied simultaneously.

1 Select any task-board-card rounded rectangle.

2 On the **Effects Panel**, check **Outer Shadow** and adjust the settings below.

Adding colour gradients

I had the idea that all the cards would be colour coded, with each being very vibrant. In doing so, each card needs to be edited independently, so synchronisation of symbols is not needed. Think of this as being a temporary unlinking process. The cards will also look great with a linear gradient, suggesting directional lighting from the right of the screen.

1 On the **Symbols Panel,** click **Sync** to disable synchronisation.

2 Select the task-board-card rounded rectangle in the My Personal Tasks Card.

3 With the **Fill Tool**, drag a gradient across the card from top to bottom diagonally, and colour the gradient from *#051D72* to *#2A43B8*.

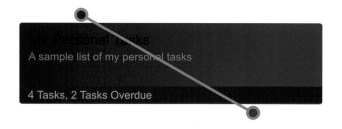

4   Repeat the process for the other cards, applying
    the following gradients:

- Work Tasks
  Orange: *#E93803* to *#FF7E00*

- My Secret Project
  Violet: *#5932AE* to *#973BBF*

To copy the gradient's path light and direction exactly
between cards, transfer the style using **Edit > Copy**,
then **Edit > Paste Style**, then simply recolour the
gradient stops.

To reinstate symbols functionality, remember to switch
synchronisation back on by enabling the **Sync** button.

Changing card objects

As well as the card, objects within the card can be
changed globally. As an example, I want to fine tune the
bottom strips on each card, making them taller and each
with a different solid fill.

1   On the **Symbols Panel**, switch **Sync** back on.

2   On any card, select the bottom-bg shape. Change the
    H value to increase the strip's height.

All cards will update with the new bottom strip size.

3   Disable sync again, then change the fill to *#061E73*,
    #EA3803, and *#6126B0* for My Personal Tasks, Work
    Tasks and My Secret Project, respectively.

Resource

tix1_08_uitextstyles.afdesign

UI:
TEXT STYLES
(MAIN SCREEN)

Previously (p. 381), the card text was edited independently so the card title, description and task counters had different text and formatting. This meant that the text type could no longer be controlled across cards. To improve this, you can create and apply **text styles** to the card text.

Creating text styles

You'll be creating three text styles for the main card text: Title, Description and Counter.

For the Title text:

1   With the **Move Tool**, select every card's title text. Select the first instance by pressing the cmd ⌘ key (Mac) or ctrl key (Win) then immediately press the shift key (⇧) to select the other card's title text in turn.

2   On the **Text Styles Panel**, select **Create Paragraph Style**.

3   In the **Edit Text Style** dialog, jump between menu options to define the text style (shown).

4   Enable **Apply style to selection** to automatically apply the style to the card title on dialog exit. Click **OK**.

- **Style: Style name** *Title*.

- **Character > Font:** *Montserrat, Bold, 12 pt*

- **Character > Colour & Decorations: Text fill** *#FFFFFF*

- **Typography > Capitals:** enable **All caps**.

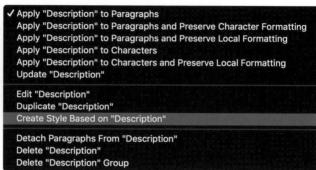

For the Description text:

1 Create as for Title text but with the following differences:

- **Style**: Rename **Style name** to *Description*.

- **Character > Font**: *Montserrat, Regular, 12 pt*

- **Character > Colour & Decorations: Text fill** *#FFFFFF*, **Opacity** *30%* (set by clicking on colour swatch; then use Colour tab)

- **Typography > Capitals**: keep **All caps** disabled.

2 Disable **Apply style to selection** and click **OK**.

For the Counter text:

1 On the **Text Styles Panel**, click the **Description** text style's options menu, select **Create style based on "Description"**. Change settings as follows:

- **Style**: Rename **Style name** to *Counter*.

- **Character > Colour & Decorations: Text fill** *#FFFFFF*, **Opacity** *60%*.

2 To apply the new Counter style to the Counter text on the page, select each Counter text object in turn with the **Move Tool** and click to select the *Counter* style in the **Text Styles Panel** (or from the **Paragraph Style** pop-up menu on the context toolbar).

The Counter style is based almost entirely on the
Description text style. As a result, the Counter style
options display as *[No change]* or as a blanked-out fill. To
see how the text style differs from its base style, view the
Style settings box in the Edit Text Style dialog.

Now you have text styles built into your design which
means that text changes can be made across all cards.
Why not try changing a text style's font colour to see
what happens?

Resource
tix1_09_uistatusbar.afdesign

UI:
STATUS BAR AND ADD TASK BOARD BUTTON (MAIN SCREEN)

We're nearing the completion of the main screen but it's time to create some more detail—a Status Bar and an Add Task Board button. Fortunately, you can use pre-built assets which can be added to the page for each.

Adding a Status Bar

1 Select the status bar rectangle.

2 On the **Assets Panel**, navigate to the **UI Bars** category and drag the *status bar standard* item over the status bar rectangle. It should snap nicely to the shape.

3 Delete the status bar rectangle from the **Layers Panel** as it's no longer needed. The new Constraints group is all you need for the Status Bar. Rename this group *status bar*.

4 While the bar looks good, I'd like to edit it to use *Affinity* as a carrier name and cut down the number of icons being shown (for a cleaner look). I'll also swap the font to be Arial for all text instances.

You may have noticed that the asset is actually a Constraints group. Don't be concerned as constraints are dealt with as a major Designer feature a little later in the project (p. 404).

> " By default, the text used in assets is San Francisco, which is only available to Apple iOS developers who are part of a paid Apple Developer Program (developer.apple.com). For the purposes of this project, I'll use Arial instead.

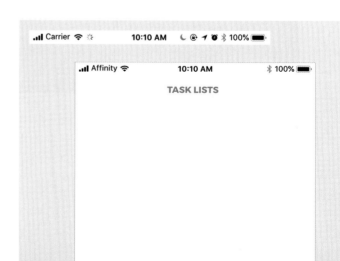

Adding an Add Task Board button

Again, you can visit the Assets panel for a replacement Add Task Board button. The original (on the nav bar) can be deleted. Go with something like a 'floating' button that pops off the page.

1   Draw a 375 x 116 pt rectangle (no stroke/fill), touching the bottom of the main screen artboard.

2   On the **Assets Panel**, navigate to the **Icons** category and drag the green Add button item to snap vertically and horizontally within the rectangle.

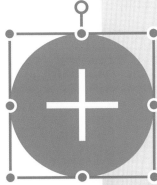

3   Resize the button about its centre by dragging a corner handle with cmd ⌘ key (Mac) or ctrl key (Win) pressed. A diameter of *56 pt* is perfect.

4   On the **Layers Panel**, clip the button inside the rectangle by dragging; ungroup the button and clip the plus sign inside the button.

5   Change the button's fill to *#979FB1*.

6   Like the other bars, apply an **Outer Shadow**.

Resource

tix1_10_uitasklistscreen.afdesign

UI: TASK LIST SCREEN

Now let's go to the second screen, the Task List Screen, and start with the background and bars, then the My Personal Tasks task list.

The idea is quite simple—every task board will have a unique colour, so when the user opens one of them, the app background changes to this colour. For My Personal Tasks, the screen background will be blue. On top of the background there will be a card with all the tasks listed, which scrolls only the content up and down.

Backgrounds and bars

1 Select the myapp-task-list-screen artboard.

2 With the **Fill Tool**, apply a linear gradient to the app background, going from *#051D72* to *#2A43B8* top to the bottom.

3 Set the fill to None on the nav bar via the **Colour Panel**, and change the My Personal Tasks title styling using the **Character Panel**.

4 Select side board fragments, fill them with white and change their layer **Opacity** to *15%*.

For the Status Bar, repeat the process for adding a Status Bar from the Assets Panel (p. 398) but instead choose the second asset in the list rather than the first (this is an inverted version that is great for adding to darker backgrounds) and remove the unwanted black background rectangles.

Task List Card

1 Change the card's background colour to *#F1F6F7*, then add an **Outer Shadow** and **Outer Glow** effects using the **Effects Panel**.

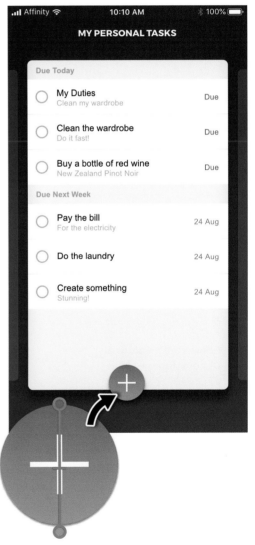

2 Copy the Add Task Board button from the previous screen, then apply a linear gradient from *#E93803* to *#FF7E00* and place it at the bottom of the card. Apply an **Outer Shadow** like the one applied to the card above.

Card text

Using the **Text Styles Panel** again, I can define text styles for each type of card text using the following settings.

For Due Today and Due Next Week.

- **Style**: Style name *Section Title*.

- **Character > Font**: *Montserrat, Bold, 11 pt*

- **Character > Colour & Decorations**: Text fill *#7C8DA8*

- **Typography > Capitals**: check All caps.

For Buy a bottle of red wine, Pay the Bill, etc.

- **Style**: Style name *Task Title*.

- **Character > Font**: *Montserrat, Regular, 14 pt*

- **Character > Colour & Decorations**: Text fill *#030C30*

For Do it Fast!, For the Electricity, etc.

- **Style**: Style name *Task Description*.

- **Character > Font**: *Montserrat, Regular, 12 pt*

- **Character > Colour & Decorations**: Text fill *#AEB3B7, Opacity 80%*

In this case, it's fine to create your text styles independently of each other and then apply the style to previously selected text of the same type.

> This is a good time to review your card text. Spend a little time on the content so your client doesn't get distracted by unclear task instructions, duplicate entries or spelling mistakes.

Creating completed tasks

I'd like my mock-up to show at least a single completed task so I'll work on the *Clean the wardrobe* task.

Add a rectangle (*#F8F8F8*) that covers the task entry. Place it inside, and at the bottom of the task's rectangle group in the **Layers Panel**. Recolour the Task Title with a fill of *#B9C1D4*, then delete the Due text.

Finally, apply a solid fill (*#B9C1D4*) to the bullet shape.

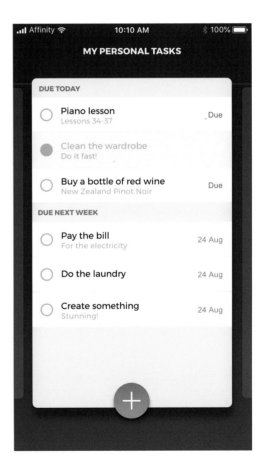

Resource
tix1_11_constraints.afdesign

CONSTRAINTS

It has long been a problem for the designer to easily envisage an app's layout on differently sized devices. Up to now, this was the moment when designers had to either redesign their projects for different screen sizes manually or have an ongoing conversation with UI developers on how to implement the design on other devices.

With the **Constraints** feature, a designer's life becomes a lot easier. Constraints mimic how the auto-layout function in Xcode works. You basically control how different design elements are **scaled** and/or **anchored** when applied to artboards that simulate differently sized devices.

Using a simple search input box as an example, it's likely that the box should remain the same height on different screen sizes, but be resizable horizontally, while keeping the same margin (*20 pt*) on both sides. That means that while it has *335 pt* width on the *375x667 pt* artboard (iPhone 6) it should be made to have a *280 pt* width on a *320x568 pt* artboard (iPhone 5).

The Constraints Panel

- Switch on the **Constraints Panel** via **View > Studio**.

As a quick recap, the panel indicates how an object will be scaled and/or anchored to its container (e.g., an artboard or shape). The inner square controls scaling; the outer anchoring, with both offering directional control. Use scaling and anchoring together or independently of each other.

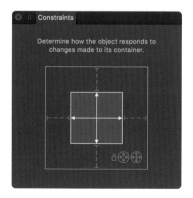

By default, all objects will scale vertically and horizontally, without anchoring.

Creating constraints

1   With the shift key (⇧) pressed, select all of the bars and Task Cards on the myapp-main-screen artboard.

2   On the **Constraints Panel**, click to enable the outer anchor lines (except bottom anchor line) and click to disable the inner vertical scaling arrow. With this configuration, the elements will scale horizontally and be anchored top, left and right to the container, if it is resized.

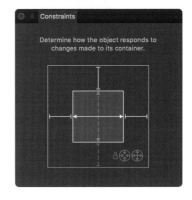

3   Repeat for the other UI elements (listed overleaf) using the constraints as indicated in the panel setups.

Object	Panel setup	Description
Add Task rectangle		The shape will scale horizontally and be anchored left and right and bottom.
Add Task Board button		Button will not scale and will be anchored to the bottom of the screen.
TASK LISTS text		Text is never scaled and will remain unanchored.
Search text (in Search bar)		Text is never scaled and will be anchored left.
All text (in any Task Card)		Text will not scale bigger but can scale down to a minimum fit (always maintaining aspect ratio). It is always anchored to the left of its container.
Bottom-bg rectangle (in any Task Card)		The shape will scale horizontally and be anchored left and right to the container. As we've used Symbols here previously, you only need to do this once on any chosen bottom-bg rectangle.
Background rectangle		The background rectangle will scale vertically and horizontally and be anchored to all sides of the container (i.e., the artboard). This will always cover 100% of the artboard.

What about the Status Bar elements? I mentioned previously that the bar elements, added from the Assets Panel, belonged to a Constraints group. This simply means that, as pre-built grouped content, Serif have already applied constraints to the asset's elements so there's nothing for you to do!

For the second artboard, apply your own constraints using what you've learnt on the main screen.

Resizing artboards

If the artboard is resized, the content will automatically reposition itself, taking into account the elements that are to be scaled and those to be anchored. The objects with applied constraints behave nicely when we've rescaled the artboard while others remain as they were.

Why not give it a go?

- Select the myapp-main-screen artboard, then resize your artboard by dragging from corner handles.

  This is a rough way of demonstrating the constraints functionality, as sizing the artboard to a custom dimension doesn't represent real device sizes.

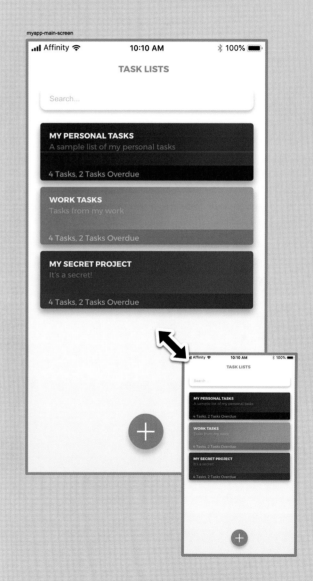

Resource
tix1_constraintstest.afdesign

Applying layouts to new device artboards

A better approach (instead of artboard resizing) allows us to perform auto-layout across device-specific artboards. To illustrate, let's create another two artboards—one for iPhone 6 Plus and another for iPhone 5.

1 With the **Artboard Tool**, select a **Size** of *iPhone 6 Plus*, then click **Insert Artboard**.

2 Repeat for an *iPhone 5* size.

3 On the **Layers Panel**, open the myapp-main-screen artboard, and select all of its content using the shift key (⇧) then **Edit > Copy**.

4 Select each new artboard and paste the contents into it using **Edit > Paste**.

Just like that, you have your design perfectly auto-scaled to other screen sizes. If you want to apply this design to any other device's dimensions, e.g., an Android phone, you just need to resize your artboard and Affinity Designer will do the magic for you.

For continuity, I reverted my edits but saved three device main-screen artboards in the tix1_constraintstest.afdesign file where you can experiment further.

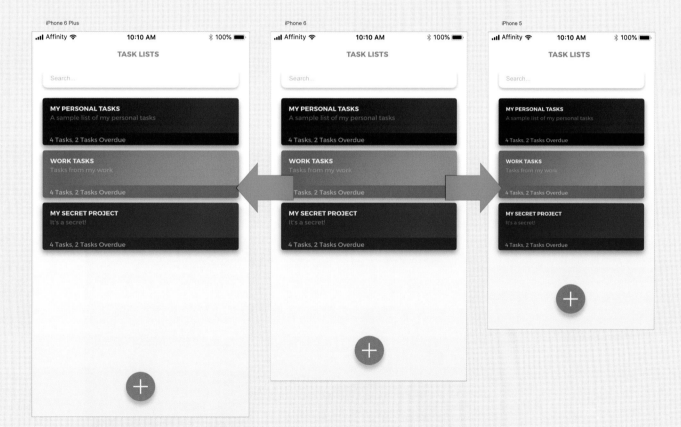

EXPORTING

It's time to prepare the design for developers. Once you've completed a final check to complete the design, you need to export design elements as **assets** then hand them off to the developer who will be responsible for interface implementation.

A developer needs to know which fonts were used, what the gradient colours are, and the dimensions of every asset. The best way to give them this information is to make another copy of Affinity Designer available to them and share your afdesign file; alternatively, you can create a style guide document.

Final check - Rename elements

Review your project and name objects and layers which you are considering exporting. Up to now, layer naming has been a design aid, but for export you'll be relying on layer names to formulate the exported graphics name. Your developer will thank you for identifying assets by their function!

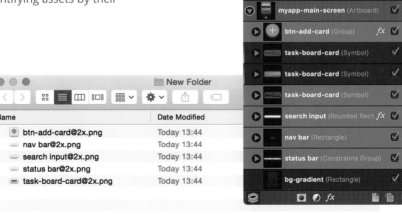

Export Persona

You'll need to export all design elements that you've used in your design so the developer can put them inside Xcode. That's where you'll use **Export Persona** (p. 17), a dedicated workspace for creating your graphic files as **slices**.

We'll focus on exporting elements as developer assets from the iPhone 6's myapp-main-screen artboard.

- On the **Toolbar**, switch to **Export Persona**.

Using the Layers Panel

This panel is a 'stepping stone' between design and slice export that is very similar to the **Layers Panel** in **Designer Persona**. It differs in that it lets you choose what objects and layers are to be exported, and generates slices from these.

1 On the **Layers Panel**, open the myapp-main-screen artboard, and select your chosen elements for export.

2 At the bottom of the panel, click **Create Slice**. On the page, a slice frame appears around chosen layers and objects.

I picked all the bars, a button and a representative card for export.

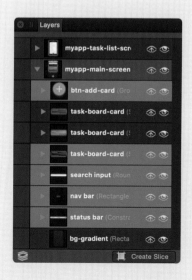

Using the Slices Panel

As slices were created, they were automatically added to the **Slices Panel**. The panel subsequently lets you choose which slices to export, in what file format, and their size scaling (1x, 2x, 3x, etc.). To keep things simple you can make use of a single preset to export all slices.

- On the **Slices Panel**, choose *Apple Universal Icon* from the **Export preset** pop-up menu.

This preset not only chooses the file format (PNG) and size scaling for you, but ensures that assets are assembled into named imageset files for Xcode JSON development.

> You export as PNG because you have a shadows applied to objects-this way you'll preserve transparency and the effect's appearance.

Exporting to folder

- Click **Export Slices (5)**, then select a folder to which you want to export your assets. Click **Export**.

Open the folder, and you'll see imageset folders for five slices, within which your graphics are saved at three different sizes, along with a supporting Contents.json file.

Contents.json file contents for btn-add-card.imageset:

Name	^	Date Modified	Size	Kind
► ▣ btn-add-card.imageset		Today 13:45	--	Folder
► ▣ nav bar.imageset		Today 13:45	--	Folder
► ▣ search input.imageset		Today 13:45	--	Folder
► ▣ status bar.imageset		Today 13:45	--	Folder
► ▣ task-board-card.imageset		Today 13:45	--	Folder

btn-add-card.png   btn-add-card@2x.png   btn-add-card@3x.png   Contents.json

```
{
  "images" : [
    {
      "idiom" : "universal",
      "filename" : "btn-add-card.png",
      "scale" : "1x"
    },
    {
      "idiom" : "universal",
      "filename" : "btn-add-card@2x.png",
      "scale" : "2x"
    },
    {
      "idiom" : "universal",
      "filename" : "btn-add-card@3x.png",
      "scale" : "3x"
    }
  ],
  "info" : {
    "version" : 1,
    "author" : "xcode"
  }
}
```

Another way to do this is to export assets as PDF files. This way, the developer can assign any size to these assets in Xcode as the PDF file can be scaled. It's becoming increasingly popular to export icons as PDF files, but a major drawback is that shadow effects will be rasterised to 1x scale only and may therefore appear blocky in 2x and 3x assets.

That's the Tix App project complete! All that's needed is an Application icon that complements this design.

See Tix App 2 (p. 416) for more information.

4

Tix App 2

Designing a complementary app icon by *Tom Koszyk*

This project looks at some of the rules governing app icon design and how you can apply them to create an icon which stands out amongst the crowd. You'll create a complementary app icon for the Tix app built in the previous project.

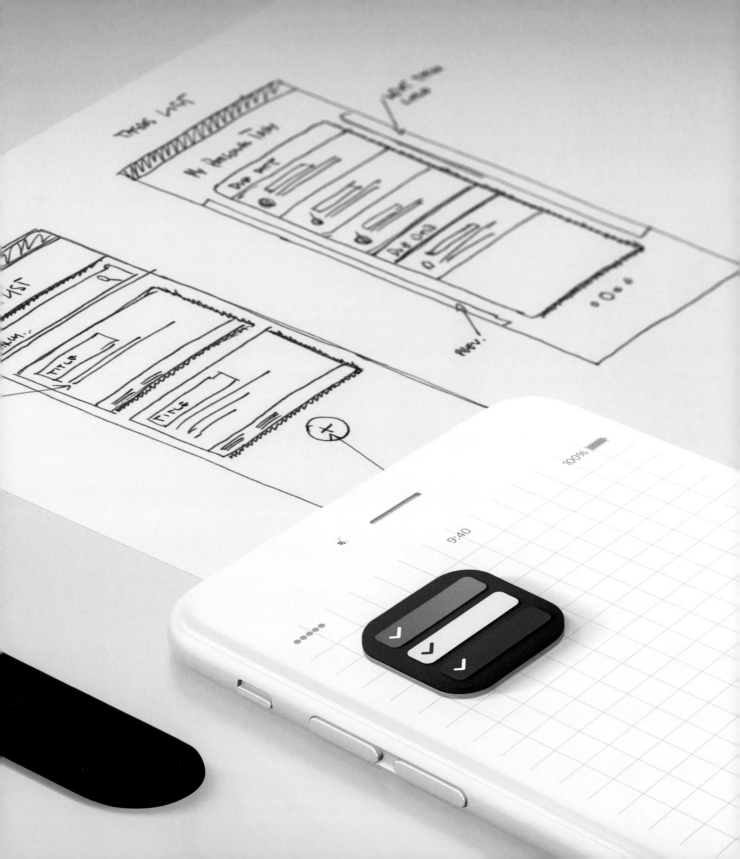

BEFORE YOU GET STARTED

Resources

 You can get all the resources that are referenced in this project from:
https://affin.co/tix2

Knowledge of Affinity Designer

To get the most from undertaking this project, you will need to:

- Be familiar with the interface of Affinity Designer. You can learn more about the interface in the Interface Tour, starting on p. 13.

- Have good core skills. See the skills table below to see which additional aspects of Affinity Designer you need to be confident with to complete this project:

Layers	p. 92
Colours & Gradients	p. 106
Effects & Adjustments	p. 112

APP ICON
DESIGN RULES

With a multitude of new applications appearing on the App Store and Google Play every day, an app's icon is key to helping browsing customers choose which one to download next. An effective app icon will draw them in long before they view screenshots, videos, and reviews.

Icons convey a specific message and act as the first touchpoint between user and app. Like a brand's logo, a good icon should be memorable and distinct—standing out from other icons in the App Store and on your home screen.

Is there any special ingredient for icon success? Not really. Popular app icons are quite different from one another, and even the Google Material Design Guidelines and Apple Human Interface Guidelines opt for quite different design solutions.

Nevertheless, there are some universal 'rules' every icon designer should follow.

Less is More

 Designs should be simple and convey a clear message.

Use simple shapes for immediate understanding and improved icon behaviour at smaller sizes.

Use recognisable metaphors, such as a camera or lens for a photography app. Users will skip an app if the meaning isn't clear with a glance. Don't make them guess!

Create a single focus point which makes it easy for users to identify the most important thing about the app.

Boldness

Even if you're not a fan of bold colours, you should implement this philosophy in your designs. Pastel and muted colours won't work well against the brighter icons on the App Store.

Apple apps have a bold design and a single focus point (pictogram) on a vivid background. They grab your attention immediately. Try emulating this style.

Consistency

Your icons should be consistent with your app design. So use the same colours and design philosophy. In my opinion, every app should use at least one strong colour to establish an information hierarchy inside the app. So go with that main colour for the icon.

Layered look

From iOS 7, Apple has been keen on flat design. However, if you look closely it's not completely flat. Subtle shadows are used to emphasise a layered appearance, i.e. one thing being shown on top of another. The same goes for Android icon designs.

With clever use of shadow effects, you can add another dimension to your icon, making it pop.

Avoid words

You might be tempted to use text in your app icon, but don't! It'll either disappear in the App Store's busy UI or be unreadable at small sizes. Remember, if the app is to be available for wearables, your icon has to work well at an extremely small size.

iOS specific rules

While Google Material Design Guidelines permit different icon shapes, all icons on iOS have the same, standard rounded rectangle shape.

> Keep your icon corners square as iOS will trim them to adhere to its standard. Don't risk giving your icon a large corner radius as it'll look terrible.

Also, Apple's Human Interface Guidelines include the following tips for icon design:

- Don't include photos, screenshots or interface elements

- Don't use replicas of Apple hardware products

- Test your icon against different wallpapers

Example icons to check out

Apple app icons provide a good example of how these rules can be applied to create some eye-catchingly simply designs.

Look at Pages, iMovie, Music Player and Control Centre icons.

What to take away from this

The rules I've discussed are not rigid. The more experience you have, the more you can experiment and find your own style.

Meanwhile, keep it consistent, simple and solid.

Resource

tix2_01_icon.afdesign

CREATING AN ICON

I'm a big fan of "layered" flat design and that's the way we'll approach our Tix app icon. I wanted to focus on a very simple representation of a task list and came up with two ideas for the icon.

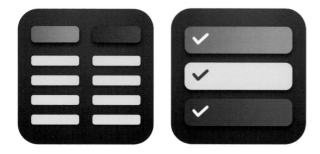

After showing these concepts to my client, we decided to go with the latter 'three tasks' design because it keeps strictly to our universal design rules.

We'll achieve a clean look by using simple shapes and a checkmark pictogram to emulate a task list. We'll colour these vividly and place them on the same blue gradient background used in the app, for consistency. The icon will stand out from the crowd, whether presented on a dark or light background.

1 Create a new document and set the **Type** to Devices then set a custom artboard size of *90x90 pt* and a **DPI** of *144*.

Snapping will definitely help when building this app icon and can be switched on from the Toolbar.

Artboard1

2   Using the **Rectangle Tool** (M), draw a square which covers the whole artboard and then, on the context toolbar, set its **Fill** to a *Radial* gradient from *RGB Hex #3341BB* to *#051E72* with a **Mid Point** of *60%*.

3   Using the **Fill Tool** (G), drag the gradient from the top of the square to bottom.

4   Draw another rectangle *72 x 18 pt* and place it at the horizontal centre of the artboard while keeping a margin of *12 pt* from top.

5 On the context toolbar, change **Corner** to *Rounded*, and change its fill to an orange gradient going from left to right, from *RGB Hex #E93803* to *#FF7E00*, respectively.

6 Now select the **Pen Tool** (P) and draw a checkmark shape then set the **Stroke** to *white* and *2 pt* and place it on the left side of the rounded rectangle.

7 With the **Move Tool** (V), select the rectangle and checkmark and group them together then, from the **Layer Menu**, select **Layer Effects** and apply an **Outer Shadow** effect.

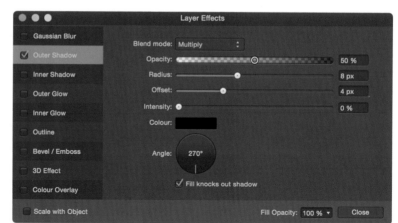

8 Duplicate the group (**Edit > Duplicate**) and position the duplicate *6 pt* below the original.

9 Hold down the cmd ⌘ key (Mac) or ctrl key (Win) and click the rectangle and change its **Fill** to *RGB Hex #EBEBEB*, then select the checkmark pictogram and set its **Stroke** to *RGB Hex #303EB6*.

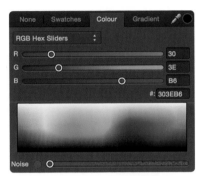

10 Duplicate the group once more and place it another *6 pt* further down and then set the new rectangle's **Fill** to a linear gradient from left to right, from *RGB Hex #5823AD* to *#973BC0*, respectively, and the checkmark pictogram **Stroke** to *white*.

You don't need to worry about rounding the icon's corners as they'll be trimmed automatically by iOS.

> To preview the iOS look, change the background's corner type to rounded with a radius of 15%.

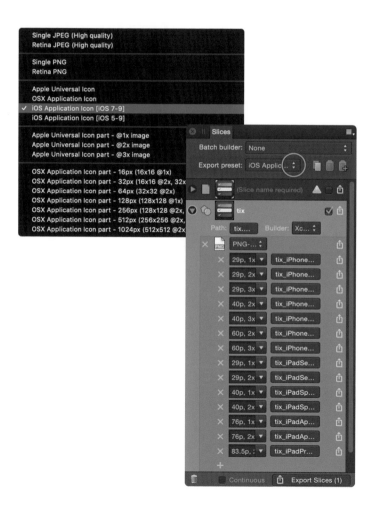

Resource

tix2_02_export.afdesign

EXPORTING

Once the design is complete, you'll need to export your icon at a range of sizes to support a variety of devices. Fortunately, Affinity Designer comes with presets to allow you to perform common export scenarios with ease.

1 Switch to **Export Persona** and, on the **Slices Panel**, rename the **Artboard1** slice to *tix*.

2 Select the **tix** slice and from the **Export preset** pop-up menu, select *iOS Application icon (iOS 7-9)*.

3 Click **Export Slices (1)**, choose a folder to export to and click **Export**.

Your icon design will be exported at various sizes for various devices and will be located in a folder titled tix.appiconset alongside a conveniently created Contents.json file for further Xcode development.

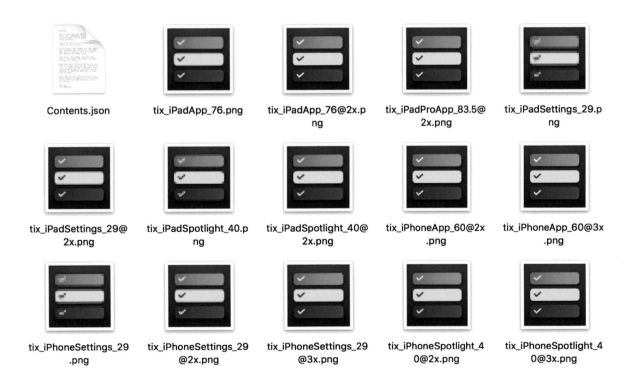

Contents.json   tix_iPadApp_76.png   tix_iPadApp_76@2x.png   tix_iPadProApp_83.5@2x.png   tix_iPadSettings_29.png

tix_iPadSettings_29@2x.png   tix_iPadSpotlight_40.png   tix_iPadSpotlight_40@2x.png   tix_iPhoneApp_60@2x.png   tix_iPhoneApp_60@3x.png

tix_iPhoneSettings_29.png   tix_iPhoneSettings_29@2x.png   tix_iPhoneSettings_29@3x.png   tix_iPhoneSpotlight_40@2x.png   tix_iPhoneSpotlight_40@3x.png

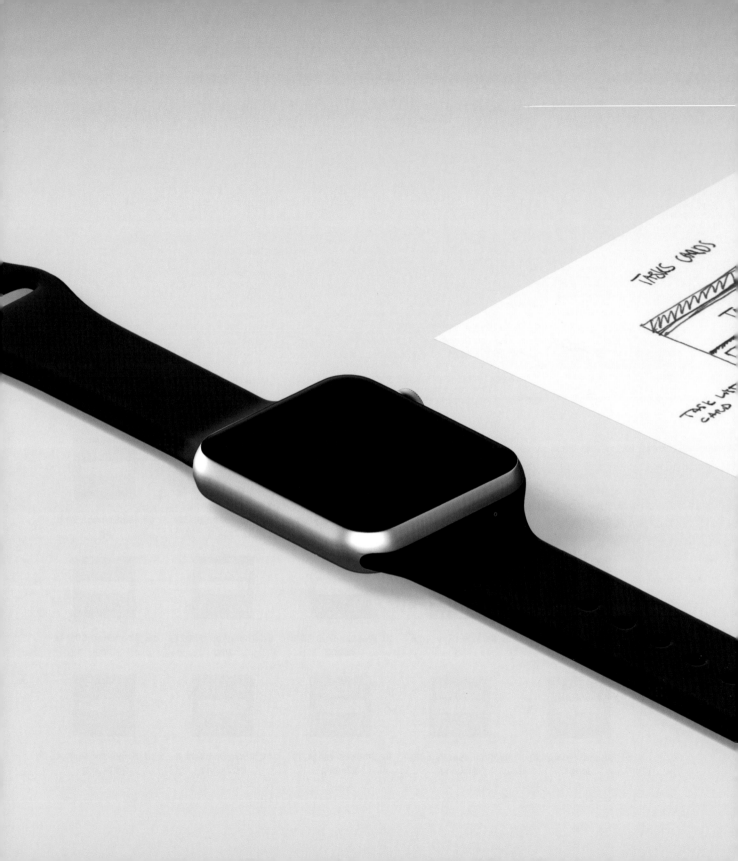

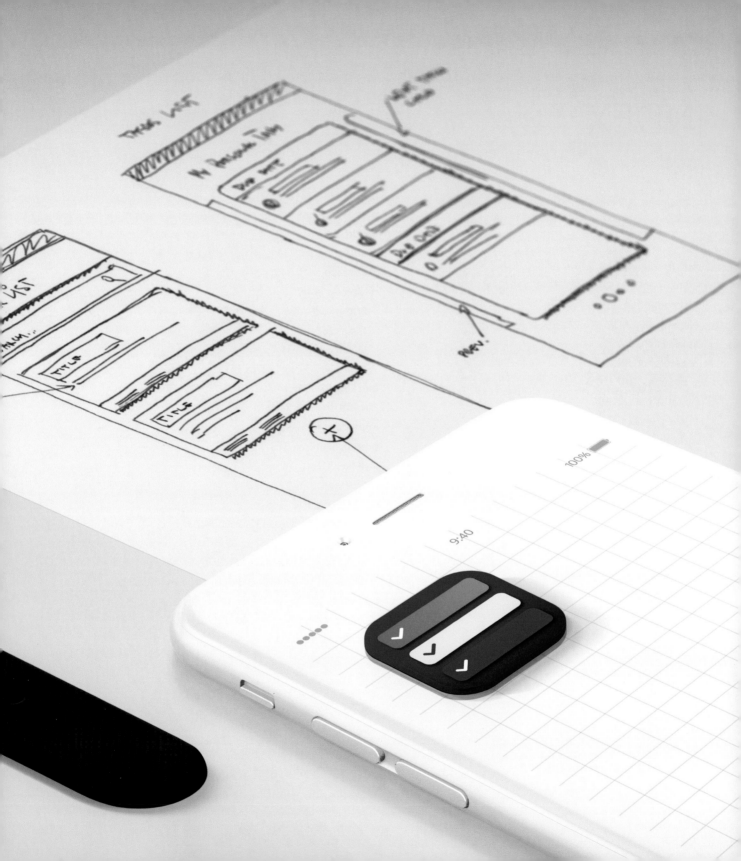

INDEX

AFFINITY
Designer

 Mac

DESIGNER PERSONA SHORTCUTS

DESIGNER PERSONA SHORTCUTS

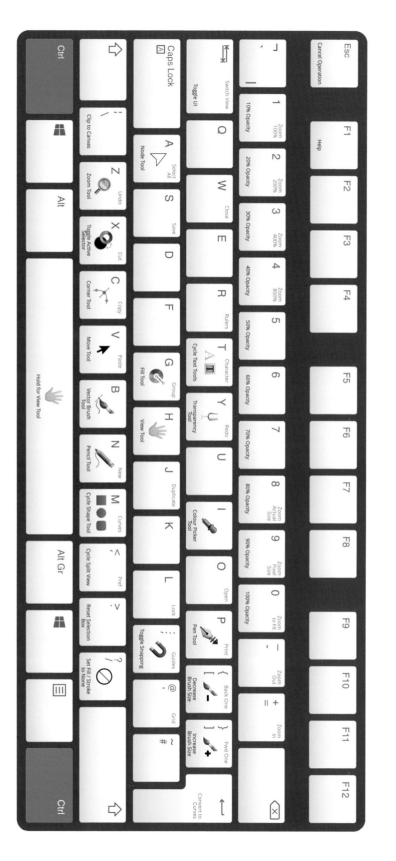

AFFINITY
Designer

Windows

AFFINITY
Designer

 Mac

PIXEL PERSONA SHORTCUTS

PIXEL PERSONA SHORTCUTS

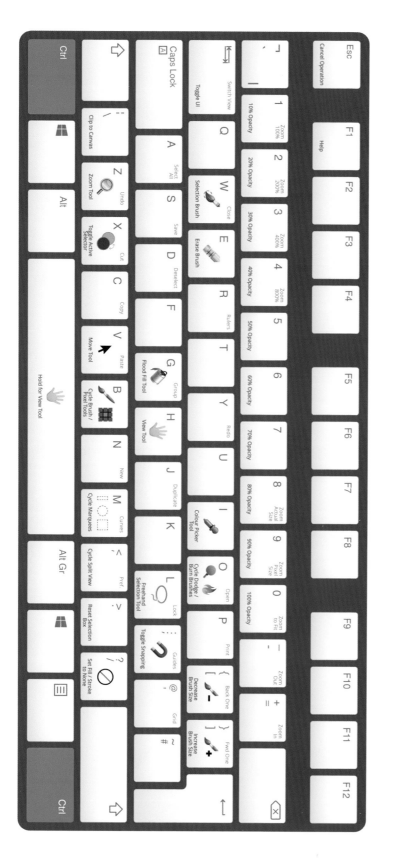

AFFINITY
Designer

Windows

AFFINITY Designer

 Mac

EXPRESSIONS

For use in input boxes in the Transform panel (and other areas of the UI)

Original

W
H

W: 120 px
H: 150 px

W: *=75% = 90 px	W: h+30 = 180 px	W: h-5 = 145 px
W: 2*h = 300 px	W: h/2 = 75 px	W: gr*h = 242.7 px
W: 118+55 = 173 px	W: 37*4 = 148 px	W: +=80 = 200 px
W: -=20 = 100 px	W: *=2 = 240 px	W: /=2 = 60 px
W: *=1.4 = 168 px		

GESTURES

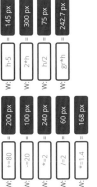

Zooming

Alt

Alt

Panning

Scrolling

Vertical   Horizontal

Shift ⇧

ADVANCED TEXT

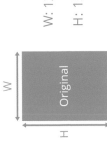

Press buttons for various actions
Alt ⌥   Cmd ⌘   Shift ⇧   Ctrl ^

Line Break

– En Dash
⇧ Em Dash
^ Subscript

⇧ Superscript

⇧ Spelling Options

⇧ Bigger

⇧ Smaller

Non-Breaking Space

^ Emoji & Symbols

ctrl   alt   cmd ⌘

⇧ Raise Baseline
Decrease Leading

▼ Lower Baseline
Increase Leading

Tighten Spacing

Loosen Spacing

(Add ⌘ to increase step size ▼ & ▲)
(Add ⌘ to decrease step size ◀ & ▶)

⌘ + T   Character Panel
⇧ ⌘ + T   Typography Dialog

⌘ + B   Bold
⌘ + I   Italic
⌘ + U   Underline

⌥ ⌘ + L   Align L
⌥ ⌘ + C   Align C
⌥ ⌘ + R   Align R

ADVANCED TEXT

Press buttons for various actions

Ctrl   Alt   Shift ⇧

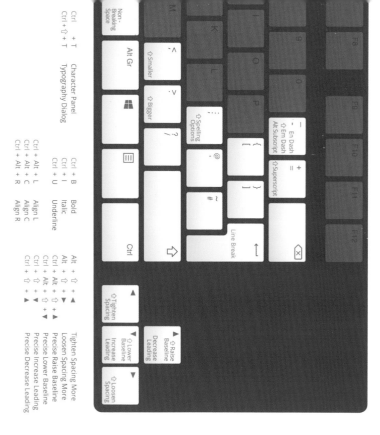

Ctrl + T	Character Panel
Ctrl + ⇧ + T	Typography Dialog
Ctrl + B	Bold
Ctrl + I	Italic
Ctrl + U	Underline
Ctrl + Alt + L	Align L
Ctrl + Alt + C	Align C
Ctrl + Alt + R	Align R
Alt + ↑ + ↑	Tighten Spacing More
Alt + ↑ + ↓	Loosen Spacing More
Alt + ↑ + ▲	Precise Raise Baseline
Alt + ↑ + ▼	Precise Lower Baseline
Ctrl + Alt + ◄	Precise Increase Leading
Ctrl + ⇧ + ►	Precise Decrease Leading

Non-Breaking Space

Keys: Alt Gr, ⇧ Smaller (^), ⇧ Bigger (ˇ), ⇧ Spelling Options, En Dash / Em Dash / Alt Subscript, ⇧ Supersript, Line Break, ⇧ Tighten Spacing, ⇧ Loosen Spacing, ⇧ Raise Baseline, ⇧ Lower Baseline, Increase Leading, Decrease Leading

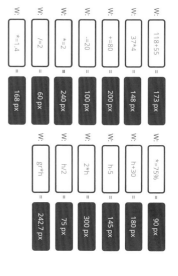

EXPRESSIONS

For use in input boxes in the Transform panel (and other areas of the UI)

W: 120 px
H: 150 px

Original

W: 118+55	= 173 px
W: 37*4	= 148 px
W: +=80	= 200 px
W: -=20	= 100 px
W: *=2	= 240 px
W: /=2	= 60 px
W: *=1.4	= 168 px
W: *=75%	= 90 px
W: h+30	= 180 px
W: h-5	= 145 px
W: 2*h	= 300 px
W: h/2	= 75 px
W: gr*h	= 242.7 px

AFFINITY **Designer**

Windows